D0200914

RATING THE PRESIDENTS

RATING THE PRESIDENTS

━━━━━━━━━━ ★ ━━━━━━━━━━

A Ranking of U.S. Leaders, From the Great and Honorable to the Dishonest and Incompetent

WILLIAM J. RIDINGS, JR.

AND

STUART B. MCIVER

A Citadel Press Book
Published by Carol Publishing Group

To my parents, Geraldine and William Ridings, Sr., for their encouragement.

To my wife, Joan, for bringing to this project her writing, editorial, and computer skills to help us pull this book together.

A Citadel Press Book
Published by Carol Publishing Group
Citadel Press is a registered trademark of Carol Communications, Inc.

Editorial, sales and distribution, and rights and permissions inquiries should be addressed to Carol Publishing Group, 120 Enterprise Avenue, Secaucus, N.J. 07094.

In Canada: Canadian Manda Group, One Atlantic Avenue, Suite 105, Toronto, Ontario M6K 3E7

Carol Publishing Group books may be purchased in bulk at special discounts for sales promotion, fund-raising, or educational purposes. Special editions can be created to specifications. For details, contact Special Sales Department, Carol Publishing Group, 120 Enterprise Avenue, Secaucus, N.J. 07094.

Manufactured in the United States of America
10 9 8 7 6 5 4 3 2 1

Library of Congress Cataloging-in-Publication Data

Ridings, William J.
    Rating the presidents : a ranking of U.S. leaders, from the great and honorable to the dishonest and incompetent / William J. Ridings Jr. and Stuart B. McIver.
        p.   cm.
    "A Citadel Press book."
    ISBN 0-8065-1799-9
    1. Presidents—Rating of—United States.   2. United States—Politics and government.
I. McIver, Stuart B.   II. Title.
E176.1.R55   1996
973' .099—dc20   95-50073
                                                                              CIP

CONTENTS

——— ★ ———

PREFACE

—— ★ ——

The Ridings-McIver Presidential Poll had its birth in 1989—the two hundredth anniversary of the first presidential administration. Thirty-nine presidents held the office during the first two centuries of the republic. The authors felt the time was right for a large poll rating the presidents across this period. By the time the poll was completed and much of this book written, two more presidents had assumed the office, and these were added to the evaluation in order to bring it up to the present election year of 1996.

William J. Ridings, Jr., an attorney with extensive experience in the field of statistics, designed the poll to build on the advances already made by previous pollsters. We sought and achieved a large and select sample, the best way to prevent a poll from being overpowered by any particular faction or school of thought. Our thanks go out to the learned, knowledgeable participants who took the time, trouble, and thought to complete our lengthy and detailed questionnaire. They made the ratings possible. Furthermore, they have added to the body of knowledge for the serious student in academia and at the same time produced information to stimulate the American citizenry's interest and curiosity in our presidential heritage. We are indeed most grateful to the participants.

INTRODUCTION

——— ★ ———

President John F. Kennedy once remarked that only the president could truly evaluate his own performance. He reasoned that the chief executive alone was in the position to experience each unique situation faced by his administration and thus judge how well he had responded to the challenges confronting him. Although a grain of truth is buried somewhere deep within the remark, the simple fact is that self-evaluation presents a problem woven into the fabric of human nature—bias. It also limits the size of the sample.

Our polling approach has been to seek a large sample from a wide range of informed opinion, primarily from people trained to look at facts objectively. The largest single group of participants has been the academic community, professors of American history, political science, or both at our nation's universities and colleges, who constituted more than 97 percent of the evaluators. Most Americans are knowledegable about presidents who hold office only during their own lifetimes, as pollster George Gallup discovered when he attempted a poll among the general population, rating past presidents. Only students of history can add to that knowledge an understanding of presidential performance in the founding years of our republic, through the turbulent period before, during, and immediately after the Civil War, and across the time when the United States was emerging as a world power.

To season the evaluations with other concerned points of view, we added a miscellaneous category consisting of elected officials, political activists, attorneys, authors, and a few knowledgeable people we knew to be students of the American presidents.

Questionnaires were mailed to potential participants in every state. Care was taken to insure that all sections of the country were represented in the ratings. We sought, too, to identify and involve women historians, who constituted 12 percent of our voting sample, and specialists in African-American studies. These points of view had not been actively sought in prior presidential polls.

The poll consisted of four parts, the most important being Quality Ratings, based on five categories: Leadership Qualities; Accomplishments and Crisis Management; Political Skill; Appointments; and Character and Integrity. Contemporary Popularity, with preassigned ratings based on the size of a president's election victory or loss or outright denial of renomination, was also included in case the participants deemed it a factor to be considered in rating a president.

The second part called for participants to assign a weighted or relative importance to each Quality Rating of the five categories plus the factor of Contemporary Popularity. Thus participants were able to determine the weight to be given to each of the categories. Accomplishments/Crisis Management and Leadership were the most important, followed by Character and Integrity, Political Skill, and Appointments. Contemporary Popularity was judged of much less importance in rating a president. These two parts constituted 60 percent of the total rating for each president.

The third part asked participants to rank the ten best presidents and the ten worst presidents. This section was weighted to account for 20 percent of the poll.

The final section, which also was weighted at 20 percent, asked participants to give a letter grade for each president: A = Great; B = Near Great; C = Above Average; D = Average; E = Below Average; or F = Failure. They were also asked to indicate their own knowledge of each president they evaluated: 1 = Large; 2 = Some; or 3 = Little. Participants were encouraged, too, to include brief comments on each president if they wished.

The comments ranged from adulation (for example, Lincoln: "a moral genius"; Franklin Roosevelt: "the Model"; and Jefferson: "towers above all other presidents in intellectual universality") to regret (for example, Carter: "character and integrity are not enough") and to insult (for example, Reagan: "too dumb" and Nixon: "a criminal").

This poll combines all of the significant and relevant methodologies heretofore used in rating the presidents, coupled with a large and widely based sample to make the poll representative of opinion in all sections of the country. This is the largest presidential poll yet produced to offer participants the opportunity to evaluate all of the country's chief executives over the more than two centuries of our nation's existence.

Seven hundred and nineteen people participated, hailing from forty-seven states as well as a small number of professors of American history at

Canadian universities, most of them with degrees from American schools. There was even participation by several historians from the United Kingdom, France, and Germany, which added the perspective of experts from outside national borders. Every region of the United States is represented. Faculty members who responded teach at such Ivy League schools as Harvard, Princeton, Columbia, and Cornell; at private schools like William and Mary, the University of Notre Dame, and Northwestern University; and at such major state universities as the University of California at Los Angeles (UCLA), the University of Oregon, the University of Texas, the University of North Carolina, the University of Nebraska, and Indiana University, among many others. Joan Hoff, of Indiana University, Nixon biographer and now president of the Center for the Study of the Presidency, gave her evaluation of the presidents, as did her predecessor as president at the center, R. Gordon Hoxie. Elected politicians who participated included Senator Richard Lugar (Republican, Indiana) and former senator Eugene McCarthy (Democrat, Minnesota), both of whom have been candidates for president. Among the celebrities who contributed were conservative activist Phyllis Schlafly and Cable News Network (CNN) commentator Judy Woodruff. Authors participating included James M. McPherson, William Bruce Catton, Hans Trefousse, and Robert Dallek.

About two-thirds of the original poll participants responded to the poll update to render a preliminary evaluation of Presidents George Bush (1989–93) and Bill Clinton, who assumed the office in 1993. The update used the exact criteria and format as the initial poll. Even though one-third of the poll participants felt that these two presidents were too close to the present to permit evaluation with the objectivity possible for earlier presidents, it was the wish of both the authors and the publisher to make this rating as up-to-date as possible.

Presidential polls date back to 1948 when Professor Arthur M. Schlesinger, Sr., of Harvard University, compiled the first poll. In the years that followed, the process of polling has been refined to incorporate more detail, objectivity, and greater participation. Steve Neal in his 1982 *Chicago Tribune* article utilized the five specific categories that we have adopted in an attempt to introduce more objectivity by considering some fixed relevant qualities in addition to the customary overall evaluation.

In his landmark book *Presidential Greatness,* Thomas A. Bailey catalogued the shortcomings of attempting to rate and evaluate the presidents. Among the many problems he observed is a preponderance of Democrats among academic experts, resulting in a political bias in favor of Democratic presidents. He observed, too, that the most famous presidents have had their reputations favorably enhanced by perpetuation in place-names and in the currency of the realm. Witness the Lincoln penny, the Roosevelt dime, and the Washington quarter.

Another critical factor that plays a significant role in rating and evaluating the presidents is the variety of situations faced by each president, ranging from serene prosperity to wrenching crises. As Dr. Bailey noted, "No two incumbents were ever dealt the same hand." Some presidents have had more opportunity to succeed than others. Or to fail.

Ratings and evaluations are further complicated by the changing nature of the institution of the presidency. Most of the pre–twentieth-century presidents felt constrained by the Constitution from taking active leadership roles. The office was initially established and viewed as an institution of much less power than it is today.

The ratings reveal that times of great national crisis or challenge produce our greatest presidents: the founding of our nation, George Washington; the Civil War, Abraham Lincoln; and the Great Depression followed by the world's most terrible war, Franklin Roosevelt.

The Ridings-McIver Presidential Poll reflects the judgment of an informed sample large enough to give Americans a balanced overview of the office of president from George Washington to Bill Clinton. Hail to the Chiefs.

The Ranking of U.S. Presidents

U.S. President in Order of Overall Ranking	Leadership Qualities	Accomplishments and Crisis Management	Political Skill	Appointments	Character and Integrity
1. Lincoln	2	1	2	3	1
2. F. Roosevelt	1	2	1	2	15
3. Washington	3	3	7	1	2
4. Jefferson	6	5	5	4	7
5. T. Roosevelt	4	4	4	5	12
6. Wilson	7	7	13	6	8
7. Truman	9	6	8	9	9
8. Jackson	5	9	6	19	18
9. Eisenhower	10	10	14	16	10
10. Madison	14	14	15	11	6
11. Polk	12	8	12	15	20
12. L. Johnson	11	12	3	10	37
13. Monroe	15	13	16	8	13
14. J. Adams	17	11	21	13	3
15. Kennedy	8	16	10	7	34
16. Cleveland	13	17	19	17	16
17. McKinley	18	15	17	18	19
18. J. Q. Adams	20	20	25	12	4
19. Carter	28	22	32	14	5
20. Taft	25	21	30	20	14
21. Van Buren	19	24	11	22	25
22. Bush	24	18	27	25	24
23. Clinton	26	23	20	24	38
24. Hoover	22	33	34	21	11
25. Hayes	29	26	23	26	22
26. Reagan	16	27	9	39	39
27. Ford	34	28	24	23	17
28. Arthur	31	25	22	27	33
29. Taylor	23	31	33	28	23
30. Garfield	30	36	26	32	26
31. B. Harrison	32	29	29	29	28
32. Nixon	21	19	18	34	41
33. Coolidge	37	34	28	31	21
34. Tyler	35	30	35	30	27
35. W. Harrison	33	39	36	35	29
36. Fillmore	36	32	31	33	31
37. Pierce	38	37	37	36	35
38. Grant	27	35	40	40	32
39. A. Johnson	39	38	41	37	30
40. Buchanan	40	41	39	38	36
41. Harding	41	40	38	41	40

RATING THE PRESIDENTS

★

George Washington

1789–1797
1st President

Overall Ranking: 3

Leadership Qualities: 3
Accomplishments and Crisis Management: 3
Political Skill: 7
Appointments: 1
Character and Integrity: 2

[F]irst in war, first in peace, and first in the hearts of his countrymen.

—Henry Lee

In his own time and in the centuries after his death, George Washington has been treated as a more-than-human symbol of America. Does Washington the man live up to Washington the myth?

George Washington was born on February 22, 1732, a British subject, on Pope's Creek Farm in Westmoreland County, Virginia. Three years later his family moved fifty miles north along the Potomac River to the large tobacco farm later to be known as Mount Vernon. As the oldest child in a second marriage, he would later inherit the smaller Pope's Creek Farm upon the death of his father. Ultimately, he would also inherit the larger Mount Vernon, which became his beloved retreat from the world.

Fatherless at age eleven, George and his five younger brothers and sisters were left in the sole care of their strong-willed mother. With a limited education, George took an interest in land surveying, eventually becoming licensed when he was seventeen. His ambition and interest in land led him in time to become one of the largest landowners in the country. In 1759, Washington married a wealthy widow, Martha Custis, who had two children and was also in her late twenties. George and Martha Washington would have no children together.

Epitomizing the citizen-soldier, Washington served in both the Virginia militia and the British army. In the French and Indian Wars, as a young captain in the British cause, he performed heroically and his name was known to King George III. Earning a reputation as a tenacious, courageous, and charismatic leader, he was given command of the American Continental army in the Revolutionary War. John Adams proposed Washington as army commander, saying, "A gentleman whose skill and experience as an officer, whose independent fortune, great talents and excellent universal character would command the approbation of all America and unite the cordial exertions of all the Colonies better than any other person in the union."

Taking command of an improvised Continental army consisting of a small untrained militia, Washington molded a fighting force. This army of patriots repeatedly lacked sufficient food, supplies, equipment, and manpower to combat the well-equipped professional world-class army of Great Britain. Britain's King George III was equally determined, through his tight-fisted rule of the American colonies, to use the might of the British Empire to put down the rebellion. The British monarch feared what we call today the domino effect. If the American colonies achieved independence, then Canada would be next, with other colonies soon to follow.

Against this fierce opposition, Washington managed through sheer willpower and charismatic leadership to keep the American fighting forces intact. He exemplified this leadership when he addressed his troops just before the Battle of Long Island with these moving words:

> The time is now near at hand which must probably determine whether Americans are to be freemen or slaves; whether they are to have any property they can call their own; whether their houses and farms are to be pillaged and destroyed, and themselves consigned to a state of wretchedness from which no human efforts will deliver them. The fate of unborn millions will now depend, under God, on the courage and conduct of this army. Our cruel and unrelenting enemy leaves us only the choice of a brave resistance, or the most abject submission. We have therefore, to resolve to conquer or die.

The American commander in chief led a weary and worn Continental army through a series of defeats, tactical withdrawals, and a few critical victories. These victories gave a measure of credibility to the American cause that prompted willing European powers to contribute decisive aid. As a result, France and Spain assisted with naval power and Holland with financial aid. In the conclusive engagement at Yorktown, Virginia, the French fleet and Washington's army, at different ends of the battlefield, sandwiched a very large and surprised British force. The trapped British army could not even escape by sea, a method the British had relied on for several other escapes.

Washington was not the most brilliant general ever to lead an American army, but through his steadfast courage and leadership he influenced the outcome of the Revolutionary War. No other American military leader has had such a personally direct impact on the successful outcome of a war.

His stint in politics included service in the Virginia House of Burgesses and in the First and Second Continental Congresses. Continuing his public service in the early struggle for national identity, Washington was elected president of the Constitutional Convention in 1787. He advocated a strong central government.

A trusted figure on the eve of the first U.S. presidential election in 1788, Washington was given one of the two votes cast by every elector in the electoral college, the constitutional body directly electing the president. Washington was able, as only war heroes can, to transcend sectional and factional loyalties. Hence, the six-foot-two, 200-pound, muscular Virginian was sworn in as the first U.S. president in 1789.

Abigail Adams characterized Washington as "polite with dignity, affable without familiarity, distant without haughtiness, grave without austerity, modest, wise, and good."

Thomas Jefferson gives us a detailed description written fifteen years after Washington's death:

> His mind was great and powerful, without being of the very first order; his penetration strong . . . and, as far as he saw, no judgment was ever sounder. It was slow in operation, being little aided by invention or imagination, but sure in its conclusion. . . . Perhaps the strongest feature in his character was prudence, never acting until every circumstance, every consideration was maturely weighed . . . but once decided, going through with his purpose, whatever obstacles opposed. His integrity was most pure, his justice the most inflexible I have ever known. . . . He was, indeed, in every sense of the words, a wise, a good and a great man.

John Adams, in his own typically blunt way, weighed in with his perspective on another aspect of the Revolutionary War hero. He wrote that Washington "was not a scholar was certain. That he was too illiterate, unread, unlearned for his station and reputation is equally past dispute."

Washington exhibited at an early age the premium he placed on ethical behavior. As a fourteen-year-old, he wrote, "Labor to keep alive in your breast that little spark of celestial fire called conscience."

However, while he was courting his future wife, Martha Custis, he wrote at least one indiscreet letter to Sally Fairfax, the wife of one of his close friends. Washington's letter clearly expresses his passion for her and his lack of passion for Martha. Four months later he married Martha. After the marriage, the Washingtons continued as frequent callers on the Fairfaxes until the Fairfaxes moved to England. This behavior reveals perhaps a little duplicity on the part of Washington in his relations with Martha and his close friend and neighbor, George Fairfax.

On one occasion in 1781, when he summoned his aide Colonel Alexander Hamilton from downstairs and was kept waiting, he greeted his longtime aide, "Colonel Hamilton, you have kept me waiting at the head of the stairs these ten minutes. I must tell you, sir, you treat me with disrespect!"

On another occasion, in 1778 at the Battle of Monmouth, General Charles Lee's forces, outnumbered by British regulars, were put to flight in an unorganized retreat. Washington confronted him on the battlefield and demanded an explanation in a fit of swearing. On the spot, Washington took control, turned the situation around, and halted the retreat.

Later, in 1791, during his presidency, Washington erupted into a rage at a private meeting with General Arthur St. Clair. An Indian ambush had taken a heavy toll on St. Clair's army, despite Washington's prior warning about such an ambush.

Another glimpse of the person of George Washington involves a congressman who arrived late at one of President Washington's official dinners. Washington greeted the tardy congressman with a glare from his blue-gray eyes, "We are obliged to be punctual here. My cook never asks whether the company has arrived, but whether the hour has."

There is evidence that Washington was not quite the rigid personality typified by his dollar bill portrait. He did enjoy some of the lighter pleasures of the day such as mixing with the ladies at tea parties, indulging in good food and wine, playing cards, and fox hunting.

Washington's contemporary reputation for honesty and integrity helped instill confidence in the office of the presidency and did greatly assist in setting the fledgling new government on track. "The indispensable man?" speculates one panel expert. He may not have been the only figure capable of serving as the first president, but he did enjoy the confidence of his countrymen and lent prestige to the office. He clearly deserves credit for making the new government and institution of the presidency work.

In terms of character and integrity, Washington is regarded today as second only to Lincoln. Comments like "vision and integrity" and "the only man in our history who had to accept the presidency" attest to the confidence his contemporaries placed in Washington the man. Although both Washington and Lincoln were great men, there were no investigative reporters back then to ferret out details concerning any possibly unflattering details of a political or personal nature. Washington's track record for courage and cautious style worked as additional insurance in founding a successful government.

The fact that Washington was a slaveholder persists as somewhat of a cloud over his reputation. However, in the context of the day, it was the norm for a wealthy Virginia planter. It is harsh to measure Washington by today's standards. Even then Washington entertained misgivings about owning slaves. In 1786 he wrote in a letter, "I never mean, unless some particular circumstance should compel me to it, to possess another slave by purchase, it being among my first wishes to see some plan adopted by which slavery in this country may be abolished."

Just what kind of leadership did Washington exercise as president? The presidency was a much weaker office in the eighteenth and nineteenth centuries compared with even the early part of the twentieth century. Washington exercised sound and cautious judgment, initiating the practice of consulting with his cabinet. The experts allude to "critical leadership," with one appraisal referring to Washington as "a rarity: a successful revolutionary and a restrained, capable executive." He deferred to the stronger legislative branch. In a letter to Alexander Hamilton in 1794, Washington wrote, "The powers of the Executive of the U. States are more definite, and better understood perhaps than those of almost any other Country; and my aim has been, and will continue to be, neither to stretch, nor relax from them in any instance whatever, unless imperious circumstances shd. [should] render the measure indispensable."

However, there were several instances when he exercised strong leadership particularly in the matters of Indian affairs, neutrality as foreign policy, the Whiskey Rebellion, the Jay Treaty, and the Pinckney Treaty. He felt himself on firm ground constitutionally in dealing with foreign affairs and putting down a rebellion challenging the authority of the new federal government. Washington's cautious leadership style was useful in avoiding blunders that could have rattled the fragile union of states.

If there was one area in which Washington did not excel, it was political skill—although even in this area he ranks well within the top 20 percent of all presidents. While his cautious style did help him avoid gaffes, as we call them today, he was not an exceptional politician in his day. Of course, Washington preferred a consensus style of getting things done. He detested politics and the political parties that were springing up during his presidency with origins in various preexisting factions. Political skill, however, was not quite as developed in our country at that time as it is today. FDR, LBJ, Reagan, and Clinton would have danced circles around the best politicians of Washington's day.

Washington believed firmly in a strong central government and, while he detested political parties, could be classified as a Federalist. He was reelected in the election of 1792 in the same way as his first election, receiving a vote from every voting elector in the electoral college.

What did Washington accomplish during his presidency? By his sheer stature and prestige, his "great looming presence" in the words of one poll participant, and through judicious leadership and governance, he allowed the roots of government to take to the soil of nationhood. Washington "made the eaglet fly, deserves to be called great," notes the expert. He steered the ship of state through the perilous waters of foreign entanglement avoiding involvement in a European war by the Proclamation of Neutrality in 1793, making peace with Britain by the Jay Treaty of 1795 and normalizing relations with Spain by the Pinckney Treaty of 1795. On the domestic front, he made peace with the Indians and acted decisively by leading a militia force of 15,000 to put down the 1794 Whiskey Rebellion involving Pennsylvania farmers. The farmers protested the federal government's right to collect a tax on alcohol distilled from their grain crop. The new government prevailed in asserting its position, and the rebellion ended.

At the conclusion of his presidency, Washington gave long-lasting advice: Avoid foreign alliances. This policy of "isolation" was to govern until the dawn of the twentieth century.

Washington especially appreciated the importance of the decisions he would be making, both procedural and substantiative. Comments one poll participant, "Defined and set precedents for the new office," with many others concurring. The new president wrote to James Madison in 1789, "As the first of everything, in our situation, will serve to establish a Precedent, it is devoutly wished on my part, that these precedents may be fixed on true principles."

No other president ever made such illustrious appointments to office, and the poll panelists rank him first in this category. Just think of the names of some of his appointees: Thomas Jefferson and Alexander Hamilton. Although at opposite ends of their contemporary political spectrum, both of these men were brilliant thinkers and spokesmen. Washington's initial appointments to the Supreme Court included the judicial activist John Jay. As chief justice he led the Court to decisions that broke new ground in asserting powers of the new federal government and of the Supreme Court as an institution. No other president ever appointed an entire court at one time.

Although overall extraordinary praise of Washington abounds, "class by himself," "a monument and really monumental," "a true giant," several dissent with comments such as "more a myth than a man," "kept prima donnas together otherwise did little," and "overrated and partisan."

Washington declined to run for a third term in 1796. Partisanship and criticism were proving too distasteful to him. While he was largely revered throughout the land, his critics believed he wanted to become another "King George." Many, objecting to the formal courtly style of entertaining reminiscent of the courts of Europe, claimed that Washington had betrayed the Revolution. The *Philadelphia Aurora*, one of the major opposition papers, in 1796 editorialized: "If ever a nation was debauched by a man, the American nation has been debauched by Washington. If ever a nation was deceived by a man, the American nation has been deceived by Washington. Let his conduct, then, be an example to future ages; let it serve to be a warning that no man may be an idol."

However, criticism came not only from partisan newspapers. Also in 1796, future president Thomas Jefferson attacked Washington's policies and internationally renowned political philosopher Thomas Paine attacked Washington's character. Jefferson opined that Washington's support for the Jay Treaty associated him with a pro-British monarchical, aristocratic party—the Federalist Party. Paine attacked Washington's character, questioning whether Washington ever had any principles. In essence, he called Washington a hypocrite.

"Cincinnatus—the model soldier turned civil leader," as one expert labels Washington, returned to Mount Vernon in 1797 and died there in 1799. On the day of his death on his deathbed he stated, "It is well. I die hard, but I am not afraid to go." After his death, his legendary reputation grew to mythic proportions.

More than any other president, the person of Washington and the character he exhibited as president, more so than his accomplishments as president, provide him with the greatness he enjoys with subsequent generations of Americans.

John Adams

1797–1801
2ND PRESIDENT

Overall Ranking: 14

Leadership Qualities: 17
Accomplishments and Crisis Management: 11
Political Skill: 21
Appointments: 13
Character and Integrity: 3

You stand nearly alone in the history of our public men in never having had your integrity called into question or even suspected. Friends and enemies agree in believing you to be an honest man.

—Benjamin Rush

"Honest John" Adams's undiplomatic frankness, courage, and brash personality no doubt limited him to only one term as chief executive. Yet, in his one term, he left a legacy of some accomplishment that did much to benefit the shaky nation in its first presidential transition.

John Adams was born on October 30, 1735, in Braintree (now Quincy), Massachusetts, the great-great-grandson of Pilgrim settlers John and Priscilla Alden. Developing an early interest in learning and reading, he graduated from Harvard and, after studying law, was admitted to the Massachusetts bar.

After a courtship, Adams married his well-educated and cultured third cousin Abigail Smith in 1764. She entertained a particular interest in politics and philosophy and became one of the most famous of all the first ladies. They had five children, including John Quincy Adams, who became the sixth president of the United States.

Adams's career as a lawyer included the successful defense of the British soldiers involved in the Boston Massacre of 1770. Six of the eight British soldiers were found not guilty, and two were found guilty of the lesser charge of manslaughter. Adams, who had been a well-known patriot, lost some popular support because of this case. He believed that all criminal defendants should have legal representation no matter how unpopular the accused or how detestable the crime the defendant is charged with. This was not the last time he would fight for an unpopular position.

Adams's interest in politics brought him into the Massachusetts legislature from 1770 until 1774 when he became a member of the First Continental Congress, serving there until 1778. He zealously promoted the cause of independence and was appointed to the committee to draft the Declaration of Independence. While an excellent writer in his own right, he deferred to Thomas Jefferson, a Virginian, to draft the document. He also nominated another Virginian, George Washington, to be commander of the colonial army.

While in the Continental Congress, he introduced the resolution that adopted the first national flag and delivered a stirring speech in favor of independence for the colonies. So active was Adams in the independence movement that Richard Stockton, a signer of the Declaration of Independence, wrote in 1776: "The man to whom the country is most indebted for the great measure of independency is Mr. John Adams of Boston. I call him the Atlas of American independence. He it was who sustained the debate, and by the force of his reasoning demonstrated not only the justice but the expediency of the measure."

During the Revolutionary War, Adams successfully negotiated with France to receive arms and financial assistance for the American cause.

As minister to the Netherlands, he successfully secured Dutch financial aid for the cause as well. Adams helped to negotiate the 1783 peace treaty with Britain and was subsequently named minister to Britain in 1785. He returned home in 1788 and finished his three-volume work, *A Defense of the Constitutions of Government of the United States of America.*

Adams became the first vice president of the United States when he took the oath of office in 1789 and served a second term beginning four years later after his reelection. Not particularly enamored with the office of the vice presidency, he wrote to his wife in 1793, "My country has in its wisdom contrived for me the most insignificant office that ever the invention of man contrived or his imagination conceived."

As vice president, the five-foot-six, blue-eyed Adams served in the shadow of the president, George Washington. Very often Adams received the brunt of the attack from enemies of the administration who would not attack Washington directly. Occasionally, these attacks took on a personal nature, such as references to the portly Adams as "His Rotundity" or criticism of his alleged monarchical views by the epithets "Duke of Braintree" and "His Superfluous Excellency." This latter criticism stemmed from Adams's attempt at establishing a more formal European style of protocol including official titles.

As a Federalist, Adams favored a strong central government. While Washington endorsed Adams for president in 1796, the acknowledged Federalist Party leader, Alexander Hamilton, felt Adams was too independent, and he therefore worked against Adams's election. This backfired when the Federalist candidate for vice president was defeated, even though Adams was narrowly elected president. This brought Thomas Jefferson, a founder of the Democratic-Republican Party, into office as vice president, the only time in American history that the president and vice president were elected from different political parties.

Known for his generally pro-British foreign policy, Adams feared the mob rule that marked the chaos and anarchy of the French Revolution of 1789.

He was strongly opposed to slavery and did not think much better of politics. Of politics he wrote, "When and where were ever found, sincerity, honesty, or veracity, in any sect or party in religion, government, or philosophy?"

Washington's foreign policy of strict neutrality rang an agreeable chord with Adams as well.

Adams was one of the more animated personalities of his day, described variously as rude, prickly, cantankerous, grumpy, stubborn, strong willed, vain, cold, aloof, ambitious, puritanical, narrow-minded, conceited, and perhaps less able to take criticism than many others. After his presidency, reflecting on the barrage of criticism he had had to endure, Adams wrote, "I could never do anything but was ascribed to sinister motives."

Jefferson described Adams in a letter to James Madison: "He is vain, irritable, and a bad calculator of the force and probable effect of the motives which govern men. This is all the ill which can possibly be said of him. He is as disinterested as the Being who made him."

Adams was public-spirited. He loved to help humankind but had difficulty relating to individuals outside his family and small circle of closest friends.

Benjamin Franklin, long acquainted with his fellow patriot activist, commented that Adams was "always an honest man, often a wise one, but sometimes, and in some things, absolutely out of his senses."

In the category of Character and Integrity, Adams enjoys a ranking behind only Lincoln and Washington. "I like his integrity, put country's good before his own popularity," commented one poll panelist, and "stubbornly honest," observed another.

As president, Adams faced his share of troubles. The young nation was going through growing pains and was navigating uncertain diplomatic waters.

The United States attempted to steer a neutral course in the war between Britain and France, but the French expected some assistance from their former ally to whom they had delivered critical aid in the American War of Independence. When the favor was not returned, the French directed privateers to interfere with American shipping. Relations between the two nations ebbed as thoughts turned to the possibility of war.

The French government wanted a multimillion-dollar loan, a $250,000 bribe, and an apology for Adams's anti-French remarks made in his message to Congress before French officials would even discuss the problem with American diplomats. This became known as the infamous XYZ Affair. The three letters represented the three French diplomats, names withheld, who were to be paid the bribe. Adams was furious and ordered the arming of all United States shipping. He initiated a building program for the navy. The Department of the Navy was established in that same year, 1798. Many enraged Americans demanded war against France, as did most of Adams's own Federalist Party members who had a built-in bias in favor of Britain. To Adams's great credit, he prudently resisted those clamoring for war and instead persisted with diplomacy. The matter was settled peacefully and honorably in 1799, thereby avoiding war.

France recognized American neutrality with the signing of the Convention of 1800, and relations were off to a fresh start—clearly a coup for the president. This episode further demonstrated his strength of character, his courage, and his independence.

Another of Adams's achievements was the 1799 passage of the Logan Act, which outlawed diplomacy by private individuals without authorization by the government.

Discussion of the Adams presidency would not be complete without reference to the notorious Alien and Sedition Acts. These acts were passed by Congress and signed by Adams as a result of deteriorating relations with France and the fear that war was an increasing likelihood. The acts gave the federal government the right, by order of the president, to deport immigrant aliens, arrest American citizens, and silence newspapers if, by their statements, they defamed or brought disrepute to the federal government. This had the effect, as was intended, of silencing opposition to government policies during the period of diplomatic crisis. Even with a war scare, these acts went too far, especially since the country was not actually at war. The acts automatically expired after two years and were not renewed. However, these acts, while never declared unconstitutional, weigh against John Adams's reputation.

Like Washington before him with the 1794 Whiskey Rebellion, Adams had to deal with his own rebellion. Again it involved Pennsylvania farmers opposing federal taxes assessed on property. The Freis Rebellion, as it is known, also failed.

Adams was the first president to move into the then unfinished White House in the new federal capital of Washington, D.C.

In his final days in office, Adams signed, and the Senate approved, the peace agreement with France that he expended so much political capital to achieve.

On the eve of the first transition of executive power to the opposition, John Adams spent the waning hours and moments of his presidency appointing loyal Federalists to federal positions such as judgeships. These became known as the "midnight appointments." Since many of the appointees served at the pleasure of the president, Adams's successor, Thomas Jefferson, replaced many with his own supporters.

Given the relatively weak power of the presidential office in his day, Adams did exercise significant leadership on a few issues he viewed as important. In the crisis with France, he effected a favorable outcome by his tenacity, even though the public mood and his own party had opposed his efforts. This probably cost him reelection. The restoration of friendly relations with France no doubt helped his successor achieve the triumph of the Louisiana Purchase, a land deal that doubled the size of the United States.

On the other hand, Adams bowed to the wishes of his fellow Federalists in Congress and signed the dubious Alien and Sedition Acts.

When it came to his worst poll category, Political Skill, Adams came up short even by the standards of his own day. He was greatly encumbered by his blunt and sometimes offensive personality. His own war secretary, James McHenry, noted, "Whether he is spiteful, playful, witty, kind, cold, drunk, sober, angry, easy, stiff, jealous, cautious, confident, close, open, it is always in the wrong place or to the wrong person." One polled expert describes Adams this way: "Brilliant man with political flaws."

Adams's appointments are considered superior and include one of the greatest jurists, John Marshall, whom he appointed to the Supreme Court position of chief justice of the United States. Marshall served on the Supreme Court for the next thirty-four years, applying his Federalist views of a strong central government in many landmark Supreme Court cases. Marshall is credited with bolstering the power of the Supreme Court, making it a branch of government coequal with the executive and legislative branches.

Adams maintained Washington's cabinet throughout most of his administration, though some of the cabinet members undermined his policies and criticized him, raising the question of just how loyal they were to him.

In being rated fourteenth in overall ranking, Adams has received a largely favorable consideration. Respondents' praise, like "brave peacemaker" and "grumpy but good," dominates over criticism such as "muddled through a dangerous period" and "narrow provincial New Englander."

Adams served one term, being defeated for reelection by the Democratic-Republican candidate, the sitting vice president, Thomas Jefferson. This marked the first transition in political power from one politi-

cal party to the opposition party. When Adams and the Federalists surrendered the reins of government, without a revolution or military coup, it
proved that the new system of constitutional government could work.

After leaving the presidency, Adams retired to his Massachusetts home
and kept an active correspondence with friends, including some of his former political colleagues. Adams and Jefferson resumed their previous cordial relationship in their postpresidential years.

This Founding Father and patriot lived to be the oldest of any president, age ninety. All the more extraordinary is that at age eighty-nine he
was the only president ever to see a son sworn in as president (John Quincy
Adams, in 1825).

Adams's life closed on one of the most astounding coincidences in history. After a long life filled with accomplishment, Adams died on July 4,
1826. His last words were "Thomas Jefferson still survives." Jefferson,
however, had in fact died earlier that day. The only two signers of the Declaration of Independence to become president, Adams and Jefferson, both
died on the fiftieth anniversary of the signing of the nation's founding document. Many Americans, then as well as now, view this as a sign that America was blessed with Divine Protection.

Thomas Jefferson

1801–1809
3rd President

Overall Ranking: 4

★

Leadership Qualities: 6
Accomplishments and Crisis Management: 5
Political Skill: 5
Appointments: 4
Character and Integrity: 7

*I think this is the most extraordinary collection of talent, of human knowl-
edge, that has ever been gathered together at the White House, with the possible exception of when Thomas Jefferson dined alone.*

> —John F. Kennedy, address at a White House dinner and
> reception honoring winners of the Nobel Prize, 1962

Thomas Jefferson would have been extraordinary enough had he only been a Virginia legislator, a member of Congress, a governor of Virginia, a minister to France, a secretary of state, a vice president, and the third president of the United States. Add to that author of the Declaration of Independence and founder of the University of Virginia. But all of this was only a part of Thomas Jefferson's world as farmer, lawyer, musician, writer, philosopher, architect, scientist, and inventor. Thomas Jefferson was the only Renaissance man to live in the White House.

The third of ten children, born on April 13, 1743, at Shadwell, near Charlottesville, in present-day Albemarle County, Virginia, he received a classical education and learned to play the violin. At fourteen, Jefferson, the oldest son, inherited the family estate and became head of the family when his father died. He studied law after graduating from the College of William and Mary, was admitted to the Virginia bar, and served in the Virginia legislature from 1769 to 1775 and from 1776 to 1779.

In 1772 he married the prosperous widow Martha Skelton. They moved in to their new home at Monticello, which he later improved into one of the nation's residential showpieces and which included many of his own inventions. Monticello housed one of the largest private libraries in the country. Jefferson farmed his land, experimented in his gardens, and recorded meteorological observations.

During 1775 and 1776 he served in the Continental Congress and was active in the independence movement. He set forth the founding principles of a nation when he wrote the Declaration of Independence in 1776. He then devoted his energies to Virginia politics, molding the statute on religious freedom and fighting for rights of the citizens against the state government. Jefferson served as Virginia's governor from 1779 to 1781. After recovering from the death of his wife in 1782, he served in the Continental Congress in 1783 and 1784. There, he drafted a bill setting forth a plan for organizing the Northwest Territory. Congress passed this Land Ordinance in 1784, but it defeated by one vote a clause in his bill that would have excluded slavery from all new territory after 1800. (Jefferson's 1784 plan served as the basis for the Northwest Ordinance of 1787, which detailed how the territory north of the Ohio River would be governed and how states could be formed from the territory and which prohibited slavery from the Northwest Territory.)

Serving as minister to France from 1785 to 1789, he was greatly impressed with the French. When Jefferson returned to America a few months after the beginning of the French Revolution, he joined the successful fight to add the Bill of Rights as the first ten amendments to the Constitution, further guaranteeing rights of the people.

The six-foot-two-and-a-half, thin-figured Jefferson served as the first secretary of state under Washington in 1789. He resigned in 1793 after repeated political disagreements with Alexander Hamilton, who led the Federalist Party and whose advice Washington consistently heeded. Some of the basic disagreements with Washington included Jefferson's emphasis on states' rights rather than a strong central government, and his advocacy of a pro-French policy at the expense of Britain. Anti-Federalist supporters of these and other ideas coalesced into a political party, which in the early 1790s took as its name the Democratic-Republican Party.

To Jefferson's and almost everyone's surprise, the electoral college elected Jefferson vice president in 1796.

Jefferson detested some of what he saw happening in the Adams administration, particularly the Alien and Sedition Acts and the accretion of power to the federal government. As vice president he was powerless to change the course of these errant policies.

The "Revolution of 1800," as Jefferson called that next presidential election, was a particularly bitter campaign. At one extreme, the *Connecticut Courant*, a Federalist newspaper, warned the voters about what would happen if Jefferson was elected: "Murder, robbery, rape, adultery, and incest will all be openly taught and practiced, the air will be rent with the cries of the distressed, the soil will be soaked with blood, and the nation black with crimes." At the other extreme, the Democratic-Republicans claimed that John Adams planned to marry one of King George III's daughters and then rejoin the United States to Britain. Partisan politics had come of age.

The election of 1800 marked the first time in our nation's history a sitting president was voted out of office and the reins of the executive branch were turned over to the opposition. It proved that the new form of government could work. Federalist president John Adams was defeated, but the two Democratic-Republican candidates, Thomas Jefferson and Aaron Burr, both won in a tie. According to the Constitution, when the electoral college voting resulted in a tie, the House of Representatives was supposed to choose between the two winners. The House's choice would become president, and the other electoral-college winner would become vice president.

After lengthy deliberation and voting thirty-six times, the Federalist-dominated House finally selected Jefferson as president. As a direct result, Congress proposed and the states ratified the Twelfth Amendment to the Constitution, changing the way the president and vice president are elected. Beginning with the 1804 election, there has been separate balloting for president and vice president and the office the candidates are running for has been predetermined by each party before the general election. Jefferson was reelected president by a landslide in 1804.

In stark contrast to his impressive, public reputation, little is known about Jefferson's private thoughts. Because of his shy and reserved nature, he kept a tight lid on his personal life while at the same time writing insightful volumes about every other imaginable subject of concern to society. Jefferson's letter to John Adams gives us a hint at his inner thoughts: "He is happiest of whom the world says least, good or bad."

Jefferson's contemporary, Congressman Samuel Mitchill of New York, noted, "His dress and manners are very plain; he is grave, or rather sedate, but without any tincture of pomp, ostentation, or pride, and occasionally can smile, and both hear and relate humorous stories as well as any other man of social feelings. . . . He is more deeply versed in human nature and human learning than almost the whole tribe of his opponents and revilers."

His successor in the White House, James Madison, wrote, "It may be said of him as has been said of others that he was a 'walking library,' and what can be said of but few such prodigies, that Genius of Philosophy ever walked hand in hand with him."

Another president, John Quincy Adams, wrote of Jefferson: "His talents were of the highest order, his ambition transcendent, and his disposition to intrigue irrepressible."

Congressman William L. Smith of South Carolina had yet another opinion when he observed the following:

A ridiculous affectation of simplicity, stiling himself in the public papers and invitation cards, plain Thomas, and similar frivolities, a pretended outcry against Monarchy and Aristocracy may have had a momentary effect with the few ignorant and unsuspecting, but have long ago excited the derision of the many, who know that under the assumed cloak of humility lurks the most ambitious spirit, the most overweening pride and hauteur, and that externals of pure Democracy afford but a flimsy veil to the internal evidences of aristocratic splendor, sensuality and Epicureanism.

We do know that Jefferson had an easygoing manner. The redhead was not an eloquent speaker and, in fact, spoke with a slight lisp. He was sensitive to criticism, with much of it coming from the partisan opposition press. There was no subject off-limits for routine press criticism of a political figure in the early days of our nation. This prompted Jefferson to note, "No man will ever bring out of the Presidency the reputation which carries him into it." This certainly rings true again today in the case of our most recent presidents.

As little as is known about Jefferson the person, much is known about his beliefs. What kind of beliefs did Jefferson hold? Volumes would be necessary for a full presentation on the thoughts of this most intellectual of presidents. His core principles are set forth in the Declaration of Independence:

> We hold these truths to be self-evident, that all men are created equal, that they are endowed by their Creator with certain unalienable Rights, that among these are Life, Liberty and the pursuit of Happiness.—That to secure these rights, Governments are instituted among Men, deriving their just powers from the consent of the governed,—That whenever any Form of Government becomes destructive of those ends, it is the Right of the People to alter or abolish it, and to institute new Government, laying its foundation on such principles and organizing its powers in such form, as to them shall seem most likely to effect their Safety and Happiness.

His political spirit is embodied by his words engraved on his memorial in the nation's capital: "I have sworn upon the altar of God eternal hostility against every form of tyranny over the mind of man."

Foremost among his political beliefs was his confidence in the people. He wrote to James Madison, "The people are the only sure reliance for the preservation of our liberty." Countervailing his trust in the people is his mistrust of government, which he noted in a letter to a colleague: "The natural progress of things is for liberty to yield and government to gain ground."

A federal judiciary answerable to no one particularly disturbed him. In

1820 he wrote, "It is a very dangerous doctrine to consider the judges as the ultimate arbiters of all constitutional questions. It is one which would place us under the despotism of an oligarchy." A staunch supporter of freedom of the press, he wrote, "Where the press is free and every man able to read, all is safe."

One of Jefferson's proudest achievements was to effect strong language in the 1786 Virginia Statute of Religious Freedom, which made religious taxes illegal and allowed for religious freedom. He also supported inclusion of the First Amendment to the U.S. Constitution, which forbade Congress from passing laws setting up an official religion and laws prohibiting people from practicing their religion. Typifying his conviction, he noted, "It does me no injury for my neighbor to say there are twenty gods, or no God. It neither picks my pocket nor breaks my leg."

Even though Jefferson was on the political scene two centuries ago, his writings are extremely relevant to our current political debates. He supported balancing national budgets so that one generation would not unconscionably burden another generation. Term limits for federal officials and smaller government bureaucracy were other political viewpoints he championed. He favored states' rights over federal power unless the federal government had clear constitutional authority on a particular subject or issue. Concentration of power in a central government concerned him throughout his life. He opposed capital punishment and had an abiding mistrust of banks. Jefferson favored a strong national defense, writing, "Whatever enables us to go to war, secures our peace."

Even though he owned slaves on his Virginia plantation, Jefferson wrote to another Southerner prior to the adoption of the Constitution, "This abomination must have an end. And there is a superior bench reserved in Heaven for those who hasten it." There is little doubt of his sincerity to see the institution of slavery abolished, but he realized that there would never be a United States if the abolition of slavery were pressed. Indeed, he felt this was the one issue with the power to blow the Union apart even after adoption of the Constitution.

Few people in Jefferson's day imagined that the presidency, the executive branch of government, would evolve from a weak branch, subservient to the legislative branch, into the most formidable and powerful branch of government. Prophetically, Jefferson in 1789 wrote to Madison, "The executive in our government is not the sole, it is scarcely the principal object of my jealousy. The tyranny of the legislatures is the most formidable dread at the present and will be for many years. That period of the executive will come in its turn, but it will be at a remote period." Jefferson envisioned the development of a more powerful presidency, a development that, like any other concentration of power, he believed must be guarded against.

Jefferson, the first president to be inaugurated in Washington, D.C., took the oath of office as a widower. His daughter Martha served as hostess at the White House throughout his two terms.

As the new president took over as chief executive, the war with Tripoli thrust itself onto the national agenda. The war lasted from 1801 to 1805. Many countries, including the newly independent United States, had been paying tribute to the Barbary States in North Africa in order to prevent pirating of Mediterranean shipping. When Tripoli demanded increased tribute from the United States, Jefferson, who had been an opponent of paying any tribute, refused. He promptly dispatched American warships to successfully end the practice.

Arguably, Jefferson's greatest single achievement as president was the Louisiana Purchase in 1803. At three cents an acre, the United States bought enough land for the $15 million purchase price to double its size, encompassing most of the present-day states between the Mississippi River and the Rocky Mountains. Observed one poll participant, the "Louisiana Purchase alone makes him great." Jefferson had his doubts about his presidential power to make such a purchase of land. However, after the Senate approved, no one really complained about what was viewed as a bargain even at that time.

Jefferson was the first president to assert executive privilege when subpoenaed to testify at Aaron Burr's treason trial. While he refused to appear, he did release selected papers, and this established a precedent that insulates the executive branch from interference from the legislative and judicial branches.

The inquisitive Jefferson commissioned Meriwether Lewis and William Clark to undertake what became known as the Lewis and Clark Expedition. From 1804 to 1806 they explored the continent between the Missouri River and the Pacific Ocean, observing and reporting valuable new information about the geography, water routes, people, plant and animal life, and natural resources of that huge area.

Another milestone in America's struggle with the slavery issue was achieved when, in 1807, Jefferson signed the bill that abolished the slave trade effective January 1, 1808. This successfully ended the importation of slaves except for small numbers who were smuggled into the country right up until the Civil War.

The Embargo of 1807 to 1809 proved to be a rather poor attempt at retribution for British naval actions during Britain's war with France. British boarding of American ships and impressment of British-born American sailors provoked Jefferson to cut off all foreign trade. Unfortunately, the United States could not absorb such a financial shock as well as Great Britain could, and the embargo was partly lifted in 1809.

In political matters, Jefferson was masterful: "The consummate politician," noted one poll participant. Jefferson founded a political party, the Anti-Federalists, later renamed Democratic-Republicans, which was formed of factions that favored less federal power and more rights residing with the individual states. Jefferson and the Democratic-Republicans also had an affinity with France and the French Revolution and a matching skepticism of British intentions.

Jefferson's success was a result of his practicality. He disagreed with many of the policies and tendencies of the Washington administration, especially after he resigned the office of secretary of state in 1793. George Washington was beyond criticism, however, until near the end of his presidency. So Jefferson led the partisan fire against Washington's vulnerable vice president, John Adams. Jefferson challenged Adams in the presidential election of 1796 and fell only three electoral votes short.

So successful was Jefferson's political maneuvering that Adams and the Federalists gradually faded into political extinction, never again to have a Federalist elected president. Jefferson the politician knew that the abolition of the slave trade was possible, but that the abolition of slavery itself could not come about without breaking apart the young nation.

As a politician, he combined ideological theory with practical politics. This enabled him to be successful in accomplishing what he did, all within the limits of constitutionally designated executive power.

Our poll participants conclude that his appointments were of first-rate quality, and they rank Jefferson fourth in this category. James Madison served as an outstanding secretary of state and later was elected president. Treasury Secretary Albert Gallatin, a Swiss immigrant, was without peer in financial matters, reducing the national debt even while making the Louisiana Purchase and conducting a war with Tripoli, truly an extraordinary achievement.

The polled experts describe Jefferson as "the greatest intellectual president," an "advocate for Empire and Liberty," a "visionary," and "the philosopher President and spokesman for America's destiny." A small number of poll participants depart from overall praise by commenting: "Better theorist than president"; "Brilliant, but duplicitous and bad administrator"; and "Presidency perhaps overrated because of other accomplishments."

After leaving the presidency on March 4, 1809, the "Renaissance man, philosopher-king," as one polled expert labels Jefferson, looked forward to retirement at Monticello. Heavily in debt because of his elegant lifestyle, he eventually sold his personal library in 1815 to the Library of Congress to pay off most of that debt.

The former president carried on a vigorous correspondence with many of the renowned figures of his day, typically writing in excess of a thousand letters a year. Jefferson took particular interest and pride in his involvement in founding the University of Virginia at Charlottesville in 1819. Not only did he design the buildings, but he also assisted in composing the course of instruction.

Jefferson and John Adams both died on July 4, 1826—the fiftieth anniversary of the date they both joined in signing the nation's founding document.

The inscription that Jefferson chose for his tombstone perhaps best shows what he thought were his most noteworthy accomplishments: "Here was buried Thomas Jefferson, Author of the Declaration of American Independence, of the Statute of Virginia for Religious Freedom, and Father of the University of Virginia." There is no mention of his presidency.

Thomas Jefferson remains one of the enduring and timeless figures in American history embodying the spirit of the American nation. No president has displayed the variety of talents as has Jefferson.

Former U.S. president James Madison rendered his tribute when he wrote, "He lives and will live in the memory and gratitude of the wise and good, as a luminary of Science, as a votary of liberty, as a model of patriotism, and as a benefactor of human kind."

JAMES MADISON

1809–1817
4TH PRESIDENT

OVERALL RANKING: 10

★

Leadership Qualities: 14
Accomplishments and Crisis Management: 14
Political Skill: 15
Appointments: 11
Character and Integrity: 6

He had as much to do as any man in framing the constitution, and as much to do as any man in administering it.

—Daniel Webster

The Father of the Constitution is a title that the modest fourth president, James Madison, did not wish to claim. Nonetheless, it is undeniably true the U.S. Constitution and the Bill of Rights added to it a few years later were drafted and debated by Madison and bear his everlasting imprint. One of the great political thinkers of the ages, he distilled political theory and breathed life into one of history's most durable political documents. James Madison was another of the nation's Founding Fathers to reach the presidency, and no president understood the Constitution better than he.

Born at Port Conway, King George County, Virginia, on March 16, 1751, he would become part of the "Virginia dynasty" of presidents, both preceded and followed by a Virginian in the White House. Shortly after his birth, the family returned to the family homestead plantation at Montpelier, Orange County, Virginia, where Madison lived for the rest of his life.

The blue-eyed, five-foot-four, brown-haired Madison graduated in 1771 from the College of New Jersey at Princeton (renamed Princeton University in 1896) and decided to study law.

Madison served in the Virginia legislature during 1776 and 1777 and helped write the Virginia state constitution in 1776. As the fledgling new nation and its constituent thirteen states drifted on the tempestuous waves of chaos and visionless national purpose, Madison became a delegate to the Annapolis Convention in 1786 and to the more successful Constitutional Convention in Philadelphia in 1787. Serving as a member of the Congress of the Confederation in 1787 and 1788, he wrote many of *The Federalist* essays proclaiming the need for a stronger central government.

Madison earned a reputation for honesty, integrity, and intelligence that was the envy of his peers. Jefferson wrote of him, "I can say conscientiously that I do not know in the world a man of purer integrity, more dispassionate, disinterested, and devoted to genuine Republicanism; nor could I in the whole scope of America and Europe point out an abler head."

A Massachusetts congressman, Fisher Ames, thought a little less of Madison's strength of character: "I think him a good man and an able man, but he has rather too much theory, and wants that discretion which men of business commonly have. He is also very timid and seems evidently to want manly firmness and energy of character."

There is no real disagreement that Madison had a keen sense of morality and sobriety. He was a man of great principle. Madison ranked an exceptional sixth in our poll in Character and Integrity, his best category.

Though polite and affable, Madison was not good at making conversation, unless among a small group of his friends when he would ease up with some risqué humor. His social graces were denounced by the wife of a colleague: "Mr. Madison, a gloomy stiff creature, they say is clever in Congress, but out of it he had nothing engaging or even bearable in his manners—the most unsociable creature in existence." There is perhaps some degree of truth in the woman's exaggerated disaffection.

Madison the political thinker had opinions and ideas that form the constitutional basis of our nation. Mindful of the natural tension between power and liberty, referring to the Constitution, he wrote, "Every word decides a question between power and liberty." He maintained a suspicion of power concentrated in any form. In his series of *Federalist* essays, he wrote, "The accumulation of all power, legislative, executive, and judiciary, in the same hands, whether of one, a few, or many, and whether hereditary, self-appointed, or elective, may justly be pronounced the very definition of tyranny." The possibility of a majority treading upon the rights of a minority, even in a democratic form of government, preoccupied him in seeing to it that the rights of minorities were secure.

Critical to his view of government are the concepts of a balance of power and a system of checks and balances. He wrote, "In all political societies, different interests and parties arise out of the nature of things, and the great art of politicians lies in making them checks and balances to each other." This was essential to protect the rights and liberty of a free people.

Madison wrote, "All power is liable to be abused." His belief was a driving force in converting the theory of a constitution into a viable working government whose function is to "impartially" secure to each citizen his or her rights and property.

Even after establishment of a working constitutional government, Madison felt that freedom must be vigilantly protected not just from the obvious threats but also from a growing government power. He stated, "Since the general civilization of mankind, I believe there are more instances of the abridgement of the freedom of the people by gradual and silent encroachments of those in power than by violent and sudden usurpations." Madison's belief in freedom of religious views and practice and his concept that religion flourishes better without government support are imprinted in the Constitution.

Even though Madison owned a Virginia plantation that included slaves, he nonetheless desired to rid the nation of the slavery evil, writing to a colleague, "Our opinions agree as to the evil, moral, political, and economical, of slavery."

Madison's fiscal conservatism is evidenced by his conviction, similar to those of his predecessors, that debt is to be retired rather than extended. On this subject he wrote a fellow Virginian, Henry Lee, "I go on the principle that a public debt is a public curse."

Ahead of his time on the subject of women's rights, Madison believed that a woman's talents need not be confined to domestic affairs of the home. He observed in a letter to a friend, "The capacity of the female mind for studies of the highest order cannot be doubted, having been sufficiently illustrated by its works of genius, of erudition, and of science." Surprising for a man who grew up in the 1700s.

The great test for Madison's presidency came in the form of foreign affairs, particularly the War of 1812. In the events leading up to the war, Great Britain and France, at war with each other, had violated American sovereignty by seizure of American shipping. British impressment of American sailors had added to the grievance of the United States against Great Britain. Madison enforced the Non-Intercourse Act of 1809, which had been signed by President Jefferson three days before he left office and which permitted trade with all countries except Great Britain and France. This modified the previous Embargo Act, which had prevented all foreign trade. Like the Embargo Act, the Non-Intercourse Act failed to have an effect on its intended targets, Great Britain and France.

President Madison and Congress soon tried another approach, namely, the Macon's Bill No. 2 in 1810. This law reopened commerce with Great Britain and France; it provided, however, that if either Great Britain or France recognized U.S. neutrality and respected American sailors and shipping, the United States would impose a trade embargo on the other warring nation. This produced results. The French gave the appearance of having agreed to respect American neutrality, and the United States promptly reimposed a trade embargo against Great Britain.

American-British relations took another blow when Madison had reason to suspect the British of fomenting an Indian uprising in America. Future president William Henry Harrison received credit and a lasting reputation as a national war hero in 1811 when he led forces that crushed a growing confederacy of Indians. In mid-1812 Madison sought and obtained a declaration of war against the British in order to prevent further national humiliation. This became known as the War of 1812, referred to as "Mr. Madison's War" by his political enemies. As the election of 1812 approached, Madison favored continuing the war; he won reelection.

The United States muddled through the war and in 1813 even managed to burn government buildings and the governor's residence at York (Toronto), Canada. But the United States suffered a severe setback when the British, in retaliation, invaded the nation's capital at Washington in 1814 and burned government buildings, including the White House, Capitol, and Library of Congress. Madison had to flee. Dolley Madison, one of the most popular first ladies, saved precious documents and portraits by taking them with her.

The biggest battle of the war, a smashing victory for the United States under General Andrew Jackson, did not figure in the war's final outcome. The famous Battle of New Orleans was fought on January 8, 1815, but the Treaty of Ghent ending hostilities was signed a few weeks before, on December 24, 1814. The news had traveled too slowly to avoid further bloodshed. The success of the United States in the battle, however, restored national pride to a euphoria not seen since victory in the Revolutionary War. Jackson achieved a popularity so immense that fourteen years later it carried him into the White House.

Most of the criticism lodged against Madison's presidency by our polled experts centers around the War of 1812, and that is probably why they rank Madison only fourteenth in Accomplishments and Crisis Management. Typical comments include these: "Failed to prevent war [during the period] 1811–1812" and "Blunders led to ineptly led and unnecessary War of 1812."

On the domestic front, Madison went along with the 1816 chartering of the Second Bank of the United States (the first national bank's charter had expired in 1811) and with higher tariffs on imported woolen, cotton, and iron goods as well as paper, leather, and other products that competed with American manufactured goods. Both of these measures were advanced by the dying Federalist Party. On his last day in office, he vetoed a bill which provided for a system of roads and canals to be built to facilitate commerce between the states. Agonizing over the measure, Madison found no power in the Constitution permitting such an activity by the federal government. He concluded that this matter must be left to the various states.

After his second term Madison retired, turning over the presidency to his fellow Virginian James Monroe, whom he had supported.

Madison showed courage as president, particularly in his leadership during the first war in which American national survival was at stake. He is one of the few chief executives who as a wartime president did not tread on the Constitution. In contrast, other presidents when confronted with crises involving national survival took shortcuts, rightly or wrongly, around the Constitution: President Abraham Lincoln during the Civil War spent money not yet authorized by Congress, imposed martial law, and suspended the right of habeas corpus; and Franklin Roosevelt ordered the questionable internment of Japanese Americans during World War II. John Adams, not even in wartime but only in a war-scare situation, signed the Alien and Sedition Acts, which shut down opposition presses and jailed administration opponents. Madison at the time in 1798 wrote to Jefferson, "The Alien bill proposed in the Senate is a monster that must forever disgrace its parents." A year later he again wrote to Jefferson, "Perhaps it is a universal truth that the loss of liberty at home is to be charged to provisions against danger, real or pretended, from abroad."

To his everlasting credit, Madison did not muzzle the press, appropriate private property, or jail civilians—even as the British came ashore at Chesapeake Bay and burned the Capitol at Washington.

His principled leadership is again evident in domestic matters when, as his second term was ending, he vetoed a bill enabling the federal government to build a system of roads and canals. He believed that, despite pressuring from obvious commercial interests, this was a matter for the states to enter into and agree upon. Poll participants ranked Madison fourteenth in the category of Leadership Qualities, praising him as "good under war stress," "brainy, reliable," and possessed of "intellectual ability." Some disagreed, describing Madison as being "indecisive" and a "weak executive."

As a cofounder of the Democratic-Republican Party with Jefferson, Madison revealed excellent organizing skills in uniting factions under the new party umbrella. For his day, he possessed uncommon political skill. He worked well with Congress. Even though Congress was controlled by his party, this in no way assured a good working relationship and government accomplishments. He used tact in his political dealings and was attentive to political needs. His affable and soft-spoken manner aided him throughout his political career.

At the conclusion of the War of 1812, Madison enjoyed great popularity both in Congress and with the people. Like Jefferson, he could have had a third term for the asking, but declined.

Madison's appointments were exceptional. Included were his secretary of state, James Monroe, who became his successor in the White House, and the legendary Albert Gallatin, who as secretary of the treasury was a holdover from the Jefferson administration. Gallatin continued to call for a balanced budget. Many consider Joseph Story, appointed to the Supreme Court by Madison, to be one of the giants of the Court. He followed the trail set by nationalist John Marshall. Story helped strengthen the role of the U.S. Supreme Court by writing its landmark decision affirming the Supreme Court's right to review the constitutionality of state court decisions.

In achieving the overall ranking of tenth place in the poll, Madison received acknowledgment as "probably the most gifted in terms of political theory" and yet some criticism as "great in other roles, but not as president."

After his presidency, Madison retired to his Montpelier plantation in 1817. Like his nearby neighbor Jefferson, Madison experienced financial difficulties, in his case owing to adversities in growing tobacco and wheat on his plantation. He did manage his own Virginia plantation and, of course, had slaves. Madison felt that the Southern economy could never keep up with that of the North because of the adverse economic and moral effect the institution of slavery had on the South.

When Jefferson died in 1826, Madison took over as rector of the University of Virginia, succeeding his old friend. He also participated in the constitutional revisions in the Virginia state convention in 1829. He maintained an interest in the affairs of the nation. In 1832 a specially called South Carolina convention adopted an Ordinance of Nullification in response to a tariff act of the federal government and threatened to secede. Madison, even though a longtime proponent of states' rights, condemned the actions of the South Carolina legislature, which had passed laws supporting the Ordinance of Nullification.

Madison saw resettlement of free-born and emancipated former slaves in Liberia as a possible solution to the slavery question. The American Colonization Society actively engaged in the resettlement attempt. Madison was selected as its president in 1833. The well-intentioned program, while around for some time, eventually fizzled.

Madison wrote *Notes on the Federal Convention of 1787* while in retirement. Historians consider it the definitive version of the proceedings. This work is consulted by judges and scholars alike on constitutional issues to this very day.

Madison lived to be eighty-five, fourth longest-living U.S. president after John Adams, Herbert Hoover, and Ronald Reagan. He left a legacy of courageous leadership as president, guided by the principles of the Constitution, which he played so large a part in framing. All Americans owe him a great debt of gratitude.

JAMES MONROE

1817–1825
5TH PRESIDENT
OVERALL RANKING: 13

★

Leadership Qualities: 15
Accomplishments and Crisis Management: 13
Political Skill: 16
Appointments: 8
Character and Integrity: 13

National honor is national property of the highest value.

—James Monroe

These words contained in Monroe's first inaugural address set the tone for his presidency.

Whether in service to his country as the Revolutionary War hero, the patriot, the legislator, the diplomat, the cabinet member, or the president, the friendly and unassuming James Monroe personified that quality of honor which he found essential in a nation.

Though not the last native of Virginia to serve as president—as William Henry Harrison, John Tyler, Zachary Taylor and Woodrow Wilson would later serve—Monroe was the last of the "Virginia dynasty," the four Virginians among the first five presidents. He was also the last of the Founding Fathers to serve as president.

Monroe was born on April 28, 1758, near Colonial Beach, Westmoreland County, Virginia, the oldest son of five children to reach maturity. His face featured blue eyes and a deep cleft in his chin.

He entered the College of William and Mary in 1774. The six-foot-tall, muscular young patriot quit college to join the Continental army and served in it from 1776 to 1780. He participated in such famous Revolutionary War events as the 1776 crossing of the Delaware with Washington and the Battle of Trenton, in which he was severely wounded. Among those who suffered in the bitter winter of 1777–78 at Valley Forge, he ultimately rose to the rank of lieutenant colonel. Commander in chief George Washington commended him: "He has, in every instance, maintained the reputation of a brave, active, and sensible officer."

After the war, Monroe studied law with Thomas Jefferson as his mentor and became a practicing Virginia attorney. Serving in the Virginia assembly and Continental Congress, he married Elizabeth Kortright and moved to Charlottesville and then to Ash Lawn, establishing this as the family estate.

The marriage produced two daughters and a son who died in infancy. His younger daughter was the first woman married in the White House.

As a U.S. senator from Virginia elected in 1790, he allied himself with the Anti-Federalists, opposing the establishment of a permanent standing army and advocating the opening of Senate proceedings to the public, which came to pass in 1794. President Washington appointed him minister to France in 1794. However, Washington reprimanded Monroe, who espoused a very sympathetic view of France. Monroe had privately denounced the Jay Treaty and did not actively support the treaty; nor did he defend it in his communications with French officials. The president expressed fear that Monroe was jeopardizing American neutrality and recalled him in 1796. This left Monroe bitter over his treatment by Washington.

After he left his post and returned to the United States in 1797, the former minister defended his actions by writing a book entitled *A View of the Conduct of the Executive, in the Foreign Affairs of the United States.* In it, he criticized Washington for endangering relations with France. This was prophetic, for within two years Washington's successor, John Adams, found himself in a position of preparing for a possible war with France.

Monroe served as governor of Virginia from 1799 to 1802 and then, as a special envoy together with Minister Robert Livingston, skillfully negotiated the Louisiana Purchase in 1803. President Jefferson later in 1803 appointed Monroe minister to Great Britain. In 1807 he returned to his law practice.

Monroe was again elected governor of Virginia in 1811, but later the same year President Madison tapped him as secretary of state, the launching pad for the presidency. Four of Washington's first five successors served in that cabinet slot. Monroe served with distinction in the post from 1811 to 1817, doubling as secretary of war during 1814 to 1815.

Monroe's election as president in 1816 on the Democratic-Republican Party ticket was by a landslide over the Federalist candidate. He was reelected without formal opposition in 1820, joining only Washington in the honor. However, one elector from New Hampshire took it upon himself to ignore the voice of the people from his state and voted for John Quincy Adams. Some say the elector disagreed with Monroe's policies; others say that he wished to reserve to Washington the honor of a unanimous electoral vote. Although we may never know the answer, the former theory is more likely. The final electoral vote was 231 to 1. It is still the greatest electoral landslide in American presidential election history since the adoption of the Twelfth Amendment, which provided for the electoral college's separate balloting for the president and vice president, effective with the election of 1804.

Monroe enjoyed an exceptional reputation for honesty among his contemporaries. His straightforwardness, sincerity, courtesy, and reserved, low-key style served him well in the presidency. Jefferson observed of Monroe,

"Turn his soul wrong side outwards and there is not a speck on it."

While Monroe's integrity and motives were never questioned, Aaron Burr attacked candidate Monroe as "one of the most improper and incompetent that could be selected. Naturally dull and stupid; extremely illiterate; indecisive to a degree that would be incredible to one who did not know him; pusillanimous, and of course hypocritical; has no opinion on any subject and will always be under the government of the worst men. . . . [A]s a lawyer, Monroe was far below mediocrity. He never rose to the honor of trying a cause of the value of a hundred pounds." However, former president John Quincy Adams eulogized Monroe: "A mind, anxious and unwearied in the pursuit of truth and right, patient of inquiry, patient of contradiction, courteous even in the collision of sentiment, sound in its ultimate judgments, and firm in its final conclusions."

Monroe's supporters vastly outnumbered his critics. One was Vice President John C. Calhoun, who praised Monroe: "Tho' not brilliant, few men were his equals in wisdom, firmness and devotion to the country. He had a wonderful intellectual patience; and could above all men, that I ever knew, when called on to decide an important point, hold the subject immovably fixed under his attention, until he had mastered it in all of its relations. It was mainly to this admirable quality that he owed his highly accurate judgment. I have known many more rapid in reaching a conclusion, but few with a certainty of unerring."

A firm believer in states' rights and limited federal government, he advocated deferring to the states those rights not specifically granted to the federal government. Monroe's concern that a federal government's powers might naturally and gradually tend to grow beyond those provided in the Constitution prompted him to carefully scrutinize actions by the federal government. This reflects a continuity in viewpoint from Jefferson and Madison. Monroe was proud of a federal government that did not appropriate increased powers to itself.

Monroe opposed the concept of a standing army. He believed as he said on one occasion, "Preparation for war is a constant stimulus to suspicion and ill-will." Citizens militias, he maintained, satisfied the need for a free people to defend itself.

Monroe's second inaugural address in 1821 reflected, for its time, an advanced view on American Indians, when he said of them, "They have claims on the magnanimity and, I may add, on the justice of this nation which we must all fill. We should become their real benefactors, we should perform the office of their Great Father, the endearing title which they emphatically give to the Chief Magistrate of our Union."

On the issue of slavery, Monroe's opinions were typical of those who wished to end the practice without civil war or breakup of the Union. He believed the answer was resettlement in Africa, particularly a new nation formed for the purpose, Liberia. He, like the other Virginia plantation owners who preceded him as president, did not like slavery. His views on resettlement as an eventual solution were, in fact, enlightened for the 1820s. To this day, Liberia's capital is named Monrovia in his honor.

Monroe excelled in his handling of foreign relations, as few presidents have. Monroe not only avoided diplomatic pitfalls as had Washington and Adams, but also produced astounding diplomatic successes. Tensions were eased with our northern neighbor by the 1818 Rush-Bagot Agreement with Great Britain wherein both countries agreed to strictly limit their naval forces on the Great Lakes. Ever since, limits on military forces on the United States–Canada borders have grown, thus enabling the United States and Canada to develop a special relationship and, by 1871, unfortified borders. Further, the Convention of 1818 fixed part of the United States–Canada border at the 49th parallel and provided for the joint occupation of Oregon Country for ten years. It also resolved the thorny issue of fishing rights between the United States and Canada.

Next, Monroe turned his attention to acquiring East Florida from Spain. This had a twofold purpose: first, to increase United States territory and, second, to eliminate the presence of a European power on the United States' border.

After Florida was ceded from Spain to the United States by the terms of the Adams-Onis Treaty of 1819, the nation's leaders still worried about European influence and intervention in the Western Hemisphere. Most of Spain's Latin American colonies had recently rebelled and had set up independent countries. The United States wanted to prevent Spain from possibly retaking them and to discourage other European powers from seizing them. Monroe consulted with his secretary of state, John Quincy Adams (who eventually became his future successor in the White House), and with former president Thomas Jefferson. As a result, he enunciated a policy we know today as the Monroe Doctrine, warning European powers to keep their intrigues out of the Western Hemisphere and pledging, in turn, to keep out of European disputes and wars. At almost the same time, Great Britain for trade reasons made clear its own demands that the new Latin American countries remain independent—and had ready its powerful navy to back up this policy. The Monroe Doctrine is a landmark in United States foreign policy. The Latin American part of it is still followed to this very day and represents one of the greatest peaceful foreign policy achievements in United States history, enshrining Monroe as one of the great presidents in the handling of foreign affairs.

On the domestic front, early in his administration in 1817, Monroe was faced with Seminole Indians crossing the border from Spanish Florida to massacre American citizens in Georgia. After Spain ignored Monroe's requests to put an end to the raids, the president dispatched General Andrew Jackson to protect American citizens and property. Jackson solved the problem by attacking the Seminoles in Florida, defeating them, and seizing Spanish posts. The Spanish governor was overthrown and quickly packed for Havana, Cuba. Jackson executed two British subjects for instigating the murderous Seminole attacks on Americans.

Jackson's actions caused a firestorm in Washington, with the cabinet and Congress divided. Monroe backed his general, took appropriate diplomatic measures, and the matter was soon resolved. Jackson's victory in Florida undoubtedly had its effect on the Spanish and facilitated the agreement to transfer the rest of Spanish Florida to the United States.

Congress enacted the Missouri Compromise of 1820 during Monroe's presidency. Monroe favored admission of Missouri to the Union, even as a slave state. The Missouri Compromise provided for admission of Missouri as a slave state and Maine as a free state, maintaining an equal balance between the number of free and slave states. Additionally, it prohibited slavery in a huge part of the Louisiana Purchase north of a defined line and permitted slavery south of that line.

Monroe followed the lead and constitutional beliefs of Jefferson and Madison on the recurring issue of federal funding of roads and canals. He encouraged the adoption of an amendment in order to authorize the federal government to take action reserved for the states. Monroe, who viewed as constitutionally proper a federal government that did not attempt to enhance its own power, said, "No other example can be found of a Government exerting its influence to lessen its own powers."

In 1819 there was a financial panic, partly as a result of a collapse in foreign demand for American cotton and other farm products with a resulting rapid fall in American land values and partly as a result of the issuing of banknotes to finance the War of 1812. This became the nation's first serious economic depression since the Constitution was ratified, and it lasted for three years. Presidents did not take direct action to alleviate national financial stress until Franklin Roosevelt broke precedent to act in the Great Depression of the 1930s. In any event, Monroe in 1819 could do little, if anything, to affect economic activity.

Monroe showed not only leadership with his declaration of the Monroe

Doctrine, but also a good measure of vision. Without firing a single shot, he effectively demonstrated America's willingness to prevent European interference and further colonization in the Western Hemisphere. Rarely in history has such a policy statement been so effective—carrying into the present-day nuclear age. After all, the Monroe Doctrine was merely a statement by the president of the United States; it was not a treaty or convention. In an era of weak presidential power, Monroe used an area of exclusive federal government interest and power—foreign policy—and took a strong leadership position.

Most of Monroe's leadership, and consequently achievements, related to foreign affairs. The acquisition of Florida from Spain is another example, securing additional territory and a secure southern border. Since the Revolution, America and Great Britain were almost constantly at odds. However, Monroe arranged for the settlement of the last of the major difficulties, enabling the two countries to bury the hatchet. This settlement meant the demilitarization and disarmament on America's border with Canada which continues to this very day.

Domestic affairs were quite another matter for Monroe. Typical for presidents of his time, he deferred to Congress and applied a "states' rights" policy on such domestic issues as the proposed building of roads and canals, which he vetoed. He was also in the background in the Missouri Compromise controversy. Monroe had doubts about federal authority to legislate on the issue of slavery in the territories. However, fearing that his veto could precipitate a civil war, Monroe signed the legislation.

Monroe produced a significant accomplishment with one polled expert noting "Good in foreign policy" and another observing "Missouri Compromise and American System" to his credit.

In politics, Monroe's polite personality enabled him to resolve problems and find areas of agreement. While principled, he attempted to build a consensus and accommodate opponents as well as supporters. He was so successful at consensus building that the opposition Federalist Party vanished during his presidency. By the end of his presidency, although there was growing sectionalism, there were no opposition national parties or national factions for the only time in the history of the United States since the adoption of the Constitution. The period from 1817 to 1825 was called the Era of Good Feelings. Monroe believed that political parties and partisanship tended to disrupt the union of the nation, rather than assist it.

The polled experts gave Monroe his highest ranking for his appointments. In foreign affairs Monroe received major assistance from Secretary of State John Quincy Adams. His cabinet also included the exceptional secretary of war John C. Calhoun and two talented attorneys general, Richard Rush and William Wirt. As one poll participant concludes, Monroe was "effective in selecting good people and kept balance."

Monroe enjoys an overall ranking in the upper third of all presidents. Favorable evaluations include comments like "unprecedented unity" and "one of our most underestimated presidents. Largely responsible for 'Era of Good Feelings,' " while a small number of negative comments follow the theme of "do-nothing."

After leaving the presidency, he retired to his Virginia home at Oak Hill, near Leesburg. There, Monroe was able to call upon his close friends, Jefferson and Madison. He shared much in common with the two former presidents. With both, he served as a regent of the University of Virginia, and with Madison he served as a cochairman of the 1829 Virginia state constitutional convention.

Monroe also joined fellow Virginians Jefferson and Madison in suffering financial hardship after leaving office. All three had to sell parts of their estate to help pay off heavy debts accrued while in office. In Monroe's case, he was required to sell all of his land including his Virginia estate and live with one of his daughters in New York City. He had pressed the government without success for reimbursement of expenses he had incurred while entertaining as a diplomat in Spain and France.

Incredibly, Monroe died on July 4, 1831, five years to the day after the passing of Adams and Jefferson. Three consecutive presidents died on July 4, surely a sign that the young nation was blessed by Divine Providence.

Some presidents have demonstrated vision in foreign policy; others have demonstrated success. However, Monroe enjoys a special place in American history for the unparalleled legacy of both vision and success in the foreign affairs of the nation.

John Quincy Adams

1825–1829
6th President

Overall Ranking: 18

★

Leadership Qualities: 20
Accomplishments and Crisis Management: 20
Political Skill: 25
Appointments: 12
Character and Integrity: 4

His disposition is as perverse and mulish as that of his father.

—James Buchanan

Like his father, John Quincy Adams acted with fierce independence, reaching the point of antagonizing and alienating not only enemies—but even supporters.

Both Adamses were one-term presidents. Bitter personal attacks against each resulted in defeat for reelection. Neither attended the inauguration of his successor. John Quincy Adams followed in the basic political tenets of his father, believing in a strong, activist federal government. The younger Adams stated this clearly when as president he addressed Congress in his first annual message: "The great object of . . . civil government is the improvement of the condition of those who are parties to the social compact."

The second of four children and eldest son, John Quincy Adams was born to John and Abigail Adams on July 11, 1767. The family farm estate at Braintree (now Quincy), Massachusetts, was always home except when public duty called him away.

Accompanying his father on the various assigned diplomatic forays provided the younger Adams with a profitable educational experience. With each change in his father's diplomatic assignment, John Quincy Adams acquired knowledge of another European language and culture. As a young man, he grasped the fine and sophisticated art of diplomacy as developed and practiced in the capitals of Europe. This served him and his country well throughout his public service.

He graduated from Harvard in 1788, studied law, was admitted to the Massachusetts bar in 1790, and opened his own law office.

From 1794 to 1801, he served as a representative in several European countries, including the Netherlands and Prussia. In 1797 he married Louisa Johnson, a native of London, England, whom he originally met in France. (She was the daughter of an American diplomat and Englishwoman.) Four children were born of the marriage. As first lady, Louisa was criticized for not only her melancholy and withdrawn nature, but also for being foreign-born, especially British! She remains the only foreign-born first lady.

Adams served in the Massachusetts legislature, as United States senator from Massachusetts, and then in the Madison administration as minister to Russia and Great Britain where he led in negotiating an end to the War of 1812.

With the inauguration of President Monroe in 1817, Adams was appointed secretary of state. He served for the entire eight years of the Monroe administration and viewed the acquisition of Florida from Spain as his most significant achievement. Playing a key role in the formulation of the Monroe Doctrine and in settling outstanding disputes with Great Britain, he rates as one of the truly great secretaries of state. Characteristically, his appointments in the State Department were made on the basis of merit, rather than on patronage.

Adams was honored with the only dissenting electoral vote in the near unanimous reelection victory of Monroe in 1820.

The election of the five-foot-seven, 175-pound Adams to the presidency in 1824 occurred in a most bizarre fashion. Since the demise of the Federalist Party by about 1820, all candidates, including Adams, were Democratic-Republicans. The election of 1824 was one largely of personalities: Adams, Andrew Jackson, Henry Clay, and William Crawford. However, each candidate did represent a different sectional rivalry and differed only on varying degrees of support or opposition to a protective tariff, a national bank, and federal involvement in road and canal building.

Although Jackson received the most popular and electoral votes, none of the four candidates received a majority. As provided by the Constitution and the Twelfth Amendment, the House of Representatives was called on to select the president. Clay, one of the candidates who had been eliminated from the competition, threw his support to Adams and Adams became the sixth president of the United States. This is the only time in our history that a president was elected without a majority of electoral votes. It is ironic that John Quincy Adams, who as a U.S. senator two decades earlier had opposed adoption of the Twelfth Amendment, was eventually elected president by its application.

When Adams chose Clay to become secretary of state, this immediately brought cries from Jackson supporters who claimed that this was payback for Clay's support. Jackson's supporters vowed to avenge the injustice and made preparations for the next presidential election, even though Adams's term had only just begun.

A greater activist than his three immediate predecessors, Adams repeatedly and firmly condemned the evil of slavery. He wrote in 1820 in his diary, "Slavery is the great and foul stain upon the North American Union." A few months later he added, "It is, in truth, all perverted sentiment—mistaking labor for slavery and dominion for freedom." On the

House floor, while serving in Congress in 1843 after his presidency, he ignited antislavery forces with prophetic words: "If slavery must go by blood and war, let war come."

For his time, Adams had a remarkable understanding of the plight of the American Indians. During his service in the House of Representatives (1831–48), he said in Congress, "In your relations with the Indian tribes, you never declare war, although you do make and break treaties with them, whenever [it] happens to suit the purposes of the President and the majority of both houses of Congress."

He was ahead of his time with his views on women. Again, in Congress he spoke out: "Why does it follow that women are fitted for nothing but the cares of domestic life, for bearing children and cooking the food of a family? . . . I say women exhibit the most exalted virtue when they depart from the domestic circle and enter on the concerns of their country, of humanity, and of their God!"

Like many political figures of the current day, Adams had a dislike for the press. Referring to journalists, he wrote in his diary, "They are a sort of assassins who sit with loaded blunderbusses at the corner of streets and fire them off for hire or for sport at any passenger they select."

Known for his independence, honesty, and courage, Adams exhibited a character and integrity that any modern president would envy. However, Adams, like his father, paid a political price. With his aloof manner and his frosty, beady black eyes, the nearly bald Adams appeared distant and harsh in his dealings even with friends.

The one charge on his character has been the "corrupt bargain," as his opponents called it, with Clay to secure the presidency. More than likely Clay backed Adams through elimination of the other two candidates. Crawford was a physically weak and ill man, and Clay harbored a combined dislike and distrust of Jackson. Clay viewed Adams as a known and safe quantity. As for Adams, he likely, without prior commitment, named Clay as secretary of state both in order to widen his own political base in order to govern more effectively and to utilize the very considerable talents which Clay brought to any position he held. This view is supported by the importance Adams placed on honesty when he wrote: "I had much rather you should impute to me error of judgment than the smallest deviation from sincerity."

Clay was favorably impressed with Adams, noting: "I have found in him since I have been associated with him in the executive government as little to censure and condemn as I could have expected in any man."

Needless to say, Adams was not without his critics. William Henry Harrison, the ninth president, commented, "It is said he is a disgusting man to do business. Coarse, Dirty and clownish in his address and stiff and abstracted in his opinions, which are drawn from books exclusively." Congressman Samuel D. Ingham of Pennsylvania stated, "He was educated as a monarchist, has always been hostile to popular government, and particularly to its great bulwark the right of suffrage, . . . he affected to become a Republican only to pervert and degrade the Democratic party; and to pave the way for such a change in the Constitution as would establish the United States an aristocratic and hereditary government."

In Character and Integrity, Adams rates an exceptional fourth in the poll behind only Lincoln, Washington, and his father, John Adams. "Unquestioned integrity!" remarks one polled expert, reflecting a consensus of opinion.

In 1825 Adams took over the reins of a rapidly growing nation, on the upswing from the modest depression of 1819 to 1822. The issue of federal involvement in internal improvements, especially roads and canals, did not trouble John Quincy Adams as it had his predecessors Madison and Monroe. In fact, he advocated an ambitious plan for road and canal construction. Congress went along only with a westward road known as the Cumberland Road and one waterway, the Chesapeake and Ohio Canal.

Adams also proposed a national university located in Washington, D.C., and an astronomical observatory. In addition, he favored maintaining the charter of the national bank. This reflected Adams's developing nationalistic view of the country and the way the federal government should function, clearly a departure from the Jefferson, Madison and Monroe path of nation development.

In order to protect domestic manufacturing mostly in New England and New York, Adams obtained passage of a high tariff on imported manufactures. This proved extremely unpopular in the South and West, and the Tariff of 1828 became known in those areas as the Tariff of Abominations. The historical importance of this legislation lies in the response of Adams's vice president, John C. Calhoun of South Carolina, who openly declared the federal act as unconstitutional and subject to nullification by any state. Adams's successor, Jackson, faced the task of dealing with Calhoun and the South Carolina legislature on this issue.

As active as he was in foreign affairs as secretary of state, Adams's diplomatic talents went largely unused as president. For the first time the United States was not preoccupied with dealing with delicate issues affecting relations with a European power. Adams was unsuccessful in achieving the United States' attendance at the Panama Congress in 1826. The concept was fostered by South American liberator Simon Bolívar to promote cooperation among Western Hemisphere nations. Southern congressmen, fearing condemnation of slavery at such a gathering, managed to delay approval of a delegation until too late for the appointees to attend on time.

Adams's accomplishments as president were modest. His narrow base of support, primarily New England and New York, made it very difficult to achieve more than he did, so that he governed tenuously. On a lighter note, Adams, an avid billiards player, installed the first billiard table in the White House.

Adams demonstrated a fair amount of leadership, but his political base was shaky. Because of his inability or unwillingness to finesse friends in Congress, Adams displayed a clear lack of political skill. His bluntness and seeming unfriendly manner rarely won him converts to his position. Consequently, most of his plans and programs were not passed even though some, like a national university and a national observatory, might have served the national interest, if the role of the federal government had been accepted in these limited areas as it had been with road and canal building. In the category of Political Skill, his worst category, he places twenty-fifth in the poll, drawing comments such as "politically incompetent" and "no political common sense."

Adams's appointments include Henry Clay as secretary of state, as well as Richard Rush in treasury and William Wirt as attorney general, both from the Monroe administration and both very well qualified. Priding himself in selecting the best, John Quincy Adams appointed cabinet members who were free from scandal and incompetence or even the claim of it by his enemies. The poll participants endorse his fine appointments by ranking him a lofty twelfth in this category.

In the election of 1828, Adams proved no match for the popular war hero, General Andrew Jackson, whose supporters had campaigned for nearly four years. Jackson soundly beat Adams.

With an overall middling ranking as an average president, polled experts both praise and criticize Adams as reflected in remarks such as "vastly underrated," "even a lesser Adams is an adornment of our history," "had a true national vision—a great man, but not a great president," and "brilliant mind, outstanding public servant; bad president."

Adams, as would be expected, withdrew to his Massachusetts farm. When neighbors nominated and elected him as their congressman in 1830, he was greatly honored by being given a second political life.

As an elder statesman and congressman, he became an exponent of the antislavery movement. The Mexican War met with Adams's strong opposition because he saw the plan of conquest as merely a provocation by the Southern states to expand slavery. Adams fought for years in Congress to eliminate the "gag rule," adopted by the House in 1830, which provided that no antislavery petition would be recognized for discussion or action. Later, Congress expanded the rule, banning even the receipt of antislavery petitions by the House of Representatives. Believing this to be unconstitutional as a violation of the First Amendment's right to petition, Adams fought and eventually succeeded in overturning this House rule in 1844. Years earlier, House supporters of his position presented him with a patriotically designed cane inscribed "Right of Petition Triumphant." The space providing for a date remained unengraved. However, as soon as the "gag rule" fell to repeal, that date was then inscribed "December 3, 1844." Adams then bequeathed the cane to the American people, proudly presenting it to the commissioner of patents.

The opening of the Cincinnati Observatory in 1843, which Adams attended, gave him great satisfaction. The opportunity was finally at hand to promote exploration and discovery. This he envisioned nearly two decades earlier when he proposed his national observatory.

In 1841 Adams successfully fought before the Supreme Court to win freedom from slavery for African mutineers of the Spanish ship *Amistad,* which had escaped from Cuban to American waters near New York State. He also convinced Congress that the federal government had the power to accept a bequest from an English scientist, James Smithson, for the United States to create the Smithsonian Institution, which it did in 1846.

In his postpresidential years, Adams remained active and accomplished more in public life than any other former president.

This highly intellectual former president wrote two books, *Dermot Mac-Morrogh or, The Conquest of Ireland: An Historical Tale of the Twelfth Century* and *The Lives of James Madison and James Monroe.*

While protesting against the Mexican War, he suffered a stroke and fell to the floor of the House of Representatives. Old Man Eloquent, as he had been known, died two days later on February 23, 1848. His last words were, "This is the last of earth! I am content."

Adams possessed both a brilliant mind and great knowledge. Very few were as well prepared for the presidency as was Adams. He had a vision for America. However, Adams lacked the ability to convert his vision into reality owing to insufficient leadership and particularly poor political skills. He was further undermined by an inadequate base of political support.

Andrew Jackson

1829–1837
7th President

Overall Ranking: 8

Leadership Qualities: 5
Accomplishments and Crisis Management: 9
Political Skill: 6
Appointments: 19
Character and Integrity: 18

An overwhelming proportion of the material power of the nation was against him. The great media for the dissemination of information and the molding of public opinion fought him. Haughty and sterile intellectualism opposed him. Hollow and outworn traditionalism shook a trembling finger at him—all but the people of the United States.

—Franklin D. Roosevelt

Jackson, known as "Old Hickory" and the "People's President," blazed the trail with strong presidential leadership for the causes he held dear. Just how did a man entering adulthood nearly illiterate, a man born in a log cabin, rise to the highest office in the land? And what kind of enemies opposed this national war hero?

Jackson exercised power in the office of the presidency as the guardian of the rights of the people. He saw the presidency not as a position of status but as an opportunity for action. He used the presidential veto more frequently than all of his six predecessors combined. Jackson made the most of his opportunity in those formative years of our nation.

Born on March 15, 1767, in a remote log cabin at the Waxhaw district on the border between North Carolina and South Carolina, Andrew Jackson became the first "log cabin president." Jackson was born to parents who arrived from Ireland just two years before his birth.

Receiving little formal education, he suffered sabre wounds at thirteen while a prisoner during the Revolutionary War for refusing to clean the boots of a British officer. After studying law in Salisbury, North Carolina, he was admitted to the practice of law in North Carolina in 1787.

Although some members of his party were killed by American Indians, Jackson survived the trip to Nashville in 1788 as part of one of the first groups of settlers to move westward on the Cumberland Road.

In 1791 he married Nashville resident Rachel Donelson Robards, who, at the time, was thought by both to have been divorced from her estranged husband living in Kentucky. As it turned out, her Kentucky husband delayed finalizing the divorce until 1793, whereupon Jackson promptly remarried his dear love. Anyone who hinted at the slightest impropriety in this matter was sure to incur the wrath of Jackson as well as his challenge to a duel. Jackson became the first president to marry a divorcee. They had no natural children, but did adopt a son—a nephew of Mrs. Jackson's—and called him Andrew Jackson, Jr.

He served as congressman and then as U.S. senator from Tennessee, aligning himself with Jefferson's Democratic-Republican Party, and then as a Tennessee state judge (1798–1804) at which time he established his permanent home, a plantation called The Hermitage, near Nashville.

On one occasion, the governor of Tennessee made unflattering remarks about Jackson's wife when he met Jackson on the courthouse steps. Jackson, a sitting judge, challenged him to a duel. Friends intervened to prevent bloodshed.

However, on another occasion, when a lawyer cast disparaging words against Mrs. Jackson in 1806, Jackson met him for a duel and shot him dead. In this duel, before he returned his own fatal shot, Jackson was shot near his heart, too close to permit removal of the bullet. He carried it with him the rest of his life. Jackson nearly died when he was shot again and severely wounded in 1813 in yet another dispute over unkind remarks made about him.

Later that year, while recovering from his wounds, Jackson learned that a group of the Creeks, who were allied with the British in the War of 1812, had brutally murdered 250 settlers in the Mississippi Territory about thirty-five miles north of Mobile, not even sparing women or children. Incensed, he organized a militia force to combat the Creeks. In 1814 Jackson defeated the Creek force, killing about 800 warriors, only after allowing the Creek women and children to evacuate to safety. In the ensuing treaty, the United States gained more than half of Alabama and part of Georgia. During the Creek engagement Andrew Jackson was given the nickname Hickory, reflecting his toughness in comparison to that of a hickory stick.

For his success in quelling the Creeks, President Madison appointed him a major general. He continued to serve in the military during the rest of the War of 1812. His next mission: to protect the southern border from British attack. Jackson's ultimate triumph was at the very end of the war when he became the man of the hour as British forces approached New Orleans.

Outnumbered by two to one in the celebrated Battle of New Orleans of 1815, Jackson inflicted on the enemy one of the worst military defeats in the history of the British army. The professional British force lost 2,600 dead, and Jackson's force lost only 8. Old Hickory, as Jackson's men now fondly called him, had become a national war hero and was compared favorably with the revered General George Washington. This most astounding American victory over a world power instilled new national pride into its citizens. Not since General Washington had accepted British surrender more than thirty years before had American spirits soared so high.

In the First Seminole War, Jackson was given the mission by President Monroe to halt the Seminole incursions into Georgia from across Georgia's border with Spanish Florida. In 1818, Jackson, like a massive powerful hurricane, crossed into Spanish Florida, crushed the Seminoles, devastated their villages, and put the Spanish authorities to flight. While Georgians slept easier, Jackson's actions caused a stir in Washington. President Monroe realized that Jackson had faced circumstances that probably justified the drastic action taken, and he did not wish to second-guess the famous general. However, some in his cabinet and in Congress were clearly unhappy and even demanded Jackson's arrest.

The furor quickly died down when the United States assuaged the feelings of the Spanish government and completed the transfer of Florida from Spain to the United States by assuming up to $5 million in legal claims of American citizens against Spain. No doubt, Jackson's initial conquest of Florida convinced the Spanish government of just how untenable their position was in holding Florida.

President Monroe appointed him to be the first governor of Florida in 1821, and after serving briefly there he returned to the U.S. Senate.

Even though Jackson received more popular and electoral votes than any of the other three active candidates in the presidential election of 1824, he did not have a majority of electoral votes, and so the election went to the House of Representatives, which chose John Quincy Adams.

Four years later, when Jackson challenged President John Quincy Adams for the presidency in the election of 1828, the campaign deteriorated into one of mutual personal attacks by each candidate's supporters. Adams's supporters assailed Jackson's wife as an adulteress, his mother as a prostitute, and his father as a mulatto. They attacked Jackson as an illiterate and a murdering hangman. The last charge stemmed from Jackson's trial and execution of six militiamen for desertion in the Creek War.

Jackson's supporters, in turn, claimed Adams and his wife had premarital relations; that Adams, a Unitarian, lacked religious conviction; that he installed gaming furniture, a billiard table, in the White House; and that Adams, while serving as minister to Russia, procured an American prostitute for the Russian czar.

This time Jackson decisively beat his only major opponent. Personal tragedy struck just as Jackson was about to savor his election triumph: his beloved wife died suddenly while they were making preparations for their victorious trip to the capital.

In his 1832 reelection bid, Jackson defeated longtime rival Henry Clay by a landslide in a campaign that, unlike the 1828 election, largely centered on issues. Jackson opposed rechartering the national bank and supported a high tariff to protect a growing manufacturing industry; Clay took opposing positions and also criticized Jackson's frequent veto use to defy Congress.

Jackson's political beliefs centered on his interest in protecting the rights of the working class and the poor. He viewed government, and particularly the presidency, as a vehicle to look after those most in need of help. The People's President, as he was called, stated his basic political credo: "I . . . believe . . . that just laws can make no distinction of privilege between rich and poor, and that when men of high standing attempt to trample upon the rights of the weak, they are the fittest objects for example and punishment. In general, the great can protect themselves, but the poor and humble, require the arm and shield of the law."

Unlike his six urbane predecessors, the energetic Jackson enjoyed the simple pleasures. His successor, Martin Van Buren, stated, "I never knew a man more free from conceit, or one to whom it was to a greater extent a pleasure, as well as a recognized duty, to listen patiently to what might be said to him upon any subject." Aaron Burr thought highly of Jackson when he remarked, "A man of intelligence, and one of those prompt, frank, ardent souls whom I love to meet."

Although Jackson's famous statement, "One man with courage makes a majority," exemplifies his feeling on character, the poll participants rate Jackson little better than average at eighteenth in Character and Integrity— significantly lower than his overall eighth ranking. He drew contrasting comments from "conviction/courage" and "a tough frontiersman . . ." to "very dangerous" and "insensitive and overrated."

Martin Van Buren, vice president during Jackson's second term, wrote of Jackson, "Never could it have been said with as much truth that heaven and earth and the other place too are raised to defeat him." As Van Buren stated, Jackson had powerful enemies, including Henry Clay, who said that Jackson was "[i]gnorant, passionate, hypocritical, corrupt and easily swayed by the base men who surround him." Another powerful and eloquent contemporary, John Quincy Adams, Jackson's immediate predecessor, commented of Jackson that he was "a barbarian who could not write a sentence of grammar and hardly could spell his own name."

Jackson displayed a combination of lively personality, charisma, and charm that would have served him well in today's political arena.

Among the highlights of Jackson's presidency were the battles over tariffs. In 1828, the year before he took office, Congress had passed the so-called Tariff of Abominations, with the highest-yet tariffs on many raw materials as well as on imported manufactured goods. It created discord between the federal government and the Southern states, particularly South Carolina. They claimed the tariffs favored the manufacturing Northeast over the agricultural South. In 1832, Congress passed and Jackson signed a new law that somewhat lowered tariffs, but not far enough for many Southern states. Jackson and his vice president, John C. Calhoun, himself from South Carolina and an eloquent states' rights advocate, locked horns when that state passed an Ordinance of Nullification declaring the federal tariff null and void in South Carolina. Jackson promptly labeled this an act of treason. At his request, Congress passed a law giving him the right to use the army and navy to enforce the federal tariff law if necessary and to repudiate South Carolina's Ordinance of Nullification.

Ironically, the crisis dissolved when Jackson's bitter enemy, Henry Clay, the Great Compromiser as he was called, proposed the Tariff of 1833, which both Jackson and South Carolina, as well as the rest of the South, found acceptable. South Carolina withdrew its Ordinance of Nullification. Jackson's resolve and willingness to use overwhelming federal force against South Carolina and the subsequent compromise pushed the states' rights issue onto the back burner.

Jackson harbored a festering hatred of the national bank, known as the Second Bank of the United States, during its entire existence. Jackson viewed all banks, particularly the national bank, as monopolistic vehicles established solely to line the pockets of the rich and, often by fraud, to cheat the working people and the poor. The bank's charter was due to run out in 1836. Its supporters in Congress did not want to wait until then to be sure the charter would be renewed, so in 1832 Congress passed a bill renewing the charter. When vetoing this bank renewal bill in 1832, Jackson said, "Many of our rich men have not been content with equal protection and equal benefits, but have besought us to make them richer by act of Congress." He added that he believed Congress lacked the constitutional authority to institute such a "monster," as he labeled it. The powerful Daniel Webster attacked Jackson, stating his veto "manifestly seeks to influence the poor against the rich. It wantonly attacks whole classes of the people, for the purpose of turning against them the prejudices and resentments of other classes." Jackson's veto prevailed.

Since the national bank's old charter lasted until 1836, Jackson greatly reduced the bank's power, depositing all new federal government funds in state banks, instead. These state banks, however, began issuing a flood of paper money and easy credit, which fueled land speculation. Jackson then reacted by requiring gold or silver in payment for public land purchase. This contributed to the Panic of 1837, which hit just after Jackson left office, saddling his successor, Martin Van Buren, with a financial mess. Even so, Jackson still believed that public money should not be in the private hands of the stockholders of a national bank.

The nation continued to grow and expand under Jackson's presidency as did the need for roads and canals. Like his predecessor, John Quincy Adams, Jackson had no problem with a federal role in constructing internal improvements between the states. However, he vetoed the Maysville Road bill, which provided for road building entirely within Kentucky.

Jackson's Indian policy provoked controversy. In 1830, the Bureau of Indian Affairs was established to handle Indian matters. In the same year, Congress passed the Indian Removal Act mandating relocation of various American Indian tribes in the East to territories west of the Mississippi River. Indian fighting continued with the Black Hawk War in 1832 in which the Sac and Fox nations in Illinois and Wisconsin were defeated by U.S. forces.

Today, many decry Jackson's resettlement policy. However, no amount of revisionism can change the fact that American Indians were a defeated people blocking the advance of a burgeoning nation. No doubt, Jackson's personal experiences witnessing American Indian attacks and atrocities on U.S. citizens and settlers colored his vision and made empathy to the plight of American Indians more difficult.

Jackson defied Chief Justice John Marshall's 1832 Supreme Court decision favorable to the Cherokee nation in Georgia. In essence, he told Marshall to enforce the decision himself.

Through tough leadership, Jackson strengthened the navy when France refused to continue installment payments on a debt to the United States. War was averted when France agreed to continue payments and Jackson indicated he intended no insult to France.

More than most presidents, Jackson evoked both adoration and hatred. Largely idolized by the working class and poor, he drew animosity from intellectuals, businesspeople, and the wealthier caste of society.

As one might expect, a mentally deranged man took a couple of point-blank shots at the war-hero president. Miraculously, the pistol did not fire, even though it was found to be in perfect working condition when tested afterward.

The polled experts note of Jackson's accomplishments: "first to breathe life into the Presidency" and "key to modern party system." While one commented, "Administration stained by its Indian policy," another observed, "Not 'politically correct' today but a great president."

A strong leader who usually knew what he wanted and how to achieve it, Jackson left the theoreticians to their books. Designated the People's President by his supporters and branded King Andrew I by his enemies, Jackson relished his role as an active and effective chief executive. Ranking an outstanding fifth in the Leadership category, his strongest quality, the poll participants describe him as "decisive," "Aggressive, tough," and "stubborn to a fault but highly skilled leader." His strong leadership style transformed the presidency. Jackson combined his belief in the presidency as a tool to effect policy, primarily through the veto power, with active leadership.

The novel approach of "Old Hickory" to the presidency not only enabled him to do battle against the "monster" national bank but also impelled him to swift, decisive action against South Carolina's Ordinance of Nullification. But unlike his predecessors, he took bold action in opening vast areas for safe American settlement by relocating American Indians farther west. Said Jackson: "Toward the aborigines of the country no one can indulge a more friendly feeling than myself. . . . [However,] the waves of population and civilization are rolling westward, and we now propose to acquire the countries occupied by the Red Men of the South and West by a fair exchange."

This founder of the Democratic Party exhibited an uncanny political savvy for his day. By greatly expanding the "spoils system," that is, political rewards for friends and supporters, he projected another dimension onto the presidency, namely, that of undisputed party leader. He, the Democratic president, not congressional party leaders, dispensed political favors of the day. Making his point, he once commented to a cabinet member, "If you have a job in your department that can't be done by a Democrat, then abolish the job."

But, there is the story of the war veteran who had lost a leg in battle and sought a government position to support his family. Advised that the soldier voted against him, the lean-framed Jackson replied: "If he lost a leg fighting for his country, that is vote enough for me."

Jackson proved to be first in another area, that of using his own trusted advisers, the "kitchen cabinet," and relegating the official cabinet to their roles as department heads enforcing policy. This foreshadowing of the modern presidency allowed Jackson to seek advice from those who enjoyed his confidence.

His appointments largely lacked luster except for his four secretaries of state, who included his successor, Van Buren. Jackson's two secretaries of war had a certain degree of notoriety; one was John H. Eaton, whose controversial wife Peggy, of questionable moral upbringing, caused such turmoil in Washington social circles, and the other was Lewis Cass, the future Democratic presidential candidate in 1848. Our polled experts rated the quality of Jackson's Appointments category as his weakest, at nineteenth in ranking.

Concluding one of the country's most successful presidencies, Jackson returned home to his plantation, the Hermitage. Even though he retired in poor health, he maintained his interest and involvement in party politics. Jackson advised his handpicked successor, Van Buren, on fiscal policy and intervened in order to help his friend and "dark horse" candidate, James K. Polk, win the 1844 Democratic presidential nomination and, subsequently, the election.

Jackson was in debt until his final days. On June 8, 1845, at the Hermitage, Jackson passed quietly away. Having cheated death so many times, he uttered his final words: "I hope and trust to meet you in Heaven, both white and black—both white and black."

"Old Hickory" was one of those rarities in American politics: a national war hero and folk hero who had unwavering core political beliefs and who also could politically outmaneuver the best of the professional politicians of his day. Often, he got things done by his sheer leadership. Jackson, perhaps more than anyone since the Founding Fathers, shaped the course of American democracy by his strong "popular" democratic leadership and party building during his presidency. In the contemporary view, he has become so powerful a symbol that his time is known today as the Age of Jackson.

Martin Van Buren

1837–1841
8th President
Overall Ranking: 21

★

Leadership Qualities: 19
Accomplishments and Crisis Management: 24
Political Skill: 11
Appointments: 22
Character and Integrity: 25

I . . . believe him not only deserving of my confidence but the confidence of the Nation. . . . He . . . is not only well qualified, but desires to fill the highest office in the gift of the people, who in him, will find a true friend and safe repository of their rights and liberty.

—Andrew Jackson

Although Martin Van Buren served in the shadow of Jackson, they were two very different men. Both shared similar political views, being the founders of the modern Democratic Party. But unlike Jackson, who could excite a throng of ordinary folk with his charisma and strong personality, Van Buren did not relate well with the people. He relied on his party machine and dealt with fellow politicians in a tactful and clever manner. When an action or event did not turn out well, Jackson could rely on his immense personal popularity to avoid personal political disaster. Van Buren had no such popularity. When the economy suffered and did not recover by the following election, President Van Buren was out of a job.

The son of a farmer and tavern owner, Van Buren was born on December 5, 1782. (He eventually became the first U.S. president born an American citizen.) The redhead was admitted to the New York bar in 1803 and commenced the practice of law.

In 1807, he married Hannah Hoes. They had four sons. Van Buren was grief stricken in 1819 when she died, leaving him a widower who never remarried.

The five-foot-six, blue-eyed Van Buren was active in New York State politics serving in the New York Senate and as state attorney general, and then in national politics in the U.S. Senate and as an able secretary of state accepting that appointment in 1829 in the Jackson administration.

In 1831, Van Buren resigned to make it easier for President Jackson to clear his cabinet of Vice President John C. Calhoun's sympathizers. Jackson and Calhoun had had a falling-out over the social acceptability of Peggy Eaton, a cabinet member's wife with a questionable moral past. Jackson promptly named Van Buren minister to Great Britain. The president's enemies, including Calhoun, who cast the tie-breaking vote in the Senate, prevented the Senate purely for political reasons from confirming the appointment.

Jackson, as usual, outflanked his enemies. He picked Van Buren as his running mate on the ticket to replace Calhoun as vice president in the election of 1832. Calhoun, because of his differences with Jackson over Peggy Eaton and South Carolina's assertion of states' rights with nullification of the tariff, became the only vice president besides Spiro Agnew to resign from the office. With Jackson's reelection, Van Buren became vice president (presiding over the same Senate that had rejected his appointment as Minister to Great Britain) and Jackson's closest adviser.

Jackson helped Van Buren obtain the 1836 Democratic presidential nomination. In the general election Van Buren faced opposition from three different Whig Party candidates, one from each section of the country: Daniel Webster from Massachusetts, William Henry Harrison then living in Ohio, and Hugh L. White from Tennessee.

The election centered on personalities, with a discussion of a few important issues of the day. Van Buren won by taking on the mantle of Jackson as that popular president's successor.

Van Buren was the first of a long line of national Democratic leaders required to walk the political high wire. Although personally opposed to slavery, he had at the same time to maintain support from those who favored and those who wanted to abolish the institution of slavery. This political tension tearing at the Democratic Party from the North and the South, symptomatic of the underlying national tension, increased gradually until the nation erupted into civil war a quarter century later.

As a shrewd but principled politician, Van Buren had no interest in ideological crusades. Our poll participants rank the "Little Magician," as he was nicknamed, eleventh in Political Skill, his best category. Poll comments include "professional politician" and "first political animal."

When Van Buren served as vice president and presided over the Senate, Henry Clay implored Van Buren in an impassioned speech to tell President Jackson that his policy against the national bank would inflict financial ruin on the country. At the conclusion of his speech, Clay returned to his seat emotionally drained, yet hoping for some response by Van Buren. When Clay saw Van Buren immediately approaching him, he, Clay, thought his message had finally produced a reaction. Clay's hopes, however, were dashed when Van Buren merely asked for a pinch of snuff and returned to his podium completely unaffected by Clay's pleading.

Van Buren served in the U.S. Senate when the tariff controversy became a hotly debated political litmus test. He gave a speech indicating he would not oppose any tariff that equally shared the burdens of economic sacrifice. At the conclusion, one political observer turned to another and asked

whether Van Buren favored or opposed the tariff, to which the other confessed his confusion as well. With stories like this to support their criticism,
his enemies called him the Red Fox of Kinderhook after his hometown of
Kinderhook, New York.

Van Buren's critics were harsh. The caustic John Quincy Adams wrote,
"There are many features in the character of Mr. Van Buren strongly re-
sembling that of Mr. Madison—his calmness, his gentleness of manner, his
discretion, his easy and conciliatory temper. But Madison had none of his
obsequiousness, his sycophancy, his profound dissimulation and duplicity."
The colorful folk hero and Tennessee congressman Davy Crockett assessed Van Buren:

> Van Buren is as opposite to General Jackson as dung is to diamond.
> . . . [He] travels about the country and through the cities in an En-
> glish coach; has English servants, dressed in uniform—I think they
> call it livery . . . ; no longer mixes with the sons of little tavern-
> keepers; forgets all his old companions and friends in the humbler
> walks of life . . . ; eats in a room by himself; and is so stiff in his gait,
> and prim in his dress, that he is what the English call a dandy. When
> he enters the Senate-chamber in the morning he struts and swaggers
> like a crow in a gutter. He is laced up in corsets, such as women in
> town wear, and, if possible, tighter than the best of them. It would
> be difficult to say, from his personal appearance, whether he was a
> man or woman, but for his large red and gray whiskers.

Senator John Randolph of Virginia, a contemporary of Van Buren's, once
quipped about Van Buren's political style, noting that he "rowed to his object with muffled oars."

Unquestionably, Van Buren possessed qualities that any good politician
required: tact, shrewdness, geniality, and caution. These very traits, however, often provoke images of dishonesty and weakness of character in the
minds of some. Although the record clears Van Buren of any hint of dishonesty, it does appear that he had his finger up to check the wind direction of the popular mood. "Vacillator extraordinary" and "too conniving"
are appraisals from two of the panel of experts.

At the time of his inauguration, Van Buren already faced the growing
Panic of 1837. Within two months, banks everywhere refused to honor
paper money. This, coupled with the collapse in British investments and
demand for cotton, crop failures, and the ensuing credit crunch, threw the
economy into a tailspin lasting for more than five years. Van Buren proposed, and Congress eventually adopted, the Independent Treasury Act

whereby the national treasury was empowered to hold tax collection receipts without placing them in private banks. The president could do little else to stimulate the economy. The poor condition of the economy continued into the election of 1840 and cost Van Buren reelection.

The conventional wisdom is that Jackson's policies caused the deep economic recession and that he left office just in time for Van Buren to receive the blame. In the nineteenth century economic conditions rarely changed just because a new president was inaugurated and, to this extent, Jackson's policies contributed. However, Van Buren showed no inclination to change Jackson's policies and, in fact, was party to their adoption because of his close advisory status as Jackson's trusted vice president. All this being said, the economic forces being unleashed in the 1837 panic had root causes largely beyond the control of either Jackson or Van Buren. Neither president should bear a primary responsibility for the Panic of 1837 and the resulting poor economy.

Van Buren opposed the annexation of Texas in order to appease his Northern supporters and to keep the divisive slavery issue off the national agenda. To pacify his Southern supporters, he continued Jackson's policy of relocating American Indians to the West.

American-British relations took a brief roller-coaster ride because of border incursions and border claims between the United States and Canada. The *Caroline* affair in 1837 involved an American steamship ferrying supplies to Canadian rebels. When the *Caroline* was attacked and seized on the American side of the border by Canadian militia and sent aflame over Niagara Falls killing one American, American tempers flared. However, Van Buren managed to quiet the momentary war fever with successful negotiations.

No sooner had the uproar over the *Caroline* settled down than a long-simmering Maine–New Brunswick border dispute erupted. Canadian officials arrested an American attempting to evict Canadians who were lumbering timber in the contested area. Van Buren sent General Winfield Scott to discuss peace, and again the saber rattling from both sides of the border ended without a single shot being fired.

In the Leadership category, Van Buren receives mixed reviews from our presidential poll participants: "Shrewd" notes one expert, while another remarks, "Unimaginative."

Van Buren initially carried over his predecessor's entire cabinet, but soon replaced the interim secretary of state with noteworthy appointee Joel R. Poinsett, who served during the four years of the Van Buren administration, directed the Second Seminole War, and unsuccessfully proposed a federal draft for the militia. He is also famous for his work as a botanist and for introducing into the United States the popular tropical plant renamed for him, the poinsettia.

Facing reelection during a major economic depression, Van Buren lost to the Whig Party's war-hero candidate, William Henry Harrison, in 1840. While Van Buren tried to secure his party's presidential nomination in 1844, Jackson threw his backing to dark horse James K. Polk, the eventual Democratic Party nominee and president.

Van Buren's last quest for a return to the presidency followed in the 1848 election when he carried the banner of the Free Soil Party, a party whose main agenda was its opposition to slavery. After his loss, he finally retired to Kinderhook to enjoy his often neglected pleasures of gardening and fishing.

In 1853 Van Buren became the first former president to visit Europe. During the 1856 and 1860 elections, he backed Democratic candidates James Buchanan and Stephen A. Douglas, respectively, hoping the election of each would prevent civil war. At the outbreak of the Civil War in 1861, Van Buren threw his support enthusiastically for the Union cause and offered President Abraham Lincoln his assistance.

The master politician, campaigning his last in a battle against illness, finally succumbed, passing away on July 24, 1862.

With his overall rank of twenty-first, which is in the middle of the overall presidential poll rankings, Van Buren's reputation is summed up by one poll participant: "The first truly average president."

Van Buren is best remembered for his polished political skills. This proficiency aided him in his domestic political maneuverings. More important, these skills provided the basis for successful diplomatic efforts at settling two international disputes and avoiding war with Canada and Great Britain, his major lasting accomplishment as president.

William Henry Harrison

1841
9TH PRESIDENT

OVERALL RANKING: 35

★

Leadership Qualities: 33
Accomplishments and Crisis Management: 39
Political Skill: 36
Appointments: 35
Character and Integrity: 29

It is true, the victory of 1840 did not produce the happy results anticipated; but it is equally true, as we believe, that the unfortunate death of General Harrison was the cause of the failure. It was not the election of General Harrison that was expected to produce happy effects, but the measures to be adopted by his administration. By means of his death, and the unexpected course of his successor, those measures were never adopted.

—Abraham Lincoln

Like Lincoln, we all wonder at the promise of a Harrison presidency. However, Harrison, even in his brief stint, did leave some tracks.

Youngest of seven children of Benjamin Harrison, who was a signer of the Declaration of Independence, William Henry Harrison was born into a wealthy Virginia planter family on February 9, 1773, at Charles City County, Virginia. In 1795, Harrison married Anna Symmes, from a prosperous family. They had ten children, one of whom was the father of future president Benjamin Harrison.

As governor of the Indiana Territory from 1800 to 1812, William Henry Harrison negotiated a treaty with the Sac and Fox nations as well as the 1809 Treaty of Fort Wayne, which made way for American settlement of large areas in the region.

Harrison established his reputation as a war hero in 1811 when he defeated the Shawnees in the Battle of Tippecanoe. He attained the rank of major general in the War of 1812. Near the war's end, the slim officer resigned to return home to his farm in North Bend, Ohio. The retired general served as an Ohio congressman, state senator, and U.S. senator from Ohio, and in the Jackson administration as minister to Colombia.

In the election of 1836, Harrison together with two other Whig Party candidates challenged Martin Van Buren, Jackson's handpicked successor. While Harrison garnered more votes than any of the other Whig candidates, the Whig plan of winning with a combination of regional candidates failed.

In the next presidential election, in 1840, the Whigs again turned to their hero of Tippecannoe and nominated him for president together with John Tyler of Virginia for vice president. No formal platform was adopted by the Whig convention. The campaign, dominated by the personalities of the candidates, became one of the liveliest in American history. The Whigs introduced novel electioneering techniques including the use of candidate names and party symbols on all kinds of objects such as posters, song sheets, snuff boxes, lanterns, almanacs, and badges. They also whipped up enthusiasm for Whig candidates with parades and rallies. The campaign slogan "Tippecannoe and Tyler Too" proved to be a winner.

At sixty-eight, Harrison became the oldest president to take the oath of office until Ronald Reagan became president in 1981. Harrison ironically delivered the longest inaugural address in history—about two hours—then served the shortest term—thirty days. The connection between the two records stems from the pneumonia Harrison caught from speaking so long on his rainy and gusty inauguration day without benefit of overcoat and hat. Caught in a heavy rain later the same day, he retired to his bed shortly afterward and remained there until his death on April 4, 1841.

Harrison had deliberately avoided discussion of the issues during the campaign so as not to alienate any supporters who constituted the fragile Whig coalition. We know from his time in the Senate, about a decade and a half before his ascendancy to the presidency, he largely supported the nationalist agenda of President John Quincy Adams. This included federal support of a system of road and canal building, the rechartering of the national bank, and a protective tariff.

In his inaugural address, which he largely wrote himself, he revealed his view of the use of the veto—the primary presidential power used at the time: "I consider the veto power . . . to be used only first, to protect the Constitution from violation; secondly, the people from effects of hasty legislation where their will has been probably disregarded or not well understood, and thirdly, to prevent the effects of combinations violative of the rights of minorities."

Referred to as benevolent, modest, mild mannered, and refined by many who knew him, Harrison's critics included Andrew Jackson, who stated shortly after Harrison took office, "The Republic . . . may suffer under the present imbecile chief, but the sober second thought of the people will restore it at our next Presidential election."

In one particular exchange, Harrison showed the influential party and congressional leader Henry Clay the door out of the White House when Clay sought appointments for his friends. He hastily warned Clay with a written note, "You are too impetuous." Harrison displayed strength of character and independence by defying this powerful politician.

The spokesman of the South, John C. Calhoun, observed after Harrison's election, "As unconscious as a child of his difficulties and those of his country, he seems to enjoy his election as a mere affair for personal vanity.

It is really distressing to see him." His predecessor and political opponent, Martin Van Buren, observed, "The President is the most extraordinary man I ever saw. He does not seem to realize the vast importance of his elevation. . . . He is as tickled with the Presidency as a young man with a new bonnet."

Harrison had a mere thirty days as president. He demonstrated some political savvy in his election campaign. He appointed an entire cabinet mostly with prominent members of Congress. His appointments included the very capable Daniel Webster as secretary of state and two others of note who performed in their cabinet posts well, John Bell and John J. Crittenden, both of whom are best remembered for their heroic efforts at attempting to find a peaceful compromise in 1861 as an alternative to civil war.

Harrison's ranking of thirty-ninth in Accomplishments and Crisis Management reflects his very brief term, evoking comments from the poll panelists such as, "No time to make a mark" and "Never had a chance"; one concluded, "Too old and feeble to serve." Some polled experts speculate on Harrison's presidency with, "dedicated but lacked skills," "little time in office, but even if he had a full term   a mediocre president," and "early death probably saved him more embarassment."

On his deathbed, the dying president uttered his last words, presumably advice directed to his vice president and successor, John Tyler: "I wish you to understand the true principles of government. I wish them carried out. I ask nothing more."

What kind of a mark can a thirty-day presidency leave? Obviously, not a very lasting one. Perhaps, Harrison may have had the promise of firm leadership with some independence. Harrison, however, never indicated that he had a program for his administration, nor that a president should even have a program. He believed that Congress should set the agenda. Harrison would likely have faced the same difficult Congress his successor, Tyler, faced. Tyler, a former Democrat, was not much of a Whig. Harrison, we can also see, did not buy into the Whig partisan way of doing business.

We might speculate that, had Harrison lived, he probably would have handled relations with Congress more diplomatically than Tyler did. However, under Clay's leadership, Congress attempted to assert itself even in presidential matters such as appointments and the status of a vice president succeeding to the presidency. Harrison told Clay in no uncertain terms that he would not tolerate interference in presidential appointments.

Harrison's poor presidential ranking is due to the fact that he had little time to accomplish anything. It is not because he performed poorly. The first president to be elected as a Whig was also the first president to die in office. He did appoint an entire cabinet and had an election campaign that demonstrated political skills. Harrison, like other presidents cut short in office, invites an unending discussion of "what if?"

John Tyler

1841–1845
10th President

Overall Ranking: 34

Leadership Qualities: 35
Accomplishments and Crisis Management: 30
Political Skill: 35
Appointments: 30
Character and Integrity: 27

If the tide of defamation and abuse shall turn, and my administration come to be praised, future Vice-Presidents who may succeed to the Presidency may feel some slight encouragement to pursue an independent course.

—John Tyler

With these words John Tyler previewed in 1848 what he thought as his principal legacy of his presidency: maintenance of a presidency and executive department independent of Congress, regardless of how the president achieved the office. Elected vice president as a Whig on the ticket with William Henry Harrison, who died after only one month in office, John Tyler became the first president to ascend to the office without being elected president.

Tyler was the first to grapple with a hostile Whig Congress over the succession issue. Five months after he took office, even his own cabinet, excepting one member, resigned en masse. With his former Democratic Party disowning him, he became a man without a party. Rarely was a president—or "acting president," as some insisted—ever so isolated. Yet Tyler filled out the last three years and eleven months of Harrison's term, setting some important precedents. These precedents carry to the present as unquestioned. Though a soft-spoken man, Tyler hung tenaciously to his principles, causing many in power to abandon him.

Born the sixth of eight children on March 29, 1790, at Greenway Plantation, Tyler shared similar family background with William Henry Harrison, his running mate. Both were born in Charles City County, Virginia, and both were sons of well-to-do Virginia planters who had also held office as governors of Virginia. Tyler became the great-great-great-uncle to a later president, Harry Truman.

He commenced the practice of law in 1809 and in 1813 married Letitia Christian, who also came from a family of large landowners. They had eight children. Tragically, in 1839 she suffered a stroke, which confined her to a bed and wheelchair. Completely inactive as first lady, she died in 1842, becoming the first president's wife to die in the White House.

The thin, six-foot-tall Tyler served as a supporter of Jefferson's Democratic-Republican Party in the Virginia legislature as a congressman and as governor of Virginia. In 1827 he stepped into the U.S. Senate in the

Jackson-Democrat mold. He broke with Jackson, however, in 1833 by supporting South Carolina's position declaring a federal tariff unconstitutional on the principle of states' rights, although he condemned that state's nullification ordinance. Tyler then gravitated to the Whig Party. He resigned his Senate seat in 1836.

The charming and well-bred Virginian received the Whig Party nomination as vice president on the Harrison ticket in 1840 and was elected vice president, serving only one month before hurrying to Washington to be sworn in as the tenth president on April 6, 1841. Never before had a vice president moved into the presidency after the death of a president.

While Tyler took over the reins of government just as if he were elected president, many, including Henry Clay and other powerful leaders, believed that Tyler should only serve as "acting president."

Tyler's enemies referred to him as His Accidency. This view maintained that Tyler would wield the powers of the presidency without actually being president. Tyler stood firm on this point until his opponents acquiesced, acknowledging him as president in his own right.

Tyler demonstrated a complete tolerance of other religions. He firmly opposed the bigotry of the nativist Know Nothing political movement, which espoused hatred and suspicion of immigrants, particularly the wave of Irish Catholics entering the country at the time.

Throughout Tyler's political career and regardless of his political affiliation, belief in states' rights and strict construction of the Constitution governed his actions. Unlike many other Southern slaveholding presidents, Tyler made no apologies for the institution of slavery in the Southern social and economic way of life. He observed that nearly all societies functioned with open class distinctions, including the most prosperous and advanced of all at the time, Great Britain.

Tyler is considered "stubborn" by at least one poll participant, and a contemporary of Tyler's held the same opinion: "When he thinks he is right he is obstinate as a bull, and no power on earth can move him."

Tyler clung to his Jacksonian hatred of a national bank scheme, and this earned him praise from his successor, James K. Polk: "[Tyler deserves] the lasting gratitude of his country [for] arresting the dominant majority in Congress in their career, and saving his country from the dominion and political incubus of the money-power in the form of a National Bank."

Longtime friend, congressman, and later Confederate general Henry Wise of Virginia appraised Tyler's character: "An honest, affectionate, benevolent, loving man, who fought the battles of his life bravely and truly, doing his whole great duty without fear, though not without much unjust reproach."

Of course, Tyler had his critics, including former president John Quincy Adams, who said, "Tyler is a political sectarian, of the slave-driving, Virginian, Jeffersonian school, principled against all improvement, with all the interests and passions and vices of slavery rooted in his moral and political constitution—with talents not above mediocrity, and a spirit incapable of expansion to the dimensions of the station upon which he has been cast by the hand of Providence." The editor of the *Richmond Whig*, John Pleasants, attacked Tyler's talents upon his accession to the presidency in 1841: "I could not believe that a man so commonplace, so absolutely inferior to many fifteen shilling lawyers with whom you may meet at every county court in Virginia, would seriously aspire to the first station among mankind."

The poll experts rank Tyler twenty-seventh in Character and Integrity, his strongest category.

In domestic matters, gridlock ruled the day. Whig Party members became incensed when Tyler vetoed two congressional attempts at reestablishing a national bank. Even though elected vice president on the Whig ticket, Tyler appeared to be repudiating the Whig agenda. He soon lost the confidence of his cabinet, all of whom had been appointed by Harrison, and at the same time alienated the Whig-controlled Congress. His entire cabinet, except Secretary of State Daniel Webster, resigned simultaneously. There was even a move afoot by some Whigs in the House of Representatives to impeach Tyler, but the attempt was beaten back by a vote of 83 to 27.

Tyler's greatest achievements as president were in foreign affairs. The Webster-Ashburton Treaty between the United States and Great Britain settled the Maine-Canadian border dispute peaceably in 1842. The Treaty of Wanghia in 1844 opened trade with China to American merchants.

An advocate of the annexation of Texas, Tyler had the opportunity to sign the bill of annexation when Congress, reading the popular mood, presented him with the bill days before he left office.

Tyler did establish, by his steadfastness, the precedent that a vice president succeeding to the presidency upon the death or incapacity of a president is just as much president as if he were elected himself. Tyler incurred such enmity in the political arena that he suffered the indignity of being the first president to have his veto overridden by Congress on a relatively minor matter just before leaving office.

Although ranking thirtieth in Accomplishments and Crisis Management, Tyler earns some praise from the poll experts, for example, "handled succession well" and "manifest destiny activist." On the downside, some criticized Tyler, including one poll participant who comments that Tyler "created political crisis."

As if not surrounded by enough controversy, Tyler remarried while in the White House in 1844, after his ill wife had died in 1842. At twenty-four, his new bride, Julia Gardiner, was thirty years younger than himself. This created another barrage of criticism and was the source of many jokes at the president's expense. They had seven children. Tyler, from both marriages, had fifteen children—the most of any president.

At thirty-fifth in Political Skill, Tyler ranks near the bottom of the poll. Comments include, "Had no understanding of give-and-take of politics" and "isolated himself." Like the two Adamses before him, Tyler made too many political enemies in his own party, and like them, he did not get re-elected to the presidency.

After the 1841 cabinet resignation, Tyler selected his own cabinet. Unfortunately, two of them died while demonstrating the world's largest naval gun aboard the American warship USS *Princeton.*" The gun blew apart, killing Secretary of State Abel P. Upshur, Secretary of the Navy Thomas W. Gilmer, and several others in the trial run.

After leaving the presidency, John Tyler returned to his home at Sherwood Forest, near Richmond, Virginia. The former president served as chancellor of William and Mary College, his alma mater. He later presided over a peace conference in Washington in 1861 that attempted to avert impending civil war. In 1862, he was elected as a member of the Congress of the Confederate States, the only former U.S. president to join that government, but died in Richmond in January 1862 before actually taking his seat. He was buried with the flag of the Confederacy, a cause in which he believed so deeply and which reflected the beliefs he held for a lifetime.

Unlike Andrew Jackson, and even William Henry Harrison, who enjoyed a large degree of popularity, Tyler could not appeal to the people. He was an unknown, not elected to the top office in his own right. Tyler, a man of courage and principle, made many political enemies, particularly in his own party. Lack of political support, together with an unyielding approach to politics, made his presidency a particularly difficult one.

JAMES K. POLK

1845–1849
11TH PRESIDENT

OVERALL RANKING: 11

---★---

Leadership Qualities: 12
Accomplishments and Crisis Management: 8
Political Skill: 12
Appointments: 15
Character and Integrity: 20

The acquisition of California and New Mexico, the settlement of the Oregon boundary and the annexation of Texas, extending to the Rio Grande, are results which, combined, are of greater consequence and will add more to the strength of the nation than any which have preceded them since the adoption of the Constitution.

—James K. Polk

These words of James K. Polk tell us what he considered his achievement and legacy. His administration, the "New Democracy," closely followed the wishes and aspirations of the people. Polk ran on a platform of expansion of the American nation, and he was as good as his word. Few presidents have left such a tangible and enduring legacy. When he left office, the outline of the modern United States of America was almost complete in its shape. The forty-eight states would, within three-quarters of a century, constitute the most powerful nation in the world. Yet Polk is not a household name and is probably the least known of any president of his stature. Only in relatively recent times has the importance of his presidential accomplishments been realized.

James Knox Polk was born on November 2, 1795, near Pineville, Mecklenberg County, North Carolina, in a small log home on a frontier farm. Oldest of ten children and sickly as a child, he suffered throughout his life from poor health. He was the great-great-great-grandnephew of John Knox, the Scottish religious leader. Young Polk moved with his family to Tennessee where his father became a founder of Columbia, Tennessee.

He graduated with honors from the University of North Carolina in 1818. As poor health continued to plague him, Polk decided upon a career in the law. The legal field provided him with the best opportunity to enter the realm of his real love—politics. After studying law, he was admitted to the Tennessee bar in 1820 and opened a practice in Columbia, Tennessee.

In 1824, he married Sarah Childress. They had no children. Exceptional for any woman of the time, Sarah gained an outstanding education attending and graduated from what is now known as Salem College in Salem, North Carolina. She acted as Polk's private secretary throughout his career. Sarah proved to be one of the outstanding and active first ladies, graciously entertaining political friends and foes alike. She is remembered also for not

permitting strong alcoholic beverages, card playing, or any kind of danc-
ing in the White House. The beautiful and charming first lady felt that
these activities detracted from the decorum of the noble and stately un-
dertakings in the executive mansion.

The small-statured, gray-eyed, Tennesseean served as a state legislator
and then congressman, rising to Speaker of the House of Representatives
in 1835. As Speaker, he helped pass Jackson's programs and earned the
nickname Young Hickory. Polk gained the distinction of being the only
Speaker to become president.

He served one term as Tennessee governor from 1839 to 1841. With
Jackson's help at the deadlocked 1844 Democratic convention, he received
the nomination for president. Most Americans had never heard of Polk,
even though he had been on the political scene for two decades. Thus, Polk
secured the reputation of being the first "dark horse" candidate for the
presidency by any major political party.

During the election of 1844 for the first time hand-painted lapel buttons portraying the presidential candidates and their running mates appeared. The campaign between Polk, the Democratic nominee, and Henry
Clay, the Whig nominee in his third run for the presidency, largely focused
on personalities. While there were issues, the Whig press preferred to attack Polk as the cowardly puppet of Jackson; the Democratic press labeled
Clay as a drunken opportunist. In the campaign, Polk became the first president to announce that he would serve only one term. And he kept his
promise.

The election was close, with Polk's slim margin of about 5,000 popular
votes in New York supplying the difference in the all-important electoral
vote. At the time, Polk, forty-nine, was the youngest president to take
office.

As a Democrat, Polk believed in states' rights and limited presidential
power in domestic affairs. He entertained the view of his predecessors, Jefferson and Jackson, that the president led with Congress in foreign affairs
and that Congress led in domestic matters. The president's veto power became the main weapon in his arsenal to prevent unconstitutional legislation. He felt that a president simply did not lead the way on domestic
affairs. Polk summarized this view before Congress in 1848 when he said,
"The President's power is negative merely, and not affirmative."

Polk followed Jackson's views on most matters, opposing a national
bank and federal road and canal building and supporting Texas annexation.
Polk correctly read the national mood and espoused expansionist views, a
policy that became known as manifest destiny. This view mandated the

inevitability of a continental United States from Atlantic to Pacific—a continental power. He advocated acquisition—by purchase preferably, by conquest if necessary—of Texas, the Mexican-controlled regions known as New Mexico and California, and the huge region called Oregon Country, since 1819 jointly occupied by the United States and Great Britain. This vision of America clearly contributed to the unique and untold wealth and power of the United States. Polk had been attacked as an expansionist, particularly by the slavery abolitionists. The abolitionists feared further expansion of slavery and slave state power and bitterly opposed and vilified him.

Polk, in turn, took a dim view of the abolitionists. He found them to be a danger to the national Union. Near the end of his presidency in 1848, he wrote, "The agitation of the slavery question is mischievous and wicked, and proceeds from no patriotic motive by its authors. It is a mere political question on which demagogues and ambitious politicians hope to promote their own prospects for political promotion. And this they seem willing to do even at the hazard of disturbing the harmony if not dissolving the Union itself."

In 1902, Professor Woodrow Wilson, who would ten years later become president, lauded Polk:

> James K. Polk . . . proved an excellent embodiment of the principles of the Democrats. He had been well known in the House of Representatives, over which he had presided as Speaker, and where he had served most honorably, if without distinction. He was a southerner, and fully committed in favor of annexation. Though in no sense a man of brilliant parts, he may be said to have been a thoroughly representative man of his class, a sturdy, upright, straight-forward party man. He believed in the policy for which his party had declared, and he meant, if elected, to carry it out.

On the other hand, antislavery Congressman Abraham Lincoln of Illinois took another view and, in 1848, condemned Polk: "I more than suspect that he is deeply conscious of being in the wrong,—that he feels the blood of this [the Mexican] war, like the blood of Abel, is crying to Heaven against him. . . . He is a bewildered, confounded and miserably perplexed man."

Congressional approval of the annexation of the Republic of Texas (which had won its independence from Mexico in 1836) in the last days of Tyler's administration caused a break in diplomatic relations between the United States and Mexico. Admission of Texas as a state on December 29,

1845, intensified hostility between the two nations, especially since the border of Texas was in dispute. Mexico claimed the border was at the Nueces River; the United States insisted that the Rio Grande, farther south, was the border. Finally, Polk called for war with Mexico after he learned that Mexican troops had crossed the Rio Grande into Texas and fired upon the encamped American army. Four days later, in May 1846, Congress formally declared war and the Mexican War was under way.

American forces won quick victories. Peace was concluded in early 1848 with the United States paying $15 million for more than one half million square miles of territory. The Mexican Cession included California and the New Mexico regions, which made up what are now parts of seven southwestern states. Mexico gave up its claims to Texas.

Just as the Mexican War was beginning, Polk continued his foreign policy success with settlement of the Oregon Country dispute with Great Britain. The region was divided, with the border set at the 49th parallel. This was implemented by the Oregon Treaty in 1846.

In 1847, the United States negotiated a treaty with New Granada (Colombia) granting the United States the right to cross the Isthmus of Panama by construction of either a railroad or a canal.

On the domestic front, Polk's "New Democracy" reinstated Van Buren's independent treasury system. The Independent Treasury Act of 1846 provided that federal funds were no longer to be deposited in private banks but held by the U.S. Treasury and that debt repayment to the federal government was to be made only by payment made in gold, silver, or federal notes. The Walker Tariff of 1846 lowered import duties on certain raw materials in order to stimulate industry.

Democratic president Polk had a Democratic Congress for the first two years of his term, and Congress gave him what he wanted. During the last two years, however, the Whigs took back control of the House of Representatives where Polk's proposals received little sympathy or support.

Polk's national announcement of an "abundance of gold" in California in his last annual message to Congress contributed to the gold rush and settlement of California. He established the Department of the Interior two days before he left office in March 1849.

Polk's accomplishments, more than any other feature of his presidency, provide him with the greatness he enjoys. With a poll ranking of eighth in Accomplishments and Crisis Management, Polk garners praise from poll participants with comments like, "Accomplished all he set out to do—worked himself to death," "promised, then delivered," and "expansion crucial to making USA"; however, one of a small number of critics notes, "Unjust war, vastly overrated."

In Polk's weakest category, Character and Integrity, he is ranked twentieth compared with his overall ranking of eleventh. He drew a good number of negative comments: "Many accomplishments but devious," "unprincipled," "nationalistic, a warmonger," and "wishy-washy."

The cabinet of the "New Democracy" included Secretary of State and future president James Buchanan and Secretary of the Navy George Bancroft, the most noted American historian of the day, who wrote the landmark ten-volume *History of the United States*. Polk's postmaster general, Cave Johnson of Tennessee, set in motion the use of postage stamps for mail delivery.

Polk detested the practice of making political appointments and described the practice in his diary late in his presidency: "In the midst of the annoyances of the herd of lazy, worthless people who come to Washington for office instead of going to work . . . I am sometimes amused at their applications. . . . One of these office seekers placed his papers of recommendation. . . . No particular office was specified . . . but he answered that he thought he would be a good hand at making Treaties . . . and would like to be a minister abroad. This is about as reasonable as many other applications which are made to me."

Congressman Andrew Johnson of Tennessee, a future president himself, attacked Polk on his appointments: "Polk's appointments all in all are the most damnable set that was ever made by any President since the government was organized. . . . He has a set of interested parasites about him, who flatter him until he does not know himself. He seems to be acting upon the principle of hanging an old friend for the purpose of making two new ones."

Polk ranks twelfth in Leadership Skill. Representative evaluations include "bold and visionary," "used Presidency for precise goals," and "very strong leader."

After the inauguration of Zachary Taylor, the Whig Party's candidate and Polk's successor, Democratic Party leaders requested that the popular Polk tour the South. The former Democratic president complied, thinking his popularity in that region would boost Democratic Party activity and success. He probably caught the cholera that raged in New Orleans at the time of his visit. Within a few days he was back at his home called Polk's Place in Nashville, Tennessee, suffering stomach pains. Gradually ebbing away, he died on June 15, 1849, just over three months after leaving office. James Buchanan stated, "He was the most laborious man I have ever known; and in a brief period of four years had assumed the appearance of an old man."

His death at fifty-three made him the shortest-lived former president to that time. Sarah Polk, widowed at forty-five, stood with her native South in the Civil War and looked after their Mississippi plantation until just after the war. She died in 1891, four and a half months short of her eighty-eighth birthday.

In earning an overall poll ranking at eleventh, Polk receives from our poll participants praise such as "greatest one-term presidency" and "sadly neglected, a winner."

The greatness of Polk rests on his substantial accomplishment of just one term during which the United States became a continental power, adding much of the western United States.

No other one-term president has demonstrated achievement to the extent that Polk did. He excelled as a hard and hands-on worker, planning his own policies. Polk's vision of the formation of a modern continental United States truly merits acclaim. America would not be what it is today if his opponents, the non-expansionists and slavery abolitionists, had had their way.

Polk's outstanding success was no accident. He assiduously planned his moves and carried them through to fruition. Former president Harry Truman summed it up in his own concise way in 1960. When asked what he thought about Polk, he replied, "A great president. He said exactly what he was going to do and he did it." Quite an achievement for a president of any era.

ZACHARY TAYLOR

1849–1850
12TH PRESIDENT

OVERALL RANKING: 29

Leadership Qualities: 23
Accomplishments and Crisis Management: 31
Political Skill: 33
Appointments: 28
Character and Integrity: 23

He really is a most simple-minded old man. He has the least show or pretension about him of any man I ever saw; talks as artlessly as a child about affairs of state, and does not seem to pretend to a knowledge of anything of which he is ignorant. He is a remarkable man in some respects; and it is remarkable that such a man should be President of the United States.

—Horace Mann

Taylor entered the presidency as a genuine war hero who had captured the public imagination. Yet he would have little more than a year to show us his presidential credentials.

Virginia-born Zachary Taylor entered this world on November 24, 1784, as the third of eight children. Moving in his early youth from his birthplace in Orange County, Virginia, he grew up in Jefferson County, Kentucky.

In 1810 he married Margaret Smith with whom he had six children. In 1835, one of their daughters, Sarah Knox Taylor, married Lieutenant Jefferson Davis, the future president of the Confederate States of America, but died of malaria after only three months of marriage. Taylor's only son, Richard, served in the army of the Confederacy as a lieutenant general.

Taylor's illustrious military career of nearly forty years included service in the War of 1812 and the Black Hawk War in Illinois in which he defeated Chief Black Hawk in 1832. Unusual for a military man of his day, Taylor neither drank nor smoked. He did, however, chew tobacco and possessed an excellent aim for the spittoon.

The five-foot-eight Taylor commanded the U.S. Army against the Seminoles in the Second Seminole War in Florida. By 1841 he was in charge of the southern division of the army and called Baton Rouge, Louisiana, home. Taylor's residence was located at his large plantation, which was worked by about a hundred slaves. Promoted to major general at the start of the Mexican War, the two-hundred-pound commander with hazel eyes distinguished himself in battle with a series of victories culminating in heroic triumph in the Battle of Buena Vista in 1847.

A national war hero by the time of the Whig nominating convention in 1848, Taylor received the nomination for president with vice presidential running mate Millard Fillmore of New York. The amiable and amicable

Taylor mentioned nothing of the issues and relied on his personal popularity to win the election. He wrote during his campaign for president, "If I occupy the White House, I must be untrammelled and unpledged, so as to be President of the nation and not of a party."

While Taylor opposed abolition of slavery in the Southern states, he also opposed its extension, especially if the local territorial inhabitants voted to ban the institution in their territorial constitutions.

Taylor expressed opposition to the Compromise of 1850 proposed by Henry Clay in his attempt to avoid the tragedy of a civil war. Just before presidential action on the bill was called for, Taylor died. His successor, Millard Fillmore, supported the compromise, and it became law. Had Taylor lived long enough to cast his probable veto, perhaps the Civil War might have occurred ten years earlier and on somewhat different terms. Addressing the possible secession of Southern states, Taylor had promised that he would blockade their ports, tax goods entering the South, and block goods from leaving the South. He told a congressman, "I can save the Union without shedding a drop of blood. It is not true, as reported in the North, that I said I would march an army and subdue them: there would be no need of any."

Taylor the man represented the epitome of the nonpretentious, common folk. He had the appearance of an old farmer, rarely wearing the uniform distinguishing his high army rank. Numerous are the occasions when a well-dressed lieutenant or even private mistook Taylor for an old farmer only to find out later he was the leader of their army.

Abraham Lincoln in 1850—ten years before he ran for president himself—gave these thoughts on the twelfth president: "It did not happen to General Taylor, once in his life, to fight a battle on equal terms, or on terms advantageous to himself—and yet he was never beaten, and he never retreated. . . . General Taylor's battles were not distinguished for brilliant military maneuvers; but in all he seems rather to have conquered by the exercise of a sober and steady judgment, coupled with a dogged incapacity to understand that defeat was possible." Senator Thomas Benton of Missouri added his praise: "His death was a public calamity. No man could have been more devoted to the Union, or more opposed to the slavery agitation."

Taylor's primary army rival, the flamboyant Winfield Scott, took another view: "Any illusion to literature much beyond good old Dilworth's Spelling Book, on the part of one wearing a sword, was evidence, [to Taylor] of utter unfitness for heavy marchings and combat. In short, few men have ever had a more comfortable, labor-saving contempt for learning of every kind."

Outgoing president James K. Polk observed on Taylor's inauguration day, "General Taylor is, I have no doubt, a well-meaning old man. He is, however, uneducated, exceedingly ignorant of public affairs, and, I should judge, of very ordinary capacity. He will be in the hands of others, and must rely wholly upon his Cabinet to administer the government."

Although having an easygoing manner, Taylor nonetheless came to his own decisions on issues about which he felt strongly. He proved Polk wrong on the leadership he demonstrated, during his brief tenure, on issues such as slavery and secession. In fact, far from being controlled by his cabinet, Taylor was about to make major cabinet changes, but this move was thwarted by his death.

Taylor, a Whig, served only a little more than one year and four months as president. He took office with a Democratic-controlled Congress and probably would not have proceeded very far with any of his programs if he had any. With Taylor placing thirty-third in Political Skill, his weakest category, one polled expert sums it up: Taylor "did not understand the American political system."

The war-hero general was the first president faced with the problem of how to deal with the territories acquired from Mexico in the Mexican War. California sought admission to the Union as a free state, upsetting the precarious balance of free and slave states. Taylor, a slaveholder and Southerner, nonetheless supported California's admission, but Congress could not agree on the issue. In addressing a joint session of Congress, the president asked that California and New Mexico be admitted based upon the state constitutions promulgated by the people of each territory. He reasoned that this was the guiding principle of American government. The Southern states fiercely objected. When prominent Southerners threatened to dislodge the small federal force in the New Mexico Territory, Taylor issued his steely warning: "I will command the army in person and hang any man taken in treason."

A touch of scandal singed the Taylor administration in its brief tenure. The Galphin family of Georgia had received from the U.S. government a settlement of an old claim of principal. The payment preceded Taylor's term, but the Galphins persisted in and received an interest payment of $191,000 after Taylor took office. Unknown to Taylor and the other cabinet members, Secretary of War George W. Crawford had been representing the Galphin family and shared one-half of the monies awarded them. Taylor, furious on learning about Crawford's role, planned to remove Crawford and reorganize his cabinet. He died before he had the chance.

A noteworthy accomplishment of the brief Taylor presidency is the Clayton-Bulwer Treaty of 1850. The treaty provided for the United States and Great Britain to refrain from exerting sole control over any canal to be constructed in Central America. It further directed both countries to refrain from any colonization in Central America. The treaty was effective until superseded by another treaty between the two countries fifty years later.

Taylor possessed an established record of military leadership and a potential for political leadership. His statements demonstrate that he was prepared to take decisive action on the key issue of secession; for example, he warned some Southern leaders that he would act with military force if they attempted to interfere with federal troops in the New Mexico Territory. Nevertheless, in the Leadership category, he finishes twenty-third in the poll.

Old Rough and Ready, as he was called, also ranks twenty-third in the Character and Integrity category. One poll panelist refers to him as "tough-minded but hardheaded."

Taylor died on July 9, 1850, after a sudden and brief gastrointestinal illness, probably caused by contaminated cherries and ice milk he consumed during his attendance at various Washington celebrations on a hot Fourth of July. He became the second president to die while in office. His last words were "I am about to die. I expect the summons very soon. I have tried to discharge my duties faithfully. I regret nothing, but I am sorry that I am about to leave my friends."

Taylor's failure to leave a real mark of accomplishment on his presidency stems from the brevity of his term and the lack of opportunity to act on the driving issues of the day: secession and slavery. Daniel Webster and other political leaders held the conviction that, had Taylor lived, he would have vetoed the Compromise of 1850, hurling the nation into civil war.

For those who believe that the Civil War was inevitable and necessary, and that is a debatable issue itself, Zachary Taylor might have been the ideal president to preserve the Union. According to that viewpoint, as a Southern slaveholder, he would have enjoyed a certain degree of trust in the minds of Southerners in resolving the twin issues of secession and slavery. As a military leader, he would have had credibility in threatening to use force to keep the Union together. He showed a high degree of decisiveness in this regard even while he was president. Finally, Taylor displayed a modern approach in his thoughts on how he might have dealt with secession by the South: blockade and economic warfare with minimum bloodshed. If successful, this might have avoided the most murderous war in our history. Few doubt that Taylor would have vigorously acted to keep the Union intact.

Some poll participants speculate on a completed term: "Too short a time in office but potential strong president"; "Had he lived, he might have been Lincoln"; and "Nearly started Civil War, but died."

However, in the final analysis, Taylor suffers from unfulfilled promise because of his brief time in office.

MILLARD FILLMORE

1850–1853
13TH PRESIDENT

OVERALL RANKING: 36

★

Leadership Qualities: 36
Accomplishments and Crisis Management: 32
Political Skill: 31
Appointments: 33
Character and Integrity: 31

God knows that I detest slavery, but it is an existing evil, for which we are
not responsible, and we must endure it, and give it such protection as is
guaranteed by the Constitution, till we can get rid of it without destroying
the last hope of free government in the world.

—Millard Fillmore

Those words of Millard Fillmore express the central frustration of his presidency.

This president, who actually was born in a log cabin, on January 7, 1800, at Locke Township (which later became Summerhill), New York, was the son of a frontier farmer. Second oldest of nine children, he worked on the family farm as a youth in Niles, New York.

Apprenticed to a cloth maker at fourteen, he enrolled part-time in a local academy to improve his frontier education. After four years, he worked as a law clerk while teaching school. The six-foot-tall, blue-eyed Fillmore was admitted to the New York bar to practice law in 1823 and opened an office in East Aurora, near Buffalo, New York.

Fillmore, a fastidious dresser, served in the New York State legislature and then rose to the powerful chairmanship of the House Ways and Means Committee during his eight years of service in the U.S. House of Representatives.

The Whigs pushed him as a candidate for governor of New York in 1844, but Fillmore lost. He took over as chancellor of the University of Buffalo in 1846 and during the Mexican War commanded a corps of the defensive New York Home Guard for several months.

Elected comptroller of New York State in 1848, Fillmore was picked by the Whigs as their vice presidential nominee that same year to balance the national ticket headed by Zachary Taylor, the national war hero from Louisiana. The congenial Fillmore, rewarded for being a loyal Whig, was without any noticeable vices such as drinking, smoking, or gambling.

The Whig ticket prevailed in a close election. Vice President Fillmore proved to be independent of his president. While Fillmore presided over the Senate's consideration of the Compromise of 1850, he advised President Taylor that, even though Taylor opposed the measure, he, Fillmore, would vote in favor of it if he had the opportunity to cast the tie-breaking vote as president of the Senate. Shortly afterward Taylor died and Fillmore took office as president on July 10, 1850, and had the chance, as the nation's chief executive, to sign the bills that constituted the Compromise of 1850. Rarely have the fortunes of such an important group of measures been reversed so dramatically—from threatened veto by one president to signing of the bills by his successor.

Fillmore was a party activist and believed in traditional Whig Party principles and programs. This contrasts with his predecessor, Taylor, who took no interest in politics prior to his election as president and exercised independence in his decision making during his presidency. Professor Woodrow Wilson of Princeton University, a future president, similarly noted, "Mr. Fillmore was . . . a man more amenable to the control of the leaders of Congress and of his party than the sturdy soldier had been whom he succeeded."

Although Fillmore opposed slavery, he thought that it had to be tolerated until such a time as it could peaceably be eradicated. He also believed in limited federal government.

Interior Secretary Alexander H. H. Stuart sheds light on Fillmore's decision making and resoluteness of conviction when he stated of Fillmore, "When he had carefully examined a question and had satisfied himself that he was right, no power on earth, could induce him to swerve from what he believed to be the line of duty."

Fillmore's first major act after attaining the presidential office was to accept the resignations from all of the incumbent cabinet members. For the first and only time, a vice president inheriting the presidency selected a completely new cabinet.

The most significant accomplishment of Fillmore's presidency proved to be the Compromise of 1850. The series of five bills gave the North and antislavery forces admission of California as a free state and prohibited the slave trade in the District of Columbia. On the other hand, Utah and New Mexico were organized as territories without restrictions on slavery. The South and proslavery forces obtained continuation of slavery in the District of Columbia and a stronger Fugitive Slave Law mandating federal officials to actively pursue runaway slaves.

Far from helping to settle the differences between North and South as Fillmore and other compromisers hoped, the Fugitive Slave Law poured gasoline on the raging fires of controversy. The Underground Railroad and Harriet Beecher Stowe's *Uncle Tom's Cabin* sprang forth as "inspired" or "hated" responses, depending upon the viewpoints of contemporary Americans. Subsequently, the 1857 Dred Scott decision of the Supreme Court featured the Court's proslavery interpretation of the Fugitive Slave Law, further fanning the flames. The Fugitive Slave Law also cost Fillmore the support of Northern Whigs, and eventually this cost the Whig nomination for president in 1852. A few years later, in 1854, Fillmore spoke to the issue: "The man who can look upon a crisis without being willing to offer himself upon the altar of his country is not fit for public trust."

There was indeed a crisis shortly after Fillmore succeeded to the presidency. Civil war loomed as a danger to the stability and survival of the Union of states. How can slavery, a Constitutionally recognized institution, be abolished, and yet be permitted to remain at the same time? No wonder Fillmore and the other national leaders in Congress pressed for the Compromise of 1850. In it, they saw an opportunity to forestall and possibly prevent the national catastrophe of a civil war. What we today view as the obvious moral issue of humanity and equality was not so obvious in the middle of the nineteenth century.

The mission of Commodore Matthew C. Perry, sent by Fillmore to open trade with Japan, stands as his noteworthy foreign policy accomplishment. Two Japanese ports opened for American trade as America began to look to the outside world to expand its commercial ventures and trade.

Two of Fillmore's cabinet appointees returned from the prior Whig administrations of Harrison and Taylor: Secretary of State Daniel Webster and Attorney General John J. Crittenden. Both were nationalists who fought hard for the Compromise of 1850.

As the United States became less defensive in foreign affairs, Daniel Webster became possibly the first foreign policy human rights advocate. One of America's great statesmen and one of the finest secretaries of state, Webster used his position to attack oppression around the world.

First Lady Abigail Fillmore used her influence to establish the first White House library. After leaving the White House in 1853, Fillmore returned to Buffalo and continued practicing law.

In 1856, after the death of his wife and daughter and prompted by his belief in civic activism, he reappeared on the political scene in an attempt to recapture the White House as the nominee of the anti-immigrant, anti-Catholic American Party (known popularly as the Know-Nothing Party). Fillmore used his unsolicited nomination to campaign for peaceful preservation of the Union in dealing with the sectional crisis and ignored the American Party positions on immigrants and Catholics. He wrote at the time of his reemergence: "It is better to wear out than rust out." He finished third in the popular vote and carried only one state.

In 1858 he married an affluent widow, Caroline McIntosh.

At the outbreak of the Civil War, Fillmore organized the Union Continentals, a group of prominent men too old for active service. As its commander, he urged recruitment and led fund-raising efforts for relief. However, as the war wore on and the colossal amount of bloodshed and destruction became apparent, Fillmore revealed his opinion that the Republicans caused the war and its bloody protraction. At an 1864 relief rally, he attacked the Republicans and advocated reconciliation with the Southern states. Later that year, he supported George B. McClellan, the Democratic presidential candidate challenging Lincoln's reelection.

In an 1864 hometown speech Fillmore stated, "Three years of civil war have desolated the fairest portion of our land, loaded the country with an enormous debt that the sweat of millions yet unborn must be taxed to pay; arrayed brother against brother, father against son in mortal combat; deluged our country with fraternal blood, whitened our battle-fields with the bones of the slain, and darkened the sky with the pall of mourning."

After the Civil War, the former president devoted his public life to improving the culture and prestige of Buffalo. He founded the Buffalo Historical Society and the Buffalo Fine Arts Academy and helped establish Buffalo General Hospital and the city's first high school. He died at seventy-four in his beloved Buffalo on March 8, 1874.

Harry Truman, as a former president, sized up Fillmore as a president: "I'll tell you at a time when we needed a strong man, what we got was a man that swayed with the slightest breeze. About all he ever accomplished as President, he sent Commodore Perry to open up Japan to the West, but that didn't help much as far as preventing the Civil War was concerned."

The poll shows Fillmore sixth from the bottom overall, with poor ratings in every category. "Mediocrity personified," "weak—poor leadership qualities," "party hack," and "historic joke" are used to describe him. A minority conclude that he "did well, considering his party situation and crisis of 1840s," "capable leader in tough times," "definitely underrated," and "stronger than the press he gets," citing his "role in Compromise of 1850."

None of the three immediate pre–Civil War presidents, starting with Fillmore and continuing with Franklin Pierce and James Buchanan, had easy choices. These three presidents rank near the very bottom in the poll, unmatched in their low ratings by presidents of any other single period in American history. They faced the impossible task of placating two opposing camps on the slavery issue, with each camp supporting the certain moral rectitude of its own position by citing biblical passages.

The mainstream in national political thought maintained the hope and expectation that slavery would gradually be phased out some day. A minority of vocal and active extremists on both sides demanded prompt and firm action, military if necessary.

Fillmore acknowledged that the United States was conceived with the original sin of slavery and hoped that sin would be expunged peacefully some day. Truman and modern historians condemn Fillmore for being weak and for not taking bold action on the slavery issue. It is possible that, had Fillmore known there was going to be a civil war ten years later anyway, he might have forced the issue and risked civil war in 1850. What was clear to Fillmore was that in 1850 the South would not, without a probable fight to the death, abolish slavery or tolerate an abatement in its power balance in the Union. In this case compromise, and not bold action, accomplished his aim.

Even though Fillmore thought slavery an evil, as president he took an oath to defend the Constitution, and keeping the Union intact peacefully became the paramount objective. He achieved his objective and kept the door open for peaceful resolution of the slavery issue.

FRANKLIN PIERCE

1853–1857
14TH PRESIDENT

OVERALL RANKING: 37

Leadership Qualities: 38
Accomplishments and Crisis Management: 37
Political Skill: 37
Appointments: 36
Character and Integrity: 35

It is a relief to feel that no heart but my own can know the personal regret and bitter sorrow over which I have been borne to a position so suitable for others rather than desirable for myself.

—Franklin Pierce

The handsome young president with curly black hair uttered these words on his inauguration, normally a triumphant and joyful occasion. His sad gray eyes told another story.

Franklin Pierce had lost his only surviving son just two months earlier and still carried the crushing grief at his inauguration as the fourteenth president. For the rest of his term the loss of his son weighed heavily upon him and the first lady. He frequently sought refuge in drinking, and she became reclusive. Never had any president started his term after so devastating a blow and in such a depressed state.

Pierce was born in Hillsboro, New Hampshire, on November 23, 1804, in a log cabin. One among nine children in his family, the spirited young boy played mischievously and enjoyed fishing in the scenic waters of New Hampshire.

Receiving a proper education in the nearby academies, Pierce went on to attend Maine's Bowdoin College and graduate in 1824. There he met classmate Nathaniel Hawthorne, the great novelist, and launched a lifelong friendship. Pierce studied law and in 1827 was admitted to the New Hampshire bar to practice law.

He served four years (1829–1833) in the New Hampshire state legislature, beginning at the time when his father, Benjamin Pierce, commenced his second term as New Hampshire governor. This was followed by four years in the U.S. House of Representatives as a Jackson Democrat. The congenial Pierce was then selected as a U.S. senator from New Hampshire. At twenty-nine he had married a minister's daughter, Jane Appleton. She disliked Washington and usually stayed home in New Hampshire when Pierce attended sessions of Congress. They had three children, but not one of them reached the age of twelve. Pierce resigned the Senate in 1842 to return home to New Hampshire where he practiced law.

When the Mexican War erupted in 1846, he served in battle honorably as a brigadier general.

Pierce reemerged in politics as a dark horse presidential candidate of the Democratic Party in 1852. He and his Whig Party opponent, his former Mexican War commander Winfield Scott, agreed on the important issues. So, the election contest turned on personalities, and it was a particularly nasty one.

The Whigs labeled Pierce doughface, that is, a Northern man with Southern principles. They proceeded to belittle Pierce's military service in the Mexican War by publishing a tiny one-inch-by-one-half-inch book titled *The Military Services of General Pierce*, sarcastically presenting his war record. Pierce's opponents, referring to his well-known drinking escapades, tagged him the "hero of many a well fought bottle."

The Democrats touted their man as Young Hickory of the Granite Hills, drawing on a comparison with the legendary Andrew Jackson, Old Hickory. While Pierce seriously injured himself when his horse stumbled on some rocks, the Whigs accused him of having a fainting spell in battle. Despite such slander, Pierce and the Democrats won the election by an electoral college landslide. Pierce was to become the only president from New Hampshire.

Two months before his inauguration, Pierce and his wife traveled on a train en route to the funeral of a friend. The car in which they were riding derailed and tumbled down into a ravine scattering the passengers along the landscape. The only fatality was their only surviving son, eleven-year-old Benjamin, who died right before his parents' eyes. Neither Pierce nor his wife ever recovered from the tragedy. Pierce took consolation in the bottle in between bouts of depression. Mrs. Pierce drifted into a state of permanent depression; for the first two years as first lady she confined herself to the upstairs living quarters of the White House. Never again did she socialize with friends.

Pierce was motivated throughout his term with both preserving and expanding the Union. In his inaugural address, he stated the supreme priority he placed on preservation of the Union: "With the Union my best and dearest earthly hopes are entwined. Without it what are we individually or collectively? . . . It is with me an earnest and vital belief that as the Union has been the source, under Providence, of our prosperity to this time, so it is the surest pledge of a continuance of the blessings we have enjoyed and which we are sacredly bound to transmit undiminished to our children."

He made no apologies for his desire to increase the borders of the nation. Even over the objections of the antislavery adherents, he insisted that the United States' path to continental greatness mandated acquisition of large tracts of land whether they were free or slave territories. Again he pushed home his point to Congress: "Who would wish to see Florida still a European colony? Who would rejoice to hail Texas as a lone star instead of one in the galaxy of States? Who does not appreciate the incalculable benefits of the acquisition of Louisiana? And yet narrow views and sectional purposes would inevitably have excluded them from the Union."

On the ever-present issue of slavery, Pierce reiterated his approach to the subject in his inaugural address, stating, "I believe that involuntary servitude, as it exists in different States of this Confederacy, is recognized by the Constitution. I believe that it stands like any other admitted right, and that the States where it exists are entitled to efficient remedies to enforce the constitutional provisions."

Pierce firmly believed in limited government, as this speech to Congress in 1853 attests: "The revenue of the country, levied almost insensibly to the taxpayer, goes on from year to year, increasing beyond either the interests or the prospective wants of the Government."

The Pierce presidency witnessed the filling out of the border of what would become the forty-eight contiguous states with the addition of the 45,000-square-mile Gadsden Purchase in 1853. This land purchase from Mexico cost $10 million and made possible a direct rail link from Texas to the rapidly growing state of California.

In 1855 Pierce sought to add Cuba as another state. He authorized negotiations with Spain to purchase their colony for $120 million without ruling out possible military action to acquire the island. The expansionist president terminated further designs to annex Cuba when an uproar of opposition arose from antislavery forces in the North. They feared that Pierce, sympathetic to the South, sought merely to further expand slavery and Southern power to include Cuba. That Carribean island ninety miles offshore continues to this very day to vex the United States.

Yet another slavery-related episode involved the establishment of two new territories, Kansas and Nebraska. The Kansas-Nebraska Act of 1854 repealed the Missouri Compromise of 1820, which had set a geographical line north of which, except for the slave state of Missouri, slavery could not be introduced. Pierce supported the concept known as popular sovereignty, which the 1854 act incorporated, whereby the settlers of each territory could vote slavery in or out. The settlers in Nebraska had no need or use for slavery. However, Kansas, settled by both proslavery Southerners and antislavery Northerners, became the stormy site where cold air met hot air. "Bleeding Kansas" resulted, with about two hundred people losing their lives in the ensuing fighting.

Pierce favored the Kansas-Nebraska Act and had abuse heaped upon him by antislavery forces who originally had anticipated that Kansas would be admitted to the Union as a free state. With the Kansas-Nebraska Act, antislavery advocates feared Kansas Territory could opt to become a slave state.

As the United States spread across a continent, Pierce supported and realized such growth measures as land grants to spur railroad construction, expansion of trade with Japan, and construction of the Atlantic cable for improved contact with Europe. His presidency saw a reduction in the national debt from $60 million to $11 million, in one term.

Pierce merits the distinction of having the entire cabinet that he appointed remain unchanged throughout his term. His was a corruption-free administration.

On the slavery issue, Pierce garnered the enmity of Northerners for compromising, even though he himself hailed as a Yankee from New Hampshire. Like his predecessor, Fillmore, Pierce failed to be renominated by his own party and passed an intact country and party to his Democratic successor, James Buchanan.

Pierce, although no longer holding public office, labored arduously at preventing civil war in the early crisis days of secession. He even attempted to arrange for a conference of former presidents to work out a settlement but abandoned the idea after former president Martin Van Buren declined to participate for fear of interfering with the governance of a sitting president.

The pro-Union Pierce criticized President Abraham Lincoln's management of the Civil War as well as Lincoln's treading upon the Constitution by acts such as suspending the writ of habeas corpus and issuing the Emancipation Proclamation. Appalled at the Civil War carnage, Pierce emphasized the importance of maintaining the Union. He thought Lincoln and his abolitionist Republican associates further made reconciliation, peace, and reunion with the South impossible. Nonetheless, Pierce devoted much of his energy to wartime relief.

By the conclusion of the Civil War, Pierce felt the sting of New Hampshire public opinion branding him as anti-Republican and a traitor.

Left behind by the deaths of his wife in 1863 and his lifelong friend Nathaniel Hawthorne in 1864, Pierce isolated himself and resorted again to frequent bouts of drinking. He died on October 8, 1869, in Concord, New Hampshire.

Nathaniel Hawthorne had assessed the New Hampshire–born president in this way: "He has in him many of the chief elements of a great ruler. His talents are administrative, he has a subtle faculty of making affairs roll onward according to his will, and of influencing their course without showing any trace of his action. There are scores of men in the country that seem brighter than he is, but [he] has the directing mind, and will move them about like pawns on a chess-board, and turn all their abilities to better purpose than they themselves could do."

President Theodore Roosevelt, however, dismissed Pierce as "a small politician, of low capacity and mean surroundings, proud to act as the servile tool of men worse than himself but also stronger and abler. He was ever ready to do any work the slavery leaders set him." President Harry Truman agreed: "He's got the best picture in the White House, Franklin Pierce, but being President involves a little bit more than just winning a beauty contest, and he was another one that was a complete fizzle. . . . Pierce didn't know what was going on, and even if he had, he wouldn't of known what to do about it."

Our poll participants largely agree with Truman's assessment. They cite Pierce's inability to resolve the slavery issue and quell the threats of secession; Pierce's asserting a more forceful approach in dealing with the South, even threat of military force, would have been more beneficial in resolving the national dilemma. One of the lesser known presidents, Pierce suffers from poor ratings across the board in all categories. Comments such as "did nothing to halt the rush to war," "pawn of the slavocracy," "lacked leadership as the country headed for Civil War," and "alcoholic who supported the Kansas-Nebraska Act" reflect his low assessment.

Clearly, the death of his only surviving son two months before his inauguration took a toll on Pierce during his presidency. Unlike his predecessor Fillmore, Pierce did not count himself as an opponent of slavery. But like Fillmore, he put the uppermost priority on peacefully preserving the Union drawing upon his oath of office to "preserve, protect and defend the Constitution of the United States."

Critics of Pierce, of course, emphasize that the abolition of slavery was at the time a moral imperative transcending the issue of constitutionality. Perfectly obvious today, but not so obvious to all in the 1850s. After all the Founding Fathers explicitly permitted the institution to constitutionally exist. The abolitionists and fire eaters (pro-slavery fanatics) were viewed by most Americans of the time as a lunatic fringe.

Pierce suffers heavy criticism by today's standards. Perhaps he ought to be viewed with more understanding within the context of his times.

JAMES BUCHANAN

1857–1861
15TH PRESIDENT

OVERALL RANKING: 40

★

Leadership Qualities: 40
Accomplishments and Crisis Management: 41
Political Skill: 39
Appointments: 38
Character and Integrity: 36

What is right and what is practicable are two different things.

—James Buchanan

Buchanan believed slavery was a moral evil. Yet slavery was embedded in the Constitution, and he saw no way soon of ridding the nation of it without war. But, he reasoned, if each state would tend to its own business, in time, the institution of slavery would collapse on its own.

With sectional crisis acute and the country being torn apart, he managed to prevent the outbreak of war during his presidency. He actively promoted peaceful resolution of the crisis, believing that if he and others could calm the agitation of the radical extremists in both North and South, preservation of the Union and peace might be possible. But all hope for compromise and peace vanished as he retired and the crisis passed to his successor, Abraham Lincoln.

Buchanan is one of the most maligned of all the presidents. However, few presidents had the preparation for the presidency that Buchanan had.

James Buchanan was born in a one-room log cabin at Cove Gap, near Mercersburg, Pennsylvania, on April 23, 1791. The eldest of eleven children, he was the son of an Irish immigrant. Buchanan suffered from a disability lasting his entire life, an unusual eye disorder causing him to tilt his head to focus his vision. He was nearsighted in one eye and farsighted in the other.

At five he and his family moved to Mercersburg, Pennsylvania, where he later attended local schools and a preparatory school. After graduating from Dickinson College in 1809, he moved to Lancaster, Pennsylvania, and studied law. In 1812 he began his law practice and served as part of a defensive unit in the War of 1812. Enticed by the lure of politics, the six-foot-tall, blue-eyed Pennsylvanian served in his state legislature.

In 1818 his life took a fateful turn from which he never recovered. Ann Coleman entered his life, and they became engaged a year later. Disagreeing over what Buchanan years later called a trivial matter, Ann Coleman broke the engagement and died shortly afterward under mysterious circumstances—probably suicide. Buchanan grieved for the rest of his life and never married, earning the distinction as the only bachelor president.

After this tragic episode in his life, he channeled his energies into an extraordinary political career, stretching over five different decades, as congressman (switching from Federalist to Jackson Democrat), minister to Russia, U.S. senator from Pennsylvania, secretary of state, minister to Great Britain, and president.

The Democratic Party turned to Buchanan, the seasoned and cordial elder statesman of his party, as their presidential nominee in 1856. On the hot-button issues of the day, the Democrats opposed interference with slavery, approved the Compromise of 1850, and favored the Kansas-Nebraska Act, which permitted territorial settlers to decide the issue of slavery as an element of their prospective state constitutions. Buchanan's main opponent was the newly formed Republican Party's first presidential nominee, John C. Frémont.

The Republican Party touted abolition of slavery as its issue. Many voted for Buchanan out of fear of civil war if Frémont were elected. Future president Ulysses S. Grant echoed this view when he recalled in his memoirs, "In 1856 . . . I preferred the success of a candidate whose election would prevent or postpone secession, to seeing the country plunged into a war the end of which no man could foretell. With a Democrat elected by the unanimous vote of the Slave States, there could be no pretext for secession for four years. . . . I therefore voted for James Buchanan for President."

Buchanan won the election with his vice president, John C. Breckinridge, who at thirty-six became the youngest vice president ever to serve.

As a strict constructionalist, Buchanan took only that action which the Constitution clearly permitted. The implied constitutional powers that later evolved for the federal government and the presidency had not yet developed in the middle of the nineteenth century. Referring to the president, Buchanan stated in his final congressional message: "After all, he [the president] is no more than the chief executive officer of the Government. His province is not to make but to execute the laws." So, in Buchanan's view, the president had no authority to free slaves. Nor could the president send an army into South Carolina to forcibly prevent secession absent an attack on federal property or absent a constitutional act of Congress directing him to do so.

His view on slavery in his own words early in his political career shows that he thought it "to be a great political and a great moral evil. I thank God, my lot has been cast in a State where it does not exist. But, while I entertain these opinions, I know it is an evil at present without a remedy . . . one of those moral evils, from which it is impossible for us to escape, without the introduction of evils infinitely greater."

In similarly blunt language, Buchanan, again in his final congressional message in December 1860 declared, "Let us look the danger fairly in the face. Secession is neither more nor less than revolution." But according to Buchanan a paralyzed and split Congress failed to give the chief executive the lawful mandate to move against those states that had merely proclaimed secession.

Journalist and Pennsylvanian Republican leader A. K. McClure in 1902 assessed Buchanan: "Buchanan was not a magnetic man, not a popular man in the common acceptance of the term, but he was respected by all not only for his ability, but for his integrity and generally blameless reputation."

On the other hand, Thaddeus Stevens of Pennsylvania, a contemporary Republican congressman, heaped biting criticism upon Buchanan when he noted, "There is no such person running as James Buchanan. He is dead of lockjaw. Nothing remains but a platform and a bloated mass of political putridity."

In his diary, President James Polk wrote the following about Buchanan, his secretary of state: "Mr. Buchanan is an able man, but in small matters without judgment and sometimes acts like an old maid." Yet virtually all who knew him vouch for him as a profoundly religious man, impeccably honest and generous. On many an occasion Buchanan bought slaves in the District of Columbia and took them with him to Pennsylvania, a free state, and emancipated them.

In one incident, when a merchant furnished Buchanan with a paid-in-full receipt showing three cents more than Buchanan paid him the president sent the merchant the three-cent shortfall. Buchanan consciously avoided even the appearance of impropriety. While president, he refused a free railroad pass and sent on to the Patent Office all gifts he received. He ran a clean ship as president and set himself as an example. As often is the case, events beyond his control took over.

Two days after Buchanan took the oath of presidential office, the U.S. Supreme Court announced its decision in the Dred Scott case. Finding slavery to be lawful under the Constitution, it ruled that blacks—whether free or enslaved—whose ancestors had arrived in America as slaves did not qualify as U.S. or state citizens; they, therefore, did not have a citizen's right to sue in federal courts. Moreover, an enslaved black person who escaped to a free state or territory must be returned as property to his or her owner. It further held that Congress had no right to ban slavery in a territory and that, therefore, the Missouri Compromise of 1820 was unconstitutional. Rarely had any presidential term commenced with such a firestorm. While the South was delighted, abolitionists in the North immediately excoriated the Court's decision, prompting a new round and escalation in sectional rivalry.

With Kansas poised on the verge of statehood, a state constitutional convention was held at Lecompton, Kansas, in the fall of 1857. Attended largely by proslavery delegates, the convention wrote a constitution that would guarantee the right of property in slaves and would lead to the admission of Kansas to the Union as a slave state. Buchanan supported the right of the convention to decide its own state's destiny. However, two subsequent referenda were held, the second of which overwhelmingly rejected the Lecompton Constitution in 1858. The Kansas question whipped up a furor over the slavery issue and the balance of sectional power. In 1859, Kansas adopted a constitution prohibiting slavery and entered the Union as a free state in 1861.

On the heels of the start of the controversy over Kansas's constitution, the Buchanan administration had been dealt another blow—the Panic of 1857. Bank depositors, with their confidence shaken after the collapse of the Ohio Life Insurance and Trust Company of Cincinnati, suddenly withdrew their funds and a panic ensued. As was customary before the Great Depression of the 1930s, the president did not intervene.

John Brown, an abolitionist leader, struck fear in the South in 1859 when he led fewer than two dozen antislavery followers, including five blacks, in a raid on a federal arsenal at Harpers Ferry, Virginia. Southerners often worried about slave rebellions, and John Brown hit that nerve. In the raid, one U.S. Marine, four townsmen including a free black, and ten of Brown's followers were killed before Brown and six of his raiders were captured, tried, and hanged.

Buchanan, having already declined renomination by the Democratic Party, attempted to calm the growing fears and tensions and to reconcile North and South in the hope of avoiding a calamitous civil war.

In the election of 1860, with the Democrats split between the Northern faction supporting Senator Stephen Douglas and the Southern faction supporting Buchanan's vice president, John C. Breckinridge, and a third-party candidate John Bell in the race, Republican Abraham Lincoln was elected president. At the very news of Lincoln's election, South Carolina in December—and Mississippi, Florida, Alabama, Georgia, and Louisiana in January 1861—proceeded to secede from the Union. It is ironic that Lincoln's election made the push toward civil war more likely. In the most geographically divisive presidential election in U.S. history, the Southern states were unanimous in their opposition to Lincoln. Never in American history has there been such an overwhelming regional rejection of a major party candidate—let alone an elected president. With Lincoln's election, most southerners believed that the time for negotiating was over and the time for secession at hand.

Even so, several patriots, such as John J. Crittenden and former president Franklin Pierce, heroically attempted to forestall civil war and maintain the Union by working at negotiations. Buchanan himself prevailed upon the governor of South Carolina to refrain from attacking Fort Sumter. Accordingly, Buchanan agreed not to send federal reinforcements to Fort Sumter in the hope that time might permit cooler heads to prevail and allow a negotiated settlement to the sectional differences and thereby peacefully preserve the Union.

By February 1861, seven Deep South states (Texas was the last of these) had announced secession from the Union one by one. Buchanan believed, as a strict constructionist, the Constitution gave him no authority to forcibly act upon the secession pronouncements. However, he intended to act, by force if necessary, to protect federal property, including Fort Sumter. Although Buchanan managed to prevent South Carolina state units from firing on Fort Sumter while he was president, it is clear that he, like Lincoln, would have defended it by force had it been attacked on his watch. Reflecting on the precarious national crisis not yet turned to bloodshed, Buchanan remarked to Lincoln as the new president took the reins of government, "My dear sir, if you are as happy in entering the White House as I shall feel on returning to Wheatland [Pennsylvania], you are a happy man indeed."

Old Buck, as he was called, retired to his treasured home at Wheatland, the sixteen-room brick mansion at Lancaster, Pennsylvania. With the outbreak of hostilities, he supported Lincoln's actions in the Civil War and even donated money to equip a Pennsylvania unit. Yet Republicans charged him with conspiring in favor of the Confederacy, prompting threats on his life. He felt that the Republicans made him a scapegoat for the war. After the war, in 1866, Buchanan wrote his book, *Mr. Buchanan's Administration on the Eve of the Rebellion*, which defended the actions of his administration. Nevertheless, it was the influential historians of the North who wrote the history books reflecting the prevailing Republican view that formed American opinion for the century following the war.

In his retirement at Wheatland, he enjoyed entertaining friends, reading, and corresponding with his past associates. Buchanan remained silent on political affairs except for acknowledging support for the Union and for both Presidents Lincoln and Andrew Johnson in their policies.

The only Pennsylvanian to serve as chief executive of the nation died at Wheatland on June 1, 1868.

The poll participants perceive Buchanan as having failed to effectively deal with secession and slavery. They rate him second worst of all the presidents. Comments like "failed to understand or meet the coming crisis," "fiddles while the nation divides," and "failed to counter the slide to war" abound. Most poll participants characterize Buchanan's attempt at compromise and lack of action in dealing with the secession crisis as weakness, placing him dead last in the Leadership category: "Indecisive in crisis," "lacked spunk to deal with mounting crisis," and "fails the test of leadership."

Others in the poll concede that "his situation was impossible" and that he faced "extraordinarily difficult problems." A minority expressed some positive view of Buchanan: "Tried to avoid war," "avoided sectionalism," and "master pacifier."

Buchanan, a lame-duck president upon Lincoln's election, viewed his mission as one of preserving the peace while promoting an atmosphere of negotiation in hopes of a peaceful resolution of sectional differences and restoration of the Union. Buchanan did hand over to Lincoln a shattered Union, but civil war was not necessarily inevitable. However, in order to skillfully arrange for any kind of agreement, the national leader required the confidence of both North and South. Buchanan, for the most part, was viewed as a mediator, although extremists on both sides attacked him. On the other hand, Lincoln most definitely enjoyed nothing but the mistrust and enmity of the South.

Shortly before his death, Buchanan reflected on his presidency and noted that he had no regrets and that he had discharged his constitutional duty. He felt that, despite the hostile Republican interpretation of history, some day he would be vindicated.

Perhaps that old American sage, Benjamin Franklin, reflects Buchanan's goals in his presidency with these words: "There never was a good war or a bad peace." Buchanan did avoid the devastation of civil war while he was president. One month after he left office, the nation was plunged into its most tragic and most bloody conflict.

ABRAHAM LINCOLN

1861–1865
16TH PRESIDENT

OVERALL RANKING: 1

★

Leadership Qualities: 2
Accomplishments and Crisis Management: 1
Political Skill: 2
Appointments: 3
Character and Integrity: 1

Next to the destruction of the Confederacy, the death of Abraham Lincoln was the darkest day the South has ever known.

—Jefferson Davis

Why is Abraham Lincoln rated as the greatest president? What is it about his presidency, or the man, or both, that captures the imagination of contemporary Americans? No doubt Lincoln's reputation has been enhanced by his becoming almost mythological, but even his archrival Jefferson Davis, president of the Confederate States of America, honored him with words of tribute.

Abraham Lincoln was born, the middle of three children, on February 12, 1809, near Hodgenville, Kentucky, in a rural log cabin. He and his family moved to near Gentryville, Spencer County, Indiana.

Largely self-educated, Lincoln worked as a rail-splitter and local postmaster in New Salem, Illinois, before becoming a successful attorney in the state capital of Springfield. He served as a state legislator and then as a congressman in the Whig Party.

Joining the Republican Party in 1856, the six-foot-four, 180-pound Lincoln was catapulted into national prominence as a spokesman on the slavery issue during his unsuccessful Senate election campaign against Stephen A. Douglas. The seven 1858 campaign debates gained fame as the Lincoln-Douglas debates. Lincoln captured the 1860 Republican presidential nomination and ran on the slavery issue. The Republican platform opposed extension of slavery into the territories but did not advocate the abolition of slavery in the slave states where it already existed. Republicans had support in the North but none in the South.

In August, before the November election, the *Southern Confederacy* magazine published in Atlanta, Georgia, stated the following:

> The South will never permit Abraham Lincoln to be inaugurated President of the United States; this is a settled and a sealed fact. It is the determination of all parties in the South. Let the consequences be what they may, whether the Potomac is crimsoned in human gore, and Pennsylvania Avenue is paved ten fathoms deep with mangled bodies, or whether the last vestige of liberty is swept from the face of the American continent, the South, the loyal South, the constitu-

tional South, will never submit to such humiliation and degradation as the inauguration of Abraham Lincoln.

With only 40 percent of the popular vote, Lincoln won the election with a majority of the electoral vote in a field of four major candidates. Reaction to Lincoln's election was predictable. The very election of Lincoln ended any realistic hope of maintaining the Union by peaceful negotiation. South Carolina announced its secession, and other Southern states soon followed. Before Lincoln took office, Alabama, Florida, Georgia, Louisiana, Mississippi, and Texas had also declared secession.

President Buchanan attempted to forestall irrevocable action on the part of the seceding states by buying time for negotiations to keep the Union together peacefully. He agreed with the governor of South Carolina not to reinforce Fort Sumter if South Carolina forces agreed not to attack it, thereby preserving an atmosphere of possible negotiation.

Lincoln was inaugurated on March 4, 1861. He took no military action until April 12, 1861, when, with provisions starting to run low at Fort Sumter, he decided to reprovision the fort. In response, Confederate forces fired on the fort that same day and occupied it the next.

Acting swiftly, Lincoln called for 75,000 volunteers on April 15 and ordered a blockade of Southern ports on April 19.

Four more states seceded and joined the newly formed Confederacy between May 6 and June 8: Arkansas, North Carolina, Tennessee, and Virginia. The critical border state of Virginia had previously voted against secession, but, after the breakdown of the understanding over Fort Sumter and subsequent firm action by Lincoln, voted to join the Confederacy.

On the burning issue of the day—slavery—Lincoln voiced his strong opposition. In his first Senate campaign in 1854 he had spoken directly to the issue: "If the Negro is a man, why then my ancient faith teaches me that 'all men are created equal,' and that there can be no moral right in connection with one man's making a slave of another."

Four years later, at Ottawa, Illinois, in one of the 1858 Lincoln-Douglas debates, Lincoln had said the following:

> I have no purpose, directly or indirectly, to interfere with the institution of slavery in the States where it exists. I believe I have no lawful right to do so, and I have no inclination to do so. I have no purpose to introduce political and social equality between the white and black races. There is a physical difference between the two, which, in my judgment, will probably forever forbid their living together on terms of respect, social and political equality, and inasmuch as it becomes

a necessity that there must be a superiority somewhere, I, as well as Judge Douglas, am in favor of the race to which I belong having the superior position.

In fairness to Lincoln, this still reflected enlightened thinking in the middle of the nineteenth century; it was still, politically, a white man's country. Lincoln clarified his position in the debates: "In the right to eat the bread, which his own hand earns, he, the Negro, is my equal and the equal of Judge Douglas, and the equal of every living man."

Lincoln further emphasized his position during his presidency in 1864: "If slavery is not wrong, nothing is wrong."

During his presidency, Lincoln viewed presidential powers broadly in order to cope with the war crisis: "As commander-in-chief of the army and navy, in time of war I suppose I have a right to take any measure which may best subdue the enemy." He also thought that even though they were not constitutionally provided, a government had certain implied powers to protect its own existence.

Lincoln possessed a brilliant wit, probably the most humorous of any president, particularly noted for its homespun nature. Once, after a prominent senator had chided Lincoln for his military blunders in the Civil War and complained that Lincoln was on the road to hell, almost there, just a mile away, Lincoln replied, "Senator that is just about the distance from here to the Capitol, is it not?"

On another occasion, a group of Chicago ministers came to Washington to volunteer advice to the president. After one minister told Lincoln that they carried "a message to you from our Divine Master" about Lincoln's handling of the issue of slavery, Lincoln looked at them with his soft gray eyes and retorted that he thought it "odd that the only channel he could send it by was the roundabout route of that awful wicked city of Chicago!"

Once, a senator who was extremely upset over being shortchanged on patronage for his friends visited Lincoln at the White House and unleashed a barrage of cussing. After the verbal cannon fire ceased, the plainspoken Lincoln inquired, "You are an Episcopalian, aren't you, Senator?"

"Yes, sir, I belong to that church."

"I thought so," remarked Lincoln. "You Episcopalians all swear alike. But [Secretary of War] Stanton is a Presbyterian. You ought to hear him swear!" Through this exchange, Lincoln, not a member of any organized church, humorously made his point about the hypocrisy of swearing by those who professed to be churchgoers.

Lincoln, the man, possessed an extraordinary amount of compassion. He was a softy when it came to setting aside execution orders, exasperating his military commanders. Invariably, he would find some excuse to permanently delay shooting a deserter.

A woman once begged Lincoln to release her husband from the army to help support his needy family. Lincoln gave in to her request. Of the incident, Lincoln said to Joshua Speed, a friend, "It is more than many can often say, that in doing right one has made two people happy in one day. Speed, die when I may, I want it said of me by those who know me best, that I have always plucked a thistle and planted a flower when I thought a flower would grow."

It is truly ironic that probably the most compassionate of presidents presided over the bloodiest term of presidency. This no doubt contributed to Lincoln's bouts of mental depression. As he himself said on numerous occasions, had it not been for his joke-telling and good humor, he would not have survived the many tragedies and pains he had experienced.

Abraham Lincoln lost one son in infancy and later lost his beloved son, William, in 1862. He never ceased to grieve for Willie, and the fragile Mary Todd Lincoln was probably driven to madness by this loss.

One hundred years after Lincoln's birth, future president Woodrow Wilson described Lincoln, the man: "Lincoln was a very normal man with very normal gifts, but all upon a great scale, all knit together in loose and natural form, like the great frame in which he moved and dwelt."

However, Democratic senator Willard Saulsburg of Delaware viewed Lincoln differently: "I never did see or converse with so weak and imbecile a man; the weakest man I ever knew in high place. If I wanted to paint a despot, a man perfectly regardless of every constitutional right of the people, I would paint the hideous, apelike form of Abraham Lincoln."

At various times during his presidency, some of the press labeled Lincoln a despot, tyrant, monster, ape, buffoon, traitor, idiot, and lunatic. He was called "that hideous baboon at the other end of the avenue" by a New York newspaper, which added, "Barnum should buy and exhibit him as a zoological curiosity."

His home-state *Illinois State Register* unmercifully tabbed him the "craftiest and most dishonest politician that ever disgraced an office in America." Even his very hometown paper verbally lashed him: "How the greatest butchers of antiquity sink into insignificance when their crimes are contrasted with those of Abraham Lincoln!"

It was no wonder Lincoln relayed the following story when asked how he liked being president: "You have heard about the man tarred and feathered and ridden out of town on a rail? A man in the crowd asked him how he liked it, and his reply was that if it wasn't for the honor of the thing, he would much rather walk."

The first major engagement of the Civil War, the Battle of Bull Run, took place in July 1861, resulting in a Confederate victory. The following month Lincoln signed the Confiscation Act freeing slaves forced to fight for the Confederacy. Union forces had to wait until February 1862 for their first important victory: General Ulysses S. Grant captured Fort Donelson in Tennessee. Later that month, the president signed the Legal Tender Act, which provided for $150 million in paper money to help finance the Union war effort.

The Homestead Act signed by Lincoln in May 1862 gave, for the cost of a nominal fee, 160 acres of public land to settlers in order to populate the frontier. The following month, slavery in U.S. territories was prohibited. With the Union position uncertain, Lincoln called for another 300,000 in volunteers in July 1862. The Morrill Act, setting up a system of government grants to finance agricultural and mechanical arts colleges, was signed into law by Lincoln the same month.

The Union cause was dealt another setback when federal troops were routed in the Second Battle of Bull Run in August 1862. However, in a battle that included the bloodiest single day of fighting in the war, Union forces turned back Confederate troops at Antietam, Maryland, in September 1862.

Lincoln, long pressured by abolitionists and Republicans, announced the Emancipation Proclamation, freeing all slaves in areas in open rebellion, effective January 1, 1863.

With no real progress visible toward a favorable conclusion of the war, Lincoln signed the Conscription Act in March 1863, and the drafting of men to fight for the Union cause began. But in July of that year there occurred the most deadly riots in U.S. history, the worst of which took place in New York City, where rioters were mainly Irish immigrants who did not see the Civil War as their struggle. Coming after the Confederate victory at Chancellorsville, Virginia, in May and on the heels of the Gettysburg, Pennsylvania, bloodbath just ten days before, the antidraft riots reflected the growing unpopularity of the war. During the four-day insurrection, about a thousand people were killed.

In June 1863, breakaway counties in western Virginia were admitted to the Union as the state of West Virginia.

Union forces halted the Confederate offensive in the North in the landmark Battle of Gettysburg in July and also seized control of the Mississippi Valley, splitting the Confederacy in half.

At a memorial service on November 19, 1863, honoring the fallen heroes at Gettysburg, Lincoln followed one of the great orators of the day, Edward Everett, who spoke for two hours. Yet Lincoln's Gettysburg Address, only a few minutes long, remains one of the great American speeches. Its concluding lines are among the most moving words ever spoken: "It is rather for us here to be dedicated to the great task remaining before us—that from these honored dead we take increased devotion to that cause for which they gave the last full measure of devotion; that we here highly resolve that these dead shall not have died in vain; that this nation, under God, shall have a new birth of freedom; and that government of the people, by the people, for the people, shall not perish from the earth."

A few days later, Union troops proved victorious at the Battle of Chattanooga, Tennessee. However, Union troops were stalled, despite numbers, equipment, and supplies vastly superior to those of Confederate forces. A frustrated Lincoln turned command of the Union army over to General Grant in March 1864.

As the months rolled on, the Union war effort showed little progress. Even staunch Republicans talked of dumping Lincoln from the ticket as they began to think of the upcoming November 1864 presidential election. Some suggested replacing Lincoln with General Grant, especially if Grant could capture the Confederate capital, Richmond, Virginia. Lincoln reacted to this speculation with his usual allegorizing: "Well I feel very much like the man who said he didn't want to die particularly, but if he had to die that was precisely the disease he would like to die of." General Grant communicated his adamant refusal to be considered as a presidential candidate.

On June 7, 1864, Lincoln was nominated by the Republicans under the coalition banner of the National Union Party. He surprised many by replacing incumbent vice president Hannibal Hamlin with Tennessee War Democrat and Union supporter Andrew Johnson as vice presidential candidate.

At this point, Lincoln's reelection looked doubtful. Many, including former president Millard Fillmore, who supported the Union, were wondering why Lincoln could not lead the North to victory over the outnumbered, undersupplied, and underprovisioned South. They were also horrified by the carnage. Lincoln felt it necessary to have each member of his cabinet sign a statement agreeing to cooperate with his successor for the sake of the country.

Former president Franklin Pierce attacked Lincoln's ineptness, saying "[Lincoln] is to the extent of his limited ability and narrow intelligence [the abolitionists'] willing instrument for all the woe which [has] thus far been brought upon the Country and for all the degradation, all the atrocity, all the desolation and ruin."

The Democrats nominated the popular general George B. McClellan for president. He had been given command of the Union army by Lincoln and was subsequently removed by him for what Lincoln viewed as lack of action. McClellan proposed to wind down the war and take a more conciliatory approach to the Confederacy—perhaps negotiate a deal. The Republicans attacked McClellan's patriotism, calling him a coward and a defeatist lacking loyalty to the Union and engaging in treasonous activities.

The Democrats responded by saying Lincoln's butchery of Americans was a result of his incompetence and stupidity, and they charged that graft permeated the entire government and war effort.

A series of Union victories by Grant and General William Sherman brightened the outlook of the Union war effort. This gave a sense of progress, with prospects of victory in sight. Lincoln's fortunes similarly changed, resulting in his reelection in 1864. Within a week after the election, Sherman started his march of devastation through Georgia.

The beginning of 1865 saw the Confederate forces on the run. On April 9 the main Confederate army under General Robert E. Lee surrendered to General Grant at Appomattox Courthouse, Virginia. By May, the remaining Confederate armies surrendered, and the Civil War became a tragedy of America's past.

On April 14, 1865, Lincoln was shot by John Wilkes Booth, a Confederate sympathizer, while attending a play at Ford's Theater in Washington. He died the next morning, the first president to be assassinated. Strangely, Lincoln had been haunted by this possibility. In 1864 he stated, "If it is [God's] will that I must die at the hand of an assassin, I must be resigned. I must do my duty as I see it, and leave the rest with God."

Lincoln left much unfinished business, including reconstruction after the devastating war. He had planned a lenient reconstruction of the South with emphasis on healing rather than retribution. He had summed up his approach: "I have always found that mercy bears richer fruits than strict justice."

Years later, former president Ulysses Grant, referring to Lincoln, noted in his own memoirs, "He always showed a generous and kindly spirit toward the Southern people, and I never heard him abuse an enemy." An integral part of Lincoln's greatness as a man and a leader was the wisdom he displayed by being magnanimous in victory. He felt that this was the quickest and most efficient political healing cure.

The Supreme Court handed down a post–Civil War opinion in 1866 in the case of Ex Parte Milligan, which touched on Lincoln's handling of Constitutional rights. The opinion was delivered by Lincoln's old friend and appointee to the Court, David Davis. The Court found that Lincoln had violated the Constitution in court-martialing civilians during the Civil War in areas in which the civil courts were functioning.

Our poll rates the category of Lincoln's Character and Integrity the highest of any president's. The poll also lauds his appointments, including Secretary of State William H. Seward, Secretary of the Treasury Salmon P. Chase, Secretary of War Edwin M. Stanton, and Secretary of the Navy Gideon Welles.

His steady leadership, rated second among the presidents, kept the Union cause alive during the Civil War's darkest days for the Union. Our experts describe this with remarks like "took America through it's greatest crisis," "great moral leader," "had broad strategic vision and a poet's wisdom," "skillful leadership under very adverse circumstances," and "started badly but ended grandly."

The poll shows nearly unanimous agreement on Lincoln's shrewd and disarming political style, rating him number two in the Political Skill category. He could handle the most vociferous of his opponents in classic diplomatic manner. The master politician made no unnecessary enemies and would be at home with today's political leaders in working a crowd and perhaps a television audience as well. "The democratic potential fulfilled" writes one expert.

The poll participants also rate Lincoln as tops in Accomplishments and Crisis Management. He collects accolades like "created a nation—master crisis manager," "grew in the job, saved the Union, ended slavery," and "the greatest achievement of U.S. political culture." However, there are those who do not consider America's bloodiest conflict, the Civil War, to be an accomplishment—nor his handling of the war to have been efficient. It took four years for the vastly superior Union forces, together with the overwhelming industrial and economic might of the North, to subdue the Confederacy. Some experts' comments include these: "[He] brought about Civil War"; "He precipitated the most tragic experience of our nation"; "It is disconcerting that an obsession for Union made him great"; and "He did violate civil rights." Then there is the issue of the unfinished business in the aftermath of the Civil War cataclysm. Lincoln died before he could bring into reality his vision for the future of the devastated nation. That legacy is lacking from his presidency. Perhaps this is why one expert describes Lincoln as "greatly overrated."

Doubtless, the top position is reserved to Lincoln in some part because of his tragic assassination and martyrdom.

Nevertheless, Lincoln was truly a great man. He possessed qualities of kindness and compassion. Lincoln also had the wisdom of magnanimousness in victory, especially needed for the national healing after the Civil War. Many of the men reaching the august office of the presidency have lacked these simple but uncommon virtues, which play so important a part in governing a nation. Lincoln, like Washington, possessed extraordinary strength of character. It is due in large part to the personal qualities of each that their reputations have survived the changing attitudes on political issues that often affect the reputations of presidents.

So, almost apart from his presidential performance, Lincoln enjoys those noble and intangible qualities of a martyred saint that assure him greatness and top ranking in the poll.

Andrew Johnson

1865–1869
17th President

Overall Ranking: 39

★

Leadership Qualities: 39
Accomplishments and Crisis Management: 38
Political Skill: 41
Appointments: 37
Character and Integrity: 30

No man has a right to judge Andrew Johnson in any respect who has not suffered as much and done as much as he for the Nation's sake.

—Abraham Lincoln

These words of President Abraham Lincoln at the time Andrew Johnson was his choice for vice president have not stopped the heap of criticism unleashed upon the seventeenth president. Much of the attack stems from Johnson's virtual war with a Congress whose policies he opposed. Congress, in turn, tried to thwart his opposition, first by encroaching on his presidential power and then by trying to remove him from office altogether by impeachment.

With the Civil War over and the strong emergency powers of the president no longer necessary, Congress reasserted itself as the predominant branch of government. To Johnson, Congress overstepped its constitutional limits. Although Johnson did not win the policy struggle, he did win the power struggle. His reputation, however, was lost in the process.

Andrew Johnson was born into utter poverty in a small log home on December 29, 1808, at Raleigh, North Carolina. With no formal education Johnson spent time in Carthage, North Carolina, Laurens, South Carolina, and Columbia, Tennessee, and settled in Greeneville, Tennessee, where he plied his craft as a tailor. The five-foot-ten tailor with the swarthy complexion and black eyes rose from Greeneville alderman and mayor to a seat in the Tennessee House of Representatives as a Jackson Democrat and then to the Tennessee Senate.

Johnson, a good speaker, represented Tennessee in the U.S. House of Representatives and then served as governor of Tennessee. In 1857 he took office as U.S. senator from Tennessee.

Johnson had been a lukewarm defender of slavery but an enthusiastic defender of the Union. In 1861, he declared, "Away with slavery, the breeder of Aristocrats. Up with the Stars and Stripes, symbol of free labor and free men." The only U.S. senator from a secessionist state to support the Union cause, he condemned secession in his typically simple, direct, and blunt way in 1860, stating, "Secession is hell-born and hell-bound." Later, after Lincoln's election as president, referring to the secessionists, he added, "I would have them arrested and tried for treason, and, if convicted, by the eternal God, they should suffer the penalty of the law at the hands of the executioner."

President Lincoln appointed him military governor of Tennessee with the army rank of brigadier general in 1862. Johnson promptly resigned his U.S. Senate seat to accept the appointment. As military governor, seeing the handwriting on the wall, he advocated abolition by state constitutional amendment, and Tennessee became the only seceding state to end slavery by state law. Johnson added his observation: "Slavery is dead, and you must pardon me if I do not mourn over its dead body."

At the 1864 national convention of the Republican Party, renamed National Union Party for the wartime effort, Lincoln was renominated for president and selected Johnson, a War Democrat and strong Unionist from Tennessee, as his vice presidential running mate. Tense over his inauguration as vice president in March 1865, Johnson fortified himself with a bit too much whiskey and embarrassed himself by appearing drunk. His enemies seized on the occasion thereafter to label him a drunkard.

Johnson served as vice president only a month. Stunned, as was the entire nation, at the death of President Lincoln, he was promptly sworn in as the seventeenth president on April 15, 1865.

Like Lincoln, Johnson believed in a mild Reconstruction policy with each state adopting a new state constitution renouncing secession, slavery, and the Confederate war debt. Each state also had to ratify the Thirteenth Amendment, which abolished slavery. Citizens of the former Confederate states, upon swearing an oath of allegiance to the United States, would receive full restoration of their citizenship. In a speech on the reconstruction debate, Johnson said, "If a State is to be nursed until it again gets strength, it must be nursed by its friends, not smothered by its enemies." Like Lincoln, he preferred magnanimity in victory to harsh military occupation. Like Lincoln, Johnson prided himself on his humble origins. Jefferson Davis, president of the Confederacy, in 1865 observed of Johnson, "One of the people by birth, he remained so by conviction, continually referring to his origin. . . . He was indifferent to money and careless of praise or censure." He took up the causes of the workingman and fought privilege where he found it. Johnson was not particularly fond of aristocrats, the wealthy class that included owners of large plantations worked by slaves. On one occasion, Johnson stated, "Some day I will show the stuck-up aristocrats who is running the country. . . . A cheap purse-proud set they are, not half as good as the man who earns his bread by the sweat of his brow."

Like many presidents, Johnson was treated cruelly by the press. Upon his election to the vice presidency, the *New York World* remarked of him,

"To think that one frail life stands between this insolent, clownish creature and the presidency! May God bless and spare Abraham Lincoln." A contemporary acquaintance of his, Ohio governor Jacob Cox, had another view and remarked early in Johnson's presidency, "If you could meet his straightforward honest look and hear the hearty tone of his voice, as I did, I am well assured you would believe with me, that although he may not receive personal assaults with the equanimity and forbearance Mr. Lincoln used to show, there is no need to fear that Andrew Johnson is not hearty and sincere in his adhesion to the principles upon which he was elected." Senator Charles Sumner of Massachusetts, another contemporary of Johnson and one of the Radical Republicans in Congress, derided him: "Johnson is an insolent drunken brute in comparison with which Caligula's horse was respectable." Senator Sumner alluded to the time the Roman emperor Caligula named his horse a Roman senator.

In spite of his critics, Johnson in May 1865 granted amnesty to all former Confederates who took part in the Civil War, except for the leaders, provided they took an oath of allegiance to the United States.

While he hated the Southern aristocracy, Johnson saw no reason to punish ordinary white citizens of the South, many of whom were suffering in poverty from the ravages of the war. His intention was to implement Lincoln's plan for leniency in welcoming back the nation's white Southerners.

Congress, controlled by the Radical Republicans, felt that their mission was to punish the Southern states that had seceded, and control the state governments in order to maintain power and prevent the almost certain return of a flood of Democratic senators and congressmen from the former Confederate states. By 1866, Republicans picked up enough seats in Congress to take control and had the votes to override presidential vetoes.

The Republicans passed the Freedmen's Bureau Act in 1866 over Johnson's veto. The law extended the existence of the Freedmen's Bureau set up under the Lincoln administration. The bureau looked after the educational and medical needs of Southern blacks and provided land and jobs for them. While the Freedmen's Bureau had a noble purpose, it was also an attempt by the Republicans to harvest the votes of 4 million former slaves. The District of Columbia Suffrage Act, passed in 1867, gave the vote to District of Columbia residents.

The Reconstruction Acts of 1867 and 1868 set forth the punitive mission of the Radical Republican Congress. These acts provided for military governments to replace the civil governments controlled by white Southern Democrats. The two laws required that in order for civilian state governments to be restored the Southern states would have to call new constitutional conventions elected by universal manhood suffrage. The new state governments would have to guarantee African-American men the right to vote and hold office. Those people who had been active in the Confederacy were to be denied the right to vote and hold office. The new state governments would have to ratify the Fourteenth Amendment.

As a result, new terms were introduced into the political vernacular, such as *carpetbaggers*, Northern opportunity seekers; and *scalawags*, white Southerners cooperating with blacks, all bent on taking control of the state and local governments in the South.

Johnson vigorously opposed the congressional Reconstruction Acts, cautioning Congress that these acts were counterproductive. In his unsuccessful veto of the First Reconstruction Act, he condemned the Radical Republican plan: "Our victories subjected the insurgents to legal obedience, not to the yoke of an arbitrary despotism." The Republican Congress did not heed his advice.

The president proved to be correct. The Ku Klux Klan sprung up in 1866 to obstruct Reconstruction and advance white control in the South. When the military governments were dismantled a decade later, the seething hatred of Southern whites was so strong that the South became solidly and exclusively a Democratic Party region for a century. To be called a Republican was a vile attack. As a consequence, Southern whites enacted segregation laws victimizing blacks, and these remained in force for a century. Obviously, Southern white attitudes on race relations had not been changed by facing the end of the barrel of a gun.

Further attesting to the failure of the Radical Republican Reconstruction was the reliance upon military occupation and lack of practical assistance to African Americans in the form of land grants and a sum of money for a fresh start in life serving as reparations for their government-sanctioned enslavement. Without practical assistance, most African Americans in the South were still at the mercy of the system, this time as poorly paid laborers or impoverished sharecroppers. When the federal forces ultimately withdrew from the South, the freed slaves were left to fend for themselves in a hostile environment.

Nonetheless, the Republican Congress, surprised by the president's strong leadership and outspoken manner, targeted Johnson. In 1867, Congress passed the Command of the Army Act, which was designed to deprive the president of his command of the army by forcing him to issue all military orders through the general of the army, who could not be removed or reassigned without Senate consent. Congress also passed the Tenure of Office Act, which prevented the president from removing any federal office holder who had attained office with required Senate approval. These two laws were clearly infringements of presidential power. Johnson, not intimidated and believing the laws unconstitutional, removed Secretary of War Edwin M. Stanton, a Radical Republican, from his own cabinet. Subsequently, Johnson was impeached by the lower house, the House of Representatives, for "high crimes and misdemeanors," primarily for violating the Tenure of Office Act and the Command of the Army Act. No president had ever been impeached before—or since.

The stage in 1868 was set for Johnson's trial by the upper house of Congress, the Senate, which could vote to convict and remove the president or acquit and keep the president. Conviction and removal of the president would give the Radical Republicans in Congress free reign to run the country completely unhampered by Johnson. No other president ever faced such a hostile and powerful Congress as had Johnson.

Of the fifty-four senators, forty-two were Republicans and only twelve were Democrats. Johnson clearly faced an uphill battle, even considering that a two-thirds majority vote, thirty-six votes, was necessary to convict him. The final vote on the most serious of the impeachment charges, including the charge of violation of the Tenure of Office Act, was thirty-five to convict, nineteen to acquit. Johnson's presidency and reputation was saved by only one vote as seven Republicans switched to vote with the twelve Democrats for acquittal. Johnson noted that had his predecessor, Lincoln, lived, "the vials of wrath would have poured out upon him."

The president continued to lash out at the Republican Congress for violating the Constitution. Almost sixty years later, in 1926, the Supreme Court ruled the Tenure of Office Act unconstitutional, proving Johnson right.

In spite of the ignominy of impeachment, Johnson's presidency saw the ratification of the Thirteenth Amendment, abolishing slavery in the United States, and the Fourteenth Amendment, granting full citizenship rights to all Americans. Also noteworthy was the acquisition of Alaska from Russia for $7.2 million, with negotiations handled by the able secretary of state William H. Seward. At the time it was referred to as Seward's Folly. Contemporary Americans have a very different opinion of that purchase.

Having failed to gain the nomination of either the Democratic or Republican Party for another term as president, Johnson retired to his home in Greeneville, Tennessee. Twice beaten in elections for Congress, he aspired to the U.S. Senate seat from his home state of Tennessee as a sign of vindication. In 1872, Johnson commented, "I would rather have the vindication of my State by electing me to my old seat in the Senate of the

United States than to be monarch of the grandest empire on earth. For this I live, and will never die content without." In January 1875, the Tennessee legislature answered his plea and elected him to the U.S. Senate.

When he returned to the Senate, the Democrats, for the first time since before the Civil War, had taken control of Congress. This happened as the military governments of the Southern states were replaced by civilian governments. Johnson had the opportunity to give a Senate speech pointing out the harm done to the South and the nation by the former Republican Congress's harsh policies, which were being continued by President Grant.

Johnson was the only president to return to the Senate after the presidency. However, he served only five months, dying of a stroke on July 31, 1875, while visiting his daughter at Carter Station, Tennessee.

Poll participants render a very low rating to Johnson as president, citing the antagonism he displayed in his congressional dealings, lack of ability, and utter lack of political skill, ranking him last in the Political Skills category. The experts largely conclude that he had a "total inability to negotiate and compromise," and was "too stubborn and tactless to make an effective Chief Executive" and was "politically incompetent." Another expert notes that Johnson "lacked leadership skills; combative personality."

Most agree that he was honest and incorruptible, as the poll gives him a somewhat higher ranking in the category of Character and Integrity. In the words of one expert, he "lacked humor but had courage." Another expert adds, "Despite great courage, his battle with Congress left little opportunity for accomplishment." Yet another concludes, "Should be credited with defending Presidency."

While the overall view of Johnson is closer to the comment of "a disaster," a few note that "bad luck hounded a really pretty good leader" and that he is "a vilified figure."

At the news of Johnson's election to the Senate in January 1875, the *New York Times* noted, "Whatever his faults as President may have been, at any rate he went out of the White House as poor as he entered it and that is something to say in these times." The *New York Herald* added, "It is now generally conceded that the imaginary misdemeanors of 1868 . . . were in fact official merits."

Johnson's blunt style and tenacious defense of his principles do not reflect much political skill, and although perhaps a man of ordinary abilities, he did apply himself diligently. However, history has vindicated Johnson in his defense against a Congress attempting to usurp constitutionally delegated presidential powers. This is further reinforced by his fight against Congress's Reconstruction policy, which was proven to be a failure.

Ulysses S. Grant

1869–1877
18th President

Overall Ranking: 38

★

Leadership Qualities: 27
Accomplishments and Crisis Management: 35
Political Skill: 40
Appointments: 40
Character and Integrity: 32

He has done more than any other President to degrade the character of Cabinet officers by choosing them on the model of the military staff, because of their pleasant personal relation to him and not because of their national reputation and the public needs.

—James A. Garfield

Within this statement made in 1874 by future president James A. Garfield, a fellow Republican and congressman at the time, lies the explanation for the utter failure of the presidency of Ulysses S. Grant. Grant appointed personal friends to high office of public trust, and many of his appointees were undeserving of his naive trust. As a result, some of these men plundered and looted whatever they could for their own personal gain. This legendary war hero rose from humble beginnings and ended up by popular demand in the nation's highest elected office, only to leave by that same popular demand after a scandal-filled two-term administration. Soon afterward, he faced the end of his life in financial ruin racing the clock to complete his memoirs.

Born Hiram Ulysses Grant on April 27, 1822, in Point Pleasant, Clermont County, Ohio, and then moving to Georgetown, Ohio, the following year, the young Grant left for the U.S. Military Academy at West Point, New York, in 1839. Because of an error, Grant was accepted at West Point as Ulysses Simpson Grant. Seeing more possibilities with U. S. Grant than Hiram Grant, he adopted the change.

The blue-eyed, brown-haired West Point graduate served in the U.S. Army in the Mexican War and later in peacetime. After his dismissal from the army because of heavy drinking, the muscular Grant engaged in a series of enterprises that failed, including farming in the St. Louis, Missouri, area. On the eve of the Civil War, Grant was employed in Galena, Illinois, as a clerk in his family's store.

The future general, who enjoyed cigars, tried his hand at painting. He tolerated false teeth and sported a full beard and mustache. Migraine headaches plagued him throughout his life.

At the outbreak of the Civil War, Grant rejoined the army. "Unconditional Surrender" Grant distinguished himself in Civil War battle, including the capture of Fort Donelson, Tennessee; the Battle at Shiloh; the siege of Vicksburg, Mississippi; and the Battle of Chattanooga. President Lincoln named him commander of all Union armies in March 1864.

The untiring general pursued Confederate General Robert E. Lee's Army of Northern Virginia, ultimately securing its surrender in April 1865. At the surrender, Grant permitted Confederate officers to keep their weapons and the Confederate soldiers to keep their horses. With characteristic leniency, he told them, "Go home and you shall be unmolested while you obey the laws in force at the place where you reside."

The general was said to have lost his temper in public only once. In 1864 Grant, while out riding, took notice of a Virginia man abusing his horse by beating it about the head. Outraged, Grant grabbed the man, throttled him, and directed that he be roped to a post for six hours. Oddly, the general who saw so much bloodshed, was easily nauseated at the sight of animal blood. On the Illinois frontier, he never took to hunting or killing animals.

Honored at his appointment to the full rank of general in 1866, the first such appointment since George Washington attained the similar honor, he served until 1869 when his fame as a national war hero carried him into office as the eighteenth president.

At forty-six, Grant became the youngest president to serve up to that time and was off to a promising start as he came to office unencumbered by political favors.

Grant was a private, shy, and prudish man, and so it was with his religious practice. Not a churchgoer or an active practitioner of any of the Christian faiths to which he adhered, he kept his own religious values and practice to himself. In the larger view for the country, he believed in a strict separation of church and state, stating in his seventh annual message to Congress, "Declare church and state forever separate and distinct; but each free within their proper spheres."

Sensitive to the needs of the American Indian, he endorsed the concept of reservations as the only way to protect them from total annihilation. In his first annual message to Congress, he stated, "A system which looks to the extinction of a race is too horrible for a nation to adopt without entailing upon itself the wrath of all Christendom and engendering in the citizen a disregard of human life and the rights of others, dangerous to society. I see no substitute for such a system, except in placing all the Indians on large reservations, as rapidly as it can be done, and giving them absolute protection there."

Twelve years after Grant's death, President William McKinley, a Civil War veteran himself, noted of Grant, "Faithful and fearless as a volunteer soldier, intrepid and invincible as commander-in-chief of the Armies of the Union and confident as President of a reunited and strengthened nation, which his genius has been instrumental in achieving, he has our homage and that of the world; but brilliant as was his public character, we love him all the more for his homelife and homely virtues."

Yet the impeccably honest Grant presided over the most scandal-ridden administration in United States history. Matters got off to a quick start with the gold market cornering scheme of James Fisk and Jay Gould in 1869. They used the president's brother-in-law, Abel Corbin, to lead Grant into a policy position of encouraging gold speculation. Fisk and Gould then took full advantage until it finally dawned on Grant that he was being used. Grant then redirected U.S. fiscal policy, causing a collapse in the gold price on September 24, 1869, known as Black Friday. This resulted in financial ruin for many innocent victims.

While strictly speaking not a scandal, the dismissal of Attorney General Amos T. Akerman in 1871 by President Grant raises serious questions about the influence the powerful railroad interests had on Grant. In investigating railroad abuses, Akerman displayed courage and integrity, in fact, more than the railroad interests cared to see. Grant complied with the railroad barons' request and dismissed Akerman, offering him an appointment as a judge or ambassador, which Akerman refused.

Then, in 1872, the Crédit Mobilier episode unraveled. Federal tax money used for construction projects of the Crédit Mobilier parent company, Union Pacific Railroad, was stolen by individuals in the Crédit Mobilier company. As congressional investigation of the financial irregularities proceeded, these implicated individuals went on to bribe key members of Congress with sale of deeply discounted company stock. Grant's vice president, Schuyler Colfax, was implicated as a favor recipient from the Crédit Mobilier defrauders. The House Judiciary Committee recommended that Colfax not be impeached because Colfax's involvement predated his service as vice president. His involvement had actually occurred when he had served as the powerful Speaker of the House. He was dropped from the national ticket at the 1872 Republican nominating convention.

Grant's second term had only begun when Treasury Secretary William A. Richardson came under fire. Richardson had entered into an outrageous agreement with his special agent, John Sanborn, whom he appointed in 1873. Sanborn was given authority to collect delinquent taxes owed to the federal government, with the outlandish fee of half of all the tax dollars realized. This matter came under congressional investigation in 1874 in which it was discovered that more than $400,000 had been collected, with half going to Sanborn under Richardson's arrangement. Richardson promptly resigned when this scandal was disclosed.

The next year of 1875 found more tax dollars going astray, this time revenue collection on whiskey production. This scandal became famous as the
Whiskey Ring. Internal Revenue Service agents and whiskey distillers un-
derreported liquor production and kept the would-be tax monies for themselves. When Grant was advised of the scandal, he told the chief
investigator to see John McDonald at the St. Louis Internal Revenue Service Bureau, as the "one honest man in St. Louis on whom we can rely."
The president was dismayed to learn that McDonald was the apparent ring-
leader. Secretary of the Treasury Benjamin H. Bristow uncovered a trail of
corruption that led to Grant's own personal secretary, Orville E. Babcock.
Grant defended Babcock, and Bristow resigned. Bristow estimated that the
scandal cost the government tax revenue on up to 15 million gallons a year.

The following year, 1876, the last full year of Grant's presidency, brought
forth revelation of yet another scandal—bribery by Secretary of War William
W. Belknap. Belknap received annual kickbacks from merchants doing
business at the trading posts in Indian Territory during his entire service
as war secretary, going back to his initial appointment by Grant in 1869. As
Congress investigated, the House of Representatives impeached Belknap,
but he resigned in 1876 before he could be tried and removed by the
Senate.

Any one of these scandals might have rocked a less popular president's
administration. Their cumulative effect finally took its toll on Grant. While
expressing an interest in a third term, on the advice of Republican Party
leaders he decided not to proceed. In his final State of the Union Address
in December 1876, he confessed, "Mistakes have been made, as all can see
and I admit." He added, "My failures have been errors of judgment, not
of intent."

While scandals dominated his administration, Grant pursued the harsh
Reconstruction policy of the Radical Republican Congress and maintained
a military occupation that attempted to enforce black voting rights by
threat of military force. In battling the Ku Klux Klan in South Carolina, he
suspended the constitutional right of habeas corpus and ordered a mass of
suspects rounded up and arrested. These were only temporary measures
and did nothing to ameliorate the basic problem. In fact, it is apparent as
reflected in the ensuing century, that these policies only aggravated racial
hostility and hatred.

In February 1869, Congress passed the Fifteenth Amendment to the
Constitution and in March 1870 the states ratified it, thus codifying constitutional enforcement of black voting rights in federal and state elections.

Shortly after his second administration got under way, the Panic of 1873 hit, setting the nation into a five-year depression. The severe economic downturn resulted from a combination of economic forces, both domestic and foreign. These included overbuilding by the railroads, economic losses from the 1871 Great Chicago Fire, subsequent business failures, and an existing depression in Europe.

In 1875, Grant attempted and succeeded in strengthening the dollar by increasing the gold reserves backing the currency. This was known as the Resumption of Specie Act of 1875.

The Civil Rights Act of 1875, providing for equal access to public and business facilities by blacks, was passed by Congress but was declared unconstitutional eight years later by the Supreme Court, citing federal government involvement in social policy as not authorized by any provision in the Constitution.

After departing the White House in 1877, Grant embarked on an extravagant two-year tour of Europe and Asia. The subject of much interest, he met with several world leaders. Within a year of his return, he set out again, this time for the Caribbean.

After returning home to Galena, Illinois, in 1880, Grant eyed another run for the presidency, a then unprecedented third term. However, he lacked the votes to clinch the Republican nomination as too many remembered the legacy of scandals that tarnished the reputation of the war hero.

Disappointed, Grant turned his attention to the business world and, trustingly, invested his life savings in a brokerage firm created by his son and his partner, Ferdinand Ward, which ended up in bankruptcy in 1884. This left Grant without financial resources at a time he knew he was dying of throat cancer.

In order to provide for his family, the former president wrote of his experiences in the Civil War for magazine serialization. He also signed a book deal to write his memoirs for Mark Twain's book publishing company. Writing against the clock and often in great pain, he completed his memoirs just a few weeks before his death on July 23, 1885, at Mount McGregor, near Saratoga Springs, New York. He is buried in the famous Grant's Tomb in New York City.

Grant is ranked near the bottom in the poll overall, with one expert labeling Grant's presidency as "a complete fiasco." The poll participants give him better marks for his character and integrity: "Honorable and good intentions; tragic appointments." His strength was his leadership, perhaps carrying over from his strong military record. But the poll participants also rate him next to last in both the Political Skill and Appointments categories, describing him as "a military leader out of his element in the oval office" and a "great general—inept president, poor judge of men." One expert notes, "His choice of friends and confidants was especially poor."

Grant's presidency is most remembered for its record of scandals, undistinguished for anything else. Though honest himself, Grant misplaced his trust in many dishonest friends. Professor Woodrow Wilson of Princeton University, eleven years before entering the presidency himself, summed up Grant's administration: "The honest, simple-hearted soldier had not added prestige to the presidential office. He himself knew that he had failed . . . that he ought never to have been made President."

While the administration of President James Monroe, whose extraordinarily popular presidency governed by nearly unanimous consensus, is known as the Era of Good Feelings, Grant's administration can be said to have been the Era of Good Stealings.

RUTHERFORD B. HAYES

1877–1881
19TH PRESIDENT

OVERALL RANKING: 25

Leadership Qualities: 29
Accomplishments and Crisis Management: 26
Political Skill: 23
Appointments: 26
Character and Integrity: 22

He serves his party best who serves the country best.

—Rutherford B. Hayes

Paradoxical words coming from the president, Rutherford Hayes, who benefited more from partisan activity than any other president. His Republican Party activists are widely regarded as having stolen the presidential election of 1876 from the apparent winner, Democratic candidate Governor Samuel J. Tilden of New York, and having given it to their man, Republican candidate Rutherford B. Hayes, governor of Ohio.

Yet, Hayes appeared to have retained his honesty and integrity during the most fraudulent presidential election in United States history. Referred to as RutherFRAUD B. Hayes, and His Fraudulency, Hayes had to fight for legitimacy to prove he was the real president.

Rutherford B. Hayes was born on October 4, 1822, in Delaware, Ohio. Graduating from Kenyon College in 1842, the redheaded, blue-eyed Hayes studied law at Harvard University. He opened his law practice in Lower Sandusky, now Fremont, Ohio, moved to Cincinnati in 1849, and built a successful law practice.

The five-foot-eight, 175-pound Hayes, a voracious reader and excellent conversationalist, did not smoke, imbibed very little, and prided himself on being a good family man. He was wounded in battle several times while fighting for the North in the Civil War and moved into a seat in the U.S. House of Representatives, to which he had been elected while serving in the army.

The full-bearded Hayes was elected governor of Ohio for two consecutive terms from 1868 to 1872. He then returned to his home in Spiegel Grove, near Fremont, Ohio, and later went on to serve an unprecedented third term as Ohio governor in 1876, resigning when he was elected president. As governor, he earned a reputation for fighting corruption.

In 1876 Republicans nominated Hayes for president to run against the Democrat Governor Samuel J. Tilden of New York, who had gained a national reputation for cleaning up New York politics. At first it appeared the Democrats were successful. Tilden won the popular vote 4,287,670 to Hayes's 4,035,924, but was one electoral vote short of a majority. There were three disputed states: South Carolina, Louisiana, and Florida, the last three Reconstruction states controlled by Republican carpetbagger gov-

ernments. The Democrats held back one elector from Oregon on a tech-
nicality. Hayes needed every electoral vote, a total of 19, from the three
disputed states to win.

The day after the election, there was no agreement on any of the disputed states, since the Republican and Democratic counts each showed all
three states carried by their own respective candidate. In the case of
Florida, the Democratic attorney general certified Tilden as winner, but
the Republican governor certified Hayes. Shortly afterward, in January
1877, with the dispute still ongoing, the new governor of Florida, a Democrat, certified the court-ordered recount in favor of Tilden.

A recount was also made in Louisiana and showed Tilden carrying the
state by almost 9,000 votes. However, after a tour of that state by nationally prominent Republicans, massive "corrections" were made to the tally
sheet by the state canvassing board, which diminished the Democratic vote
by 13,000 votes. It was common knowledge that the canvasing board was
for sale to the highest bidder, and the Republicans had the money—so
Louisiana ended up showing a Republican majority.

As a result of the undisguised vote fraud, an electoral commission was
established to determine the validity of the returns for the only time in
American history. It consisted of seven Republicans, seven Democrats, and
one Independent. Five days before the commission was to meet, the Independent member resigned and was replaced by a Republican. The commission voted, eight to seven, along strictly party lines, to accept the
Republican count of the returns in the three disputed states, making the
electoral vote: Hayes, 185, Tilden, 184. There were near riots and a willingness to take up arms among Democrats around the country who saw the
obvious fraud in thwarting the choice of the people. (By the Republican
count, Tilden had 250,000 more popular votes than Hayes.)

There has been the persistent belief through the years that Southern
Democrats struck a deal with Hayes's operatives. In exchange for Democrats recognizing Hayes as the winner and not dragging the controversy
beyond the scheduled inauguration day, it is widely believed that the Republicans agreed to withdraw the last of the federal troops from the South,
appoint one Southern Democrat to the cabinet, and expand federal aid to
assist the South in the task of rebuilding.

To his long-lasting credit, Tilden, who had been cheated out of the
presidency, said, "I prefer four years of Hayes' Administration to four years
of civil war." And so, within forty-eight hours after the Senate reported the
results of the electoral commission, Hayes was inaugurated president on
schedule.

It is supreme irony that the most fraudulent presidential election, that of 1876, followed the most corrupt administration, Grant's, yet the election was between two men who were honest corruption fighters and no fraud has ever been traced to either candidate.

Hayes saw civil service reform as the cure for the widespread corruption in appointments to government jobs. A few weeks before taking the oath of office, Hayes noted his criteria for cabinet appointments: "1. A new Cabinet—no holdovers from the Grant administration; 2. no presidential candidates; 3. no appointment to 'take care' of anybody." So, Hayes was mindful of and troubled by the rampant corruption of the day when governments jobs were secured by considerations clouded by politics, friendships, and outright payoffs.

In foreign policy, Hayes believed in carrying on the policy of the Monroe Doctrine, especially in the development of a canal in Central America. Concerned over French overtures and attempts at a canal, he demonstrated his firmness on the issue when he wrote, "The United States will not consent that any European power shall control the Railroad or Canal across the Isthmus of Central America. With due regards to the rights and wishes of our sister republics in the Isthmus, the United States will insist that this passage way shall always remain under American control."

Unusual for the time was Hayes's liberal belief in a presidency with flexible powers. His interpretation of presidential power is recounted in his remark eight years after leaving office: "The executive power is large because [it is] not defined in the Constitution. The real test has never come because the Presidents have, down to the present, been conservative, or what might be called conscientious, men, and have kept within limited range. . . . But if a Napoleon ever became President, he could make the executive almost what he wished to make of it." This view is much more the current-day approach to the office and demonstrates Hayes's foresight on the development of the office.

Because of his reputation for incorruptibility, Hayes did suffer from the fallout of the most controversial presidential election in U.S. history. A later Republican president, Benjamin Harrison, evaluated Hayes: "He was a patriotic citizen, a lover of the flag and of our free institutions, an industrious and conscientious civil officer, a soldier of dauntless courage, a loyal comrade and friend, a sympathetic and helpful neighbor, and the honored head of a happy Christian home. He has steadily grown in the public esteem, and the impartial historian will not fail to recognize the conscientiousness, the manliness, and the courage that so strongly characterized his whole public career."

Another president, Woodrow Wilson, while a professor at Princeton University, critiqued Hayes: "Mr. Hayes had as little political authority as Mr. [Andrew] Johnson had had. . . . He had no real hold upon the country. His amiable character, his lack of party heat, his conciliatory attitude towards the South alienated rather than attracted the members of his party in Congress. . . . The Democrats did not like him because he seemed to them incapable of frank, consistent action."

As his first major act after being sworn in as president, Hayes ended Reconstruction in 1877 and ordered the remaining army troops out of the South. The federal government turned its attention from subduing the South to subduing labor unrest such as the railroad strike in 1877, the first significant organized strike in U.S. history. Federal troops arrived to suppress the strike and get the railroads rolling again.

The Bland-Allison Act of 1878, passed over a presidential veto, set the government on a path to purchase between $2 million to $4 million of silver a month to mint silver dollars for softening and inflating the currency. This was of great benefit to miners, farmers, and those who owed money.

The following year, after the government had built up its gold reserves, the currency strengthened when the government resumed specie payments. It was authorized to do so by the Resumption of Specie Act of 1875, which had called for redemption of all paper money with gold after January 1, 1879. This hard money counteracted some of the effects of the soft money introduced under the Bland-Allison Act.

Known for battling corruption, Hayes took his fight to a fellow Republican, Roscoe Conkling, the powerful New York political boss. Some wonder if this was payback for Conkling's support of fellow New Yorker Samuel Tilden, the Democratic candidate for president and Hayes's opponent in the 1876 election. Hayes prevailed, and Conkling lost his prestigious political appointment empire. Most notably affected by all of this was Conkling's appointee as Collector of the Port of New York. Chester A. Arthur was fired. A few years later, Arthur was president of the United States.

High on Hayes's list of priorities was reform of corrupt civil service practices. However, except for the ban he issued on federal employees' participation in partisan politics, Hayes only managed to focus attention on the problem. Action came later under a different president—ironically, a former party hack and Conkling appointee, Chester A. Arthur.

Hayes proposed a single six-year term for the president and federal financial assistance to the states for public education. Neither proposal received sufficient support to be acted upon. Hayes targeted polygamy practiced by the Mormons. In Hayes's administration, the Library of Congress found a building and the Washington Monument was at long last completed after decades of sporadic construction work. His last directive, perhaps at the prompting of his prohibitionist wife, was the executive order banning sale of alcoholic beverages at federal military installations.

The Hayeses, except for one known occasion early in the Hayes administration, entertained at the White House without alcoholic beverages. First Lady Lucy Hayes was mockingly called Lemonade Lucy. After one of the Hayeses' festive gatherings, Secretary of State William M. Evarts quipped, "It was a brilliant affair; the water flowed like champagne."

Looking forward to his retirement, the affable Hayes returned to Spiegel Grove and enjoyed family life after turning the presidency over to his fellow Republican and successor, James A. Garfield, in March 1881. A few weeks after leaving office, Hayes wrote to a friend: "The escape from bondage into freedom is grateful indeed to my feelings. . . . The burden, even with my constitutional problems, has not been a light one. I am glad to be a freedman."

He remained involved in public life by working for a variety of charitable causes and educational institutions. Hayes pressed for greater reliance on rehabilitating criminals as an integral part of the criminal justice system—quite an enlightened view for the time.

Lucy Hayes died in 1889. When Rutherford Hayes died on January 17, 1893, at Spiegel Grove, Fremont, Ohio, his last words were "I know I am going where Lucy is."

Hayes finishes in the poll as an average president, as one expert puts it, "Mr. Average in every way." The controversial election of 1876 haunts his reputation and is reflected in poll participants' comments that he had "participated in first theft of Presidency—Campaign of 1876" and that "his election [was] so clouded as to make him ineffective." Most noteworthy is his reputation for honesty. One expert notes: "Honest to a fault, he restored some of the luster to a Presidential office tarnished by the Grant scandals."

The Hayes presidency is best remembered for the tainted election that brought him to the White House, even though he seemed to have remained above the fray. His presidential term saw the closing of the Reconstruction era and the last direct effects of the Civil War upon the nation. While Hayes hoped to begin the healing process, the harsh military occupation and abuses of Reconstruction, which he supported while in Congress, took their toll on race relations in the South.

Hayes, in essence, was an honorable man who dealt competently with the issues of his day.

JAMES A. GARFIELD

1881
20TH PRESIDENT

OVERALL RANKING: 30

Leadership Qualities: 30
Accomplishments and Crisis Management: 36
Political Skill: 26
Appointments: 32
Character and Integrity: 26

*He was earnestly seeking some practical way of correcting the evils aris-
ing from the distribution of overgrown and unwieldy patronage—evils always appreciated and often discussed by him, but whose magnitude had
been more deeply impressed upon his mind since his accession to the Presidency. Had he lived, a comprehensive improvement in the mode of appointment and in the tenure of office would have been proposed by him,
and with the aid of Congress no doubt perfected.*

—James G. Blaine

And so it was that future presidential candidate James G. Blaine summarized his views of and expectations for James A. Garfield, the twentieth
president.

James A. Garfield, the second assassinated president, served only six
months of his term including his final two months during which he battled
for his life.

The last of the log-cabin-born presidents, James Abram Garfield was
born on November 19, 1831, at Orange, Ohio. He developed an appetite
for reading, particularly American history and later novels by Jane Austen.

The muscular and energetic Garfield worked at odd jobs as a teenager,
on a canal boat and as a carpenter, before attending Geauga Seminary in
Chester, Ohio, in 1849 and 1850. He dropped out to teach school, however,
and while teaching, he attended Western Reserve Eclectic Institute, later
renamed Hiram College, from 1851 to 1854.

Garfield then entered Williams College in Massachusetts in 1854, graduating with honors in 1856. There, he established himself as a debating
champion. Added to his debating skills were his exceptional talents as an
orator, necessary tools for a successful politician.

Moving to Hiram, Ohio, in 1856, he taught at Hiram College and the
following year was named as its president, serving for four years.

The amiable Garfield was elected to the Ohio state senate as a Republican in 1859 and admitted to the Ohio bar in 1860. The blue-eyed, brown-
haired state senator resigned to join the Northern war effort in the Civil
War and rose, at thirty, to become the youngest general in the Union army.
He left the army with the rank of major general in 1863 to take a seat in
the U.S. House of Representatives from Ohio. In Congress, as a backslap-

ping politician, he rose to the position of Republican minority leader before being elected to the U.S. Senate in 1880.

In 1876 he established Mentor, Ohio, as his home and resided at a home that became known as Lawnfield.

Garfield was the surprise nominee for president at the 1880 Republican national convention, winning on the thirty-sixth ballot at the deadlocked convention. The Democrats nominated Winfield S. Hancock, who had also served as a general in the Union army.

The 1880 presidential election was considerably less contentious than the 1876 one. The only significant issue of disagreement was the tariff. Republicans wanted a high tariff to protect industry, while the Democrats espoused a low tariff. The level of personal attack was mild for the times: Democrats charged that Garfield took bribes for his congressional votes, and Republicans accused the Democrats of being behind a forged letter in which Garfield supposedly supported bringing low-paid Chinese laborers into the country. Percentagewise, Garfield won by the smallest popular vote margin of any president in American history up to that time.

Immediately upon assuming office, Garfield directed his postmaster general to look into possible fraud in the awarding of contracts for mail routes. In what became known as the Star Route scandal, highly placed Republicans were incriminated in the scandal. Although there were no convictions, this scandal created more momentum for civil service reform.

On July 2, 1881, while preparing to get on a train at the Washington, D.C., railway station, Garfield was shot twice by Charles J. Guiteau, a mentally deranged man. Guiteau, a frustrated office seeker, had planned the assassination, writing earlier in the day: "The President's tragic death was a sad necessity, but it will unite the Republican party and save the Republic. . . . I had no ill-will toward the president. His death was a political necessity."

The president hung on for about two and a half months before finally succumbing at the seaside resort of Elberon, New Jersey, on September 19, 1881. Guiteau was tried in the fall and hanged the following year.

Garfield had anticipated the difficulties of being president. The day before he was inaugurated, he stated, "You may write down in your books now, the largest percentage of blunders which you think I will be likely to make, and you will be sure to find in the end that I have made many more than you have calculated, many more."

Garfield described the frustration of dealing with office seekers and making appointments: "My day is frittered away by personal seeking of people, when it ought to be given to the great problem[s] which concern the whole country. Four years of this kind of intellectual dissipation may cripple me for the remainder of my life. What might not a vigorous thinker do, if he could not be allowed to use the opportunities of a presidential term in vital, useful activity! Some Civil Service reform will come by necessity after the wearisome years of wasted Presidents have paved the way for it." It is a great irony that his assassin was just one of these disappointed office seekers.

Garfield's critics included former president Ulysses S. Grant, who stated in 1881, "Garfield has shown that he is not possessed of the backbone of an angle-worm."

Senator John Sherman, a fellow Ohio Republican, noticed another side of Garfield: "His will power was not equal to his personal magnetism. He easily changed his mind and honestly veered from one impulse to another."

In a presidency showing promise and cut short after only six months—the second briefest presidency—little can be said and much can be speculated. His predecessor, President Rutherford B. Hayes, during the election campaign, stated of Garfield, "There is a great deal of strength in Garfield's life and struggles as a self-made man. . . . From poverty and obscurity, by labor at all avocations, he became a great scholar, a statesman, a major general, a Senator, a Presidential candidate. . . . The truth is, no man ever started so low that accomplished so much, in all our history. Not Franklin or Lincoln even."

His low ranking in our poll is a reflection of his very brief presidency. As Hayes pointed out, Garfield was a self-made man, rising by his own efforts and hard work from utter poverty to the highest office in the land. He seemed willing to take on much needed civil service reform. It is likely that he would have enjoyed at least as much success in dealing with Congress and getting things done as his successor.

Chester A. Arthur

1881–1885
21st President

Overall Ranking: 28

Leadership Qualities: 31
Accomplishments and Crisis Management: 25
Political Skill: 22
Appointments: 27
Character and Integrity: 33

I may be President of the United States, but my private life is nobody's damned business.

—Chester A. Arthur

With intrusive and deeply personal questions asked of recent presidents by the press, such as whether President Ronald Reagan dyed his hair, whether President George Bush had an extramarital affair, and whether President Bill Clinton had smoked marijuana, who today would dare to respond like President Arthur? Presidents today are under a microscope of scrutiny, whereas President Arthur had most Americans and the press of his day agreeing with his statement setting the president's private life off limits to public inquiry.

While serving as president, Arthur successfully disguised as a cold his bouts with Bright's disease, a terminal kidney malfunction. Compare this with today when even the president's weight and blood pressure are reported on TV and radio and in the newspapers. Arthur was definitely a man of and for the nineteenth century.

Chester Alan Arthur was born on October 5, 1829, in North Fairfield, Vermont. After graduating from Union College in Schenectady, New York, in 1848, he taught at North Pownal Academy in Vermont during 1851 to 1852 and attended law school. Admitted to the New York State bar in 1854, the six-foot-two, stocky Arthur established his law practice in New York City. As a lawyer and slavery abolitionist, he was instrumental in desegregating public transportation in New York City when he represented a black woman, successfully suing a Brooklyn streetcar company for removing her from a white-only car.

The prominent attorney married Ellen Herndon in 1859. She died in 1880, a year before he became president. While Arthur was president, he requested fresh flowers to be placed daily at her White House portrait. He grieved over her loss until his dying day.

Active in Republican Party politics, the brown-haired Arthur with his characteristic mustache and sideburns was appointed to the politically powerful position of collector of the Port of New York during the administration of President Ulysses S. Grant. This office controlled much of New York's patronage job appointments. However, in 1878, President Rutherford B. Hayes, a fellow Republican, removed Arthur as part of his civil service reform to take politics out of government employment. Some speculate that Hayes also sought to visit a little revenge on Arthur's boss, the Republican Party boss of New York State, Senator Roscoe Conkling, for having been too friendly with Hayes's 1876 Democratic presidential opponent, New York governor Samuel J. Tilden.

When reformer James A. Garfield received the 1880 Republican presidential nomination, Conkling and other political bosses were thrown a bone by the naming of one of Conkling's men, New Yorker Chester A. Arthur, as the vice presidential candidate. After a very close election, Arthur, who had never held elective office before, found himself as vice president of the United States. When Garfield was shot and clung to life for about eleven weeks, Vice President Arthur spent most of this time in New York, not wishing to be seen as too eager to capitalize on the tragedy. After Garfield died, Arthur was sworn in as president on September 20, 1881.

In his inaugural address, Arthur stated, "Men may die, but the fabrics of free institutions remain unshaken."

When Arthur inherited the executive mantle, the boom in railroad construction was nearing an end and the vast pool of low-paid, largely Chinese immigrant, labor was in search of other employment. This caused both racial and labor unrest, especially on the West Coast. Under this pressure, Arthur signed the Chinese Exclusion Act in 1882 providing for a temporary ten-year halt to both Chinese immigration and citizenship for Chinese immigrants.

The most significant achievement of Arthur's administration was the Pendleton Civil Service Act of 1883. This act provided for exams to establish the priority of federal job applicants, rather than the spoils system of outright political patronage. It also prohibited federal job salary kickbacks to political party organizations. Arthur infuriated his political friends by signing the bill into law, even though he himself and his friends had practiced and benefited from the spoils and patronage system. It appeared that Arthur had undergone a transformation upon undertaking the presidential office. When Arthur denied the request of one of his Republican Party favor seekers, the party man protested that Arthur would be making a similar request were he in the same party position. Arthur replied, "I certainly would but since I came here I have learned that Chester A. Arthur is one man and the President of the United States is another."

When Republicans and Democrats could not agree on a solution to the ongoing tariff controversy in 1883, Arthur appointed a commission to study the issue. The commission recommended a large decrease in the tariff rates. Congress passed a bill that slightly decreased the tariff, and Arthur signed it.

Arthur addressed Congress in an attempt to strengthen the U.S. Navy, warning, "The long peace that has lulled us into a sense of fancied security may at any time be disturbed." He succeeded in prodding Congress, and a building program was instituted.

On the foreign policy front, Arthur organized an international conference that created a system of standard time zones to put the time clocks of the world on a uniform basis. He negotiated a treaty for the United States to construct a canal connecting the Atlantic and Pacific Oceans through Nicaragua which, however, was not approved by the Senate. Arthur also attempted to develop a single currency for North and South America to make financial dealings within the Western Hemisphere easier.

The charming and sociable Arthur, a connoisseur of many of life's pleasures such as food, wine, and art, disregarded Garfield's and his predecessor Hayes's penchants for simple entertaining and in Hayes's case an outright ban on alcohol. A surprised Hayes once complained, "Nothing like it ever before in the Executive Mansion—liquor, snobbery, and worse."

While Arthur did tend to the nation's business, no one accused him of being a workaholic. In fact, the *Chicago Tribune* in 1882 leveled this objection: "Mr. Arthur's temperament is sluggish. He is indolent. It requires a great deal for him to get to his desk and begin the dispatch of business. Great questions of public policy bore him. No President was ever so much given to procrastination as he is."

After leaving office, Arthur quipped to a reporter, "Well, there doesn't seem anything else for an ex-President to do but go into the country and raise big pumpkins." But he did return to the practice of law in New York City. The kidney ailment that afflicted him during his presidency grew worse and gradually curtailed his ability to practice law. He was confined to a bed in his New York City home for several months prior to his death, which occurred on November 18, 1886.

In rendering an assessment of Arthur, diplomat Elihu Root recounted, "He was wise in statesmanship and firm and effective in administration. Honesty in national finance, purity and effectiveness in the civil service, the promotion of commerce, the re-creation of the American Navy, reconciliation between North and South and honorable friendship with foreign nations received his active support. Good causes found in him a friend and bad measures met in him an unyielding opponent." Woodrow Wilson had a briefer and less flattering opinion: "A non-entity with side whiskers."

Another of the presidents rated average, Arthur draws comments like, "better than expected" and "the big surprise." One expert labels Arthur as a "machine politician." Another observes that "on taking office, [he] reformed both himself and the civil service." Arthur clearly exceeded expectations in the view of the majority of poll participants. One expert opines that he "rose to the occasion on becoming President" while another states that Arthur "displayed some real statesmanship in supporting civil service and tariff reform."

Arthur was a president without any real ideological agenda. He was a party man who transformed himself to reflect the dignity and importance of the office he held, that of the presidency, a man of ordinary abilities who rose to the occasion. The Gentleman Boss, as he was sometimes called, performed surprisingly well.

During Arthur's administration, America, for the first time in a generation, no longer dealt with the direct effects of the Civil War but rather started to look forward and outward again. At that juncture in American history, Arthur did a creditable job at keeping America going in the right direction and on the path of progress.

GROVER CLEVELAND

1885–1889
22ND PRESIDENT
1893–1897
24TH PRESIDENT

OVERALL RANKING: 16

★

Leadership Qualities: 13
Accomplishments and Crisis Management: 17
Political Skill: 19
Appointments: 17
Character and Integrity: 16

Public office is a public trust.

—Motto of the Cleveland administration

Grover Cleveland emerged in 1884 as the first Democrat to win the nation's highest office since before the Civil War; eight years later he became the only man elected to two nonconsecutive terms as president of the United States. In presidential polls, historians have consistently rated him as the most effective president between the administrations of Abraham Lincoln (1861–65) and Theodore Roosevelt (1901–9).

As president, Cleveland pushed hard for lower tariffs, sound money, and civil service reform. His most powerful weapon in combating what he viewed as the excesses of Congress was the veto. Known earlier as the Veto Mayor, then as the Veto Governor, he became the Veto President. In his first term alone, he wielded the veto more than three hundred times. From George Washington through Chester A. Arthur, twenty-one previous presidents had used the veto power just 132 times. Cleveland knew how to say no.

Stephen Grover Cleveland was born in Caldwell, New Jersey, on March 18, 1837, the son of a Presbyterian minister. After studying law at a Buffalo firm, he was admitted to the bar in 1859. Cleveland was elected sheriff of Erie County by just 303 votes in 1870. As county hangman, he executed two murderers, an unpleasant duty he refused to shirk. Elected mayor in 1881, he proved so effective at cleaning up corruption in Buffalo he won election as governor of New York by a landslide in 1882.

Cleveland's opposition to New York City's corrupt Tammany Hall bosses helped him earn the Democratic nomination for president. Within days a scandal suddenly struck the Cleveland camp. A TERRIBLE TALE, A DARK CHAPTER IN A PUBLIC MAN'S HISTORY read the banner headline on page one of the *Buffalo Evening Telegraph*. The story stated that in 1874 Cleveland had had an affair with a young Buffalo widow named Maria Halpin. Mrs. Halpin claimed Cleveland was the father of her baby boy, who bore the name of Oscar Folsom Cleveland. It was not clear who the father actually was, but Cleveland accepted the responsibility after learning that two of his married friends had also been intimate with her. He concluded that as a bachelor he had less to lose than did his friends. He agreed to pay child support but not to marry her. He continued his financial support until the child was adopted into a prominent New York family.

No presidential candidate had ever before faced a personal scandal of this magnitude. Advisers tried to persuade him to deny the story. He refused. His response was, "Above all, tell the truth."

The campaign turned not on issues but on the personal morality of the two candidates. By confronting charges honestly and openly, Cleveland kept the support of the reformers, the real source of his strength. He was helped, too, by the backing of a group of dissident Republicans called Mugwumps, a derisive moniker fastened on them by the *New York Sun*. When the votes were counted, Cleveland had won with 4,911,017 votes, just 62,683 more than James G. Blaine. His electoral vote edge was 219 to 182.

The new president challenged Congress, which had dominated the presidency since the Civil War. In reasserting the power of the chief executive, he made his most important contribution to the office. His greatest impact came from his relentless vetoing of wasteful, improper, or unjust bills. "Good negative president," one poll participant comments.

When he found that unfair land grants to powerful railroad interests prevented homesteaders from settling on western lands, he recovered much of this land and opened it to the public. After discovering that lands in the Oklahoma and Dakota Territories were being stolen from the Indians and given to land speculators, he returned ownership to the reservations.

His toughest battles were against the high tariff that he believed would in the long run destroy competition and cause serious trade imbalances. Republicans responded that high tariffs protected domestic manufacturers and jobs. The president failed to achieve tariff reform.

Cleveland entered the White House a bachelor. At first his sister Rose, a former schoolteacher, served as hostess for official occasions. In late May of 1886 the president, who was forty-nine, announced that he would marry his twenty-one-year-old ward, Frances Folsom, the daughter of one of his closest friends and law partner. On June 2, 1886, Grover Cleveland became the first president to marry in the White House. Wedding music was provided by John Philip Sousa and the U.S. Marine Band.

In October, on Bedloe's Island in New York Harbor, the president presided over the dedication of the Statue of Liberty, a gift from France.

Nominated unanimously for a second term, he faced a strong opponent in Benjamin Harrison, a Civil War general and the grandson of President William Henry Harrison. President Cleveland did not campaign actively. His only public appearance was to accept the nomination. An eloquent speaker, Harrison concentrated his campaign on attacking Cleveland's tariff policies. When the 1888 returns were in, Cleveland had won the popular vote by more than 90,000 votes, but he had lost, 233 to 168, in the electoral college. Failure to carry his home state of New York proved the margin of defeat. Tammany Hall had exacted its revenge.

Cleveland accepted his defeat calmly and seemed almost relieved to be leaving public office. The ex-president joined a law firm in New York City. On October 3, 1891, the Clevelands' first child was born. The proud father announced he had "just entered the real world." Wrote biographer Zachary Kent, "All America fell in love with Baby Ruth Cleveland."

A year later America was ready, too, to return Cleveland to the presidency. Under President Benjamin Harrison, the Republican-controlled Congress had increased tariffs, granted higher pensions for veterans, and authorized many projects that Cleveland would have been vetoed. The "Billion Dollar Congress" had left the treasury nearly empty. The United States was ready to return to the hard-money policies of Cleveland.

Tammany Hall tried to block the renomination of Cleveland, but he won a narrow victory on the first ballot. His vice presidential running mate was Adlai Stevenson, an Illinois congressman and the grandfather of the future presidential candidate. President Harrison was nominated by the Republicans on the first ballot. The sound-money issue dominated the campaign between Cleveland and Harrison until October when First Lady Caroline Harrison died. Out of respect for her, both Cleveland and Harrison stopped campaigning. Once again Cleveland won the popular vote, this time by nearly 400,000 votes; the electoral vote also fell into his column by the sizable margin of 277 to 145.

On inauguration day, a heavy snowstorm chilled the crowd and the president, an omen of hard days to come. Heavy spending and unsound money practices by the previous administration had pushed the country into the worst depression it had suffered to date. The Panic of 1893 resulted in fifteen thousand business failures and threw 4 million people out of work. Banks were failing. Stock prices were collapsing. Gold reserves had dropped to a dangerous level. Wrote the *Commercial Financial Chronicle*, "Mr. Cleveland is about all that stands between this country and absolute disaster."

President Cleveland blamed the Sherman Silver Purchase Act of 1890 for the drain on the gold supply because of its provisions that permitted investors to buy silver on the open market, then sell it to the government for gold. Anxious to reassure the American people, on June 30, 1893, he called for a special session of Congress in August to repeal the Sherman

Silver Purchase Act. Later that day he slipped quietly out of the White House and boarded a train for New York City. He was about to face in secret a dangerous operation. He had asked his White House physician to look at a sore "rough place" on the roof of his mouth. About the size of a quarter, it was found to be cancerous. Knowing the panic that might result if his illness were known, he insisted on absolute secrecy.

Oneida, the yacht of a close friend, Commodore Elias C. Benedict, was anchored in New York Harbor. During the day, crewmen, sworn to secrecy, ferried five doctors, an operating table, and medical instruments and supplies to the yacht. When Cleveland was sneaked aboard that evening, all was ready for the operation the next morning.

On July 1, the yacht cruised up the East River and on out into Long Island Sound. Below deck, President Cleveland, dressed in pajamas, sat in a straight-backed chair tied to a mast. Dr. Joseph D. Bryant cut out a large segment of Cleveland's upper left jawbone. In just half an hour the operation was over.

Oneida then sailed north to Cleveland's vacation home at Buzzards Bay, Massachusetts. Newsmen lurking nearby were told that the president had had two bad teeth extracted. On July 17, he underwent a brief follow-up operation to remove the rest of the cancer. Dr. Kasson C. Gibson fitted the president with an artificial rubber jaw that he wore inside his cheek. His face appeared normal, and his booming voice sounded natural. Vague rumors were spread, but no details on the operation were made public until nine years after his death.

Despite terrible pain, he continued to work for the repeal of the Sherman Silver Purchase Act. "The people of the United States are entitled to a sound and stable currency," he declared in his August message to Congress. He refused to compromise, and on October 30 Congress repealed the Sherman Silver Purchase Act.

In 1893 Frances gave birth to little Esther Cleveland, the first child born in the White House to a sitting president.

Cleveland's cure for the economic depression was not effective. Conditions continued to worsen, and much of his second term was beset with protest marches and labor strife. By the end of his administration, even his own party had turned against him, advocating wider circulation of silver.

He and Frances retired to Princeton, New Jersey, where they increased their children to five. Then in 1904 a tragedy struck their household: Baby Ruth, twelve, contracted diphtheria and died. Four years later, Grover Cleveland followed his firstborn daughter, dying of heart and kidney disease on June 24, 1908, at age seventy-five.

He had left the White House an unpopular and discredited president. In the century that followed, the verdict of history has been far kinder. He has held steadily to his position as the most effective president to serve the United States between the Civil War and the arrival of the twentieth century.

Participants in our poll give him highest marks in the Leadership category, ranking him thirteenth, and lowest in the Political Skill category, where they place him nineteenth. In the Character and Integrity category, he draws a ranking of sixteenth. As a sheriff, mayor, governor, and finally president it was his moral force that stamped him as one of the most incorruptible of all American presidents. One poll participant comments that Cleveland was an "honest man who fought for clean government."

Before President Cleveland's death, author Mark Twain had given well-deserved praise to him: "Your patriotic virtues have won for you the homage of half the nation and the enmity of the other half. This places your character on a summit as high as Washington."

BENJAMIN HARRISON

1889–1893
23RD PRESIDENT
OVERALL RANKING: 31

★

Leadership Qualities: 32
Accomplishments and Crisis Management: 29
Political Skill: 29
Appointments: 29
Character and Integrity: 28

[A]t the end of one hundred days of this work the President should not be judged too harshly if he shows a little wear, a little loss of effusiveness, and even a hunted expression in his eyes.

—Benjamin Harrison

Benjamin Harrison boasted an incomparable pedigee—the grandson of President William Henry Harrison and great-grandson of Virginia Governor Benjamin Harrison, a signer of the Declaration of Independence. His heritage imbued him with deep respect for public service. He was a Civil War general, a U.S. senator, and eventually the twenty-third president. Unfortunately, his remarkable "political genes" left him short in one vital area: the human touch so essential in leading a nation.

His handshake was cold; one contemporary said it was like a "wilted petunia." His official manner was so brusque and rude that detractors referred to him as "the White House iceberg" or "that damned icicle." He was able, however, with the support of Republican majorities in both houses of Congress to push through his most favored legislation—extended benefits for veterans and higher tariffs.

Cool and aloof in manner, Harrison was unable to delegate authority. This may have accounted in part for the words he wrote in 1897 about the difficulty of the job, leading to "a little wear, a little loss of effusiveness, and even a hunted expression in his [the president's] eyes."

Born August 20, 1833, on his grandfather William Henry Harrison's 600-acre farm in Ohio, young Ben was raised in a strict Presbyterian family. He attended a one-room log schoolhouse before continuing his education at Farmers' College and Miami University in Ohio.

Harrison practiced law in Indianapolis where he became active in the new Republican Party. During the Civil War, he earned a battlefield promotion to brigadier general by leading his men through heavy Confederate defenses at Peach Tree Creek, Georgia, in the pivotal battle for Atlanta. He was the last of the Civil War generals to serve as president. Harrison later wrote, "I am not a Julius Caesar nor a Napoleon but a plain Hoosier colonel with no more relish for a fight than for a good breakfast and hardly so much."

After the war, Harrison continued to be active in Republican circles, running twice, unsuccessfully, for governor before the Indiana legislature elected him unanimously to the U.S. Senate in 1881. When the Democrats gained control of the state legislature in 1887, he lost his Senate seat.

He promptly announced for president and the following year was picked to run against the incumbent Democratic president, Grover Cleveland. Unlike many office seekers during America's Gilded Age of Politics, Harrison campaigned on issues, speaking directly to the facts rather than demeaning his opponent.

A riveting speaker and Civil War hero, Harrison drew trainloads of prospective voters to hear him deliver campaign speeches from the front porch of his Indianapolis home. He spoke passionately for pensions for veterans, civil rights for blacks, and a high tariff on foreign goods to protect American industry.

His straightforward approach proved successful during the low-key 1888 presidential race, which pitted the Indiana Republican against an advocate of low tariffs. Both candidates waged campaigns notable for their dignity and decency. Harrison spoke about a "contest of great principles" and lived up to it with a notably clean campaign.

Cleveland, a conservative Democrat, captured the popular vote by more than 90,000 votes, but Harrison won the election with 233 electoral votes to 168 for Cleveland. Republican majorities in Congress supported his Dependent and Disability Pensions Act of 1890, which extended compensation to veterans disabled by nonmilitary causes and their dependents, and the McKinley Tariff Act of 1890, which placed high duties on imported products.

During the Harrison administration, six states—North Dakota, South Dakota, Montana, Washington, Idaho, and Wyoming, were admitted to the Union. By the end of his term, Harrison, recognizing Hawaii's potential, was developing a plan to bring those Pacific islands under U.S. protection.

All the new western states, though solidly Republican, by this time known as the Grand Old Party (GOP), strongly favored silver as well as gold to back U.S. currency. It was a stance Harrison opposed. Nonetheless, in return for the western states' support for high tariffs, the Harrison administration made a concession to back the Sherman Silver Purchase Act of 1890.

Passage of the law, which required the U.S. Treasury to make monthly purchases of 4.5 million ounces of silver, quickly created an economic crisis. Under the terms of the Sherman Silver Purchase Act, the Treasury used notes redeemable in gold or silver to pay for the silver. So many holders promptly redeemed their notes for gold they nearly depleted the government's reserves. The law was repealed in 1893.

In 1890 Congress passed the Sherman Antitrust Act. The legislation was the first of the antitrust laws aimed at curbing conspiracies by monopolies "in restraint of trade or commerce among the several states, or with foreign nations."

Harrison pushed for reciprocal trade agreements to strengthen the nation's ties with Latin America. He saw the need to construct a shipping canal somewhere in Central America as a shortcut between the Atlantic and Pacific Oceans. Modernization of the navy was a top priority for Harrison's administration, which began work on the creation of a "steel Navy" to replace an out-of-date wooden fleet.

Little Ben—as Harrison, a stocky five foot six in height, was known to his enemies—took every detail of his job as president seriously. Unable to delegate, he devoted many hours daily during the first sixteen months of his term interviewing candidates for some 1,700 government appointments. His Republican colleagues and the political bosses expected him to rubber-stamp their handpicked patronage nominees. Harrison's independence cost him many backers. In the 1890 congressional elections, Republicans lost eighty seats in the House of Representatives and severely eroded support for the president's programs.

Said the influential Republican senator Thomas C. Platt, "Outside the White House and at a dinner he could be a courtly gentleman. Inside the Executive Mansion, in his reception of those who solicited official appointments, he was as glacial as a Siberian stripped of his furs."

"Damn the president!" said Col. Theodore Roosevelt, who was head of the U.S. Civil Service Commission at the time. "He is a cold-blooded, narrow-minded, prejudiced, obstinate, timid old psalm-singing Indianapolis president."

In a letter to his brother, Harrison himself complained, "I am born to be a drudge." Though Harrison was indeed a born workaholic, circumstances had placed an unduly heavy burden on his husky shoulders. Unlike today, nineteenth-century presidents had to make do with an inadequate office staffing because Congress failed to budget the necessary funds. In addition, the chronic illness of Secretary of State James G. Blaine created more work for Harrison.

Among his more notable cabinet appointments were William H. H. Miller, of Indiana, a strong, principled attorney general, and Benjamin F. Tracy, who as secretary of the navy, conducted an ambitious shipbuilding and modernization program for the fleet. Harrison's postmaster general was

John Wanamaker, the famed Philadelphia department store owner, whose innovations included rural free delivery, parcel post, and the postal savings bank.

Harrison himself, depressed by the 1892 death of his wife Caroline from tuberculosis, waged a lackluster reelection campaign against Cleveland. Voter outrage over the rising cost of consumer goods brought on by the high tariff fueled a strong comeback by the "low-tariff" Cleveland. In this election, Cleveland captured sizable majorities in both the popular and the electoral votes.

After his loss in the election of 1892, Harrison returned to legal practice in Indiana. Until his death from pneumonia in 1901, Harrison stayed active in politics, gaining a solid reputation as an elder statesman. In 1894 he gave a series of lectures at Stanford University in California. Much of his legal work was devoted to serving as chief counsel for Venezuela in its boundary dispute with Great Britain over Venezuela's border with what was then British Guiana.

Harrison lacked the charisma and compelling leadership necessary to rank among the more effective presidents. But few could surpass Harrison's devotion to duty during the tumultuous era of our country's westward expansion. Harrison foresaw the need for the United States to build strong ties in South America and in the Pacific region.

Our poll participants, who give him low marks in every category, conclude that he brought to the presidency a lack of the leadership and political skills required to make this demanding office work. Comments are generally unfavorable: "lackluster," "unimaginative but competent," "cold fish," and "burly, bearded and boring."

"One of the characteristics of General Harrison always commanded my respect—his fearless independence and stand for what he believed right and just," said Hoosier poet James Whitcomb Riley, who delivered Harrison's eulogy. "A fearless man inwardly commands respect, and above everything else Harrison was fearless and just."

WILLIAM MCKINLEY

1897–1901
25TH PRESIDENT
OVERALL RANKING: 17

★

Leadership Qualities: 18
Accomplishments and Crisis Management: 15
Political Skill: 17
Appointments: 18
Character and Integrity: 19

Remember the Maine! To Hell with Spain!

—Popular slogan from the Spanish-American War

When the U.S. battleship *Maine* exploded and sank in Havana Harbor on February 15, 1898, 266 Americans died. President William McKinley heard the call for action against a Spanish regime that held the island of Cuba under its control. On April 11, 1898, the president asked Congress to declare war on Spain.

President McKinley, often criticized for his hesitancy, conducted the war forcefully and skillfully. His leadership during the war and the U.S. victory made the United States a true world power.

Voters were pleased enough to make him the first president since Abraham Lincoln to be elected to two consecutive terms. Tragically, he met the same ill fortune as President Lincoln, death at the hands of an assassin in the first year of his second term. He was, as one poll participant comments, "robbed by fate."

William McKinley, Jr., was born January 29, 1843, in the little town of Niles, Ohio, the seventh of nine children. By his eighteenth birthday, he had already seen action in the Civil War. At the Battle of Antietam, his bravery and initiative earned the respect of his commanding officer, Lt. Col. Rutherford B. Hayes, who called him "one of the bravest and finest young officers in the army."

After the war, McKinley studied law in Albany, New York, and became a lawyer, practicing in Canton, Ohio. Active in local Republican politics, he campaigned vigorously for his Civil War commander when Hayes ran successfully for governor of Ohio. In 1869, McKinley was elected county prosecutor but lost a close race for a second term.

Two years later, twenty-seven-year-old McKinley married Ida Sexton, daughter of the owner of the First National Bank of Canton. In 1873, a tragic series of events engulfed the family. Ida, overcome with grief at the death of her mother, lapsed into declining health. Then she gave birth to a second child, but the little girl died within a year. Ida suffered a severe physical breakdown, leaving her subject to fits of epilepsy. Next their four-year-old daughter Katie died of typhoid fever.

A grieving McKinley plunged into Ohio politics and in 1876 won a seat in Congress. In Washington, McKinley, convinced American industries needed protection from foreign competition, became the nation's leading expert on tariff laws.

In 1889, the Ohio congressman became chairman of the powerful House Ways and Means Committee. He pushed through the McKinley Tariff Bill of 1890, taxing nearly four thousand import items. Without foreign competition, many American companies raised prices. Angry Ohio voters took it out on McKinley, and he lost his bid for reelection by 303 votes.

The defeated congressman recovered to win election as governor of Ohio in 1891. Two years later a personal crisis threatened his career when the failure of a friend's business left McKinley with a personal debt of $130,000. A wealthy Ohio industrialist, Marcus Alonzo Hanna, known as Mark Hanna, intervened and established a trust fund to pay off the debts. Hanna had solved McKinley's problem, but there would be a price to pay.

In the 1893 race for governor, a landslide majority made McKinley the front-runner for the 1896 presidential nomination under Mark Hanna's expert guidance. At the convention in St. Louis, McKinley supporters hawked buttons and canes, waved banners, and passed out pamphlets and leaflets. Theodore Roosevelt, a young Republican from New York, saw Hanna's handiwork and said, "He has advertised McKinley as if he were a patent medicine." McKinley won easily on the first ballot.

The Republican nominee espoused the gold standard and high tariffs against William Jennings Bryan, a young Nebraska congressman. Bryan's radical economic ideas frightened America's business community into pouring large sums of money into McKinley's campaign, and Hanna managed it with rare skill. He had some $3 million to spend, compared with Bryan's $50,000. McKinley won with 271 electoral votes to Bryan's 176.

As his payoff, Hanna wanted a seat in the U.S. Senate. McKinley persuaded Ohio senator John Sherman to accept the post of secretary of state in his cabinet, then had his campaign manager appointed to Sherman's Senate seat. Approaching senility, Sherman was a poor choice to advise the new president in a sphere of emerging importance.

In 1898, the country peacefully annexed the Hawaiian Islands as a U.S. territory, but there would be no peace in the matter of the Spanish colony of Cuba. In 1895, the Cuban people had revolted against Spain. Sensational newspaper coverage charging Spanish atrocities fanned pro-Cuban sentiments into a clamor for war. McKinley resisted, patiently working toward a peaceful solution.

In January 1898, the United States sent the battleship *Maine* to Havana

Harbor. Then, on February 15, an explosion sank the battleship. Many of the nation's newspapers rushed to blame the disaster on Spain. President McKinley's navy commission, convened to investigate the sinking, failed to determine who was responsible for the explosion. Meanwhile, the country was spoiling for a fight. Even McKinley's assistant secretary of the navy, the belligerent Theodore Roosevelt, was losing patience with his commander in chief, complaining, "McKinley has no more backbone than a chocolate eclair."

On April 11, 1898, President McKinley asked Congress for war powers. Two weeks later, the United States formally declared war on Spain. The president called for 125,000 volunteers to attack Spanish forces in Spain's two Caribbean colonies, Cuba and Puerto Rico. While the army was mobilizing, the navy sent a squadron to attack the Spanish fleet at its Pacific Ocean colony, the Philippine Islands. In May, the American ships there won a stunning victory over the Spanish fleet in the Battle of Manila Bay. In July, the Spanish fleet in Cuba was destroyed. By August 12, Spain was ready to agree to Cuban independence, to cede Puerto Rico to the United States, and to leave the fate of the Philippines up to a Paris peace conference. "It's been a splendid little war," declared diplomat John Hay, as the United States emerged as a world power. The Paris talks resulted in the 1898 Treaty of Paris by which the United States acquired the Philippines from Spain for $20 million. Spain gave up its claims to Cuba and ceded Puerto Rico and the Pacific island of Guam to the United States.

In 1899 Secretary of State John Hay initiated the Open Door policy, which permitted Western powers to trade freely with China. The following year, McKinley was forced to deal with the Boxer Rebellion in China. A secret society called the Boxers had killed Western missionaries and laid siege to foreigners in Peking (now Beijing). The president ordered a force of five thousand American troops to join a relief force with seven other nations. The troops quickly ended the Boxer Rebellion and freed the westerners.

Elsewhere in the Pacific, Germany, Great Britain, and the United States agreed to divide the Samoan Islands between Germany and the United States. The treaty was signed in 1899 and ratified by the Senate in 1900.

The flexing of America's muscle made McKinley so popular he was renominated unanimously in 1900. The only real question was the choice of vice president to succeed New Jersey's Garret A. Hobart, who had died in office in 1899. McKinley left the decision up to the convention. As governor of New York, Teddy Roosevelt had upset old-guard Republicans with his vigorous reform program. They decided to get him out of New York by making him vice president. Mark Hanna, the Republican chairman, was wary. He made a prophetic complaint: "Don't any of you realize there's only one life between this madman and the White House?"

Delegates did not share Hanna's misgivings. The convention nominated Roosevelt to run with McKinley by a vote of 925 to 1. The only vote against Roosevelt was cast by the nominee himself.

Running again against Bryan, McKinley won by another landslide, 292 electoral votes to 155. He did not, however, have long to serve. In late summer, he visited the Pan-American Exposition in Buffalo and on September 6 held a brief public reception at the exposition's Temple of Music. Dressed in pin-striped trousers, a dark frock coat, and a black satin cravat, the president welcomed his admirers, using his special "McKinley grip," developed to prevent soreness and blisters from too many handshakes. Suddenly a clean-shaven man in a black suit stepped forward, his right hand covered with a white handkerchief. Two gunshots sounded. The president staggered back into the arms of a Secret Service agent. By the time he reached a chair, he was bleeding through his vest.

Before McKinley was taken to the hospital, he said to his secretary, George Cortelyou, "My wife. Be careful, Cortelyou, how you tell her. Oh, be careful."

President McKinley was carried to the hospital by an experimental electric-powered ambulance. One bullet had only grazed the president's ribs; the other had penetrated deep into his abdomen. He seemed at first to rally, then gangrene set in. Late in the afternoon of Friday the thirteenth, he whispered to his doctors, "It is useless, gentlemen. I think we ought to have a prayer." President McKinley died shortly after midnight. His assassin, Leon Czolgosz, an anarchist, confessed and was electrocuted six weeks later.

Rushing back from a camping trip in New York's Adirondack Mountains, Theodore Roosevelt arrived in Buffalo to take the oath as the twenty-sixth president. Mark Hanna was not happy: "Now look! That damned cowboy is President of the United States."

Our poll participants, ranking McKinley as a better-than-average president, give him his highest marks for the Accomplishments and Crisis Management category, rating him fifteenth. They are, however, sparing in their praise. "A pious expansionist," writes one, while another comments, "events lifted him above mediocrity."

McKinley's greatest achievements lay in ushering the country into its role as a world power. Said Secretary of State John Hay, "Under his rule Hawaii has come to us, and Tutuila [American Samoa]; Puerto Rico and the vast archipelago of the East [Philippines]. Cuba is free. Our position in the Caribbean is assured beyond the possibility of future question. . . . In dealing with foreign powers, he will take rank with the greatest of our diplomatists."

THEODORE ROOSEVELT

1901–1909
26TH PRESIDENT

OVERALL RANKING: 5

★

Leadership Qualities: 4
Accomplishments and Crisis Management: 4
Political Skill: 4
Appointments: 5
Character and Integrity: 12

The White House is a bully pulpit.

—Theodore Roosevelt

Theodore Roosevelt had been mountain climbing in the Adirondacks when a messenger brought him word that President William McKinley was dying. Before he could reach Buffalo, where the president had been shot, he learned that McKinley had died. Roosevelt arrived not to comfort a dying president but to be sworn in as the twenty-sixth president of the United States on September 14, 1901.

At forty-two, the youngest man ever to assume the office, Roosevelt brought to the presidency boundless energy and a flamboyant macho style that delighted Americans. Headline writers called him TR, the first president known just by his initials, and an adoring populace called him Teddy. His reach was so great he even gave his name to a toy animal beloved by millions of children, teddy bear.

Author, journalist, mountain climber, cowboy, big game hunter, police commissioner, war hero, governor, he saw the world as a place to be conquered. Where some presidents envisaged the office as restricted to the powers designated by the Constitution, he saw it as one in which a president could take any action in the public interest not forbidden by law or the Constitution.

Roosevelt even gave the Executive Mansion a new name—the White House—then proceeded to declare, "The White House is a bully pulpit." One of Roosevelt's favorite sayings was "Speak softly and carry a big stick, you will go far." A more accurate motto for him would have been "Speak loudly and often and back it up with a cannon." The important thing was that he backed it up.

Pale and sickly from birth, Theodore Roosevelt was born on October 27, 1858, in New York City, the second of four children of a wealthy New York banker. Bodybuilding workouts in a gymnasium in his home transformed him into a strong, energetic, athletic adult.

At twenty-one, Roosevelt graduated Phi Beta Kappa from Harvard College and three years later published his first book, *The Naval War of 1812*, and was elected to New York's state legislature.

In 1884, tragedy struck the Roosevelt household. Both his wife and his mother died on Valentine's Day, his mother from typhoid fever, his wife from Bright's disease, following the birth of their only child. Leaving his baby daughter, Alice, with his older sister, Roosevelt headed out West to the Dakota Badlands, where he bought two ranches. For three years he lived the life of a cowboy, then returned to the world he had left. He married again, this time to a childhood friend, Edith Carow.

Back East he ran unsuccessfully for mayor of New York and wrote magazine articles and books. In the course of his life he wrote thirty-eight books, more than any other president.

In 1888, President Benjamin Harrison appointed him to the U.S. Civil Service Commission. He returned to New York City as police commissioner in 1895. Disguising himself in a black cape, he at times ventured out at night checking on policemen loafing on the job. The press and the public loved him.

President McKinley named him assistant secretary of the navy in 1897. The following year an explosion sank the battleship *Maine* in Havana Harbor. Less than two weeks after Congress declared war against Spain in April 1898, Roosevelt resigned his navy post and accepted a commission as lieutenant colonel in the 1st Volunteer Cavalry, called the Rough Riders. He won fame by leading the regiment's charge up a hill near the Cuban city of Santiago.

His heroism in Cuba made TR a national hero and brought him the Republican nomination for governor and, in November 1898, victory in a close election. He quickly alienated his own party by pushing through a tax on corporation franchises. New York Republicans decided to move him out of New York and into the vice presidency where it was assumed he could do little harm. In June, delegates at the Republican National Convention nominated him as President McKinley's running mate.

As was his style, Roosevelt campaigned energetically for the ticket that won overwhelmingly in November 1900. When the assassination of President McKinley the following September elevated him to the presidency, he was already well known throughout the land. "It is a dreadful thing to come into the presidency this way, but it would be a far worse thing to be morbid about it. Here is the task and I have got to do it to the best of my ability, and that is all there is about it."

The new president pledged "to continue absolutely unbroken the policy of President McKinley for the peace, the prosperity and the honor of our beloved country." A conservative Republican senator commented, "That simple declaration immediately restored confidence in the business world."

After his reassuring comments, TR wasted little time in shaking up party conservatives. In his first message to Congress in December 1901, he declared, "Corporations engaged in interstate commerce should be regulated if they are found to exercise a license working to the public injury. It should be as much the aim of those who seek for social betterment to rid the business world of crimes of cunning as to rid the entire body politic of crimes of violence."

He called for the government's right to inspect the books and records of corporations engaged in interstate commerce. He sought the creation of a Department of Commerce and Labor. To the post of secretary of the new department he later appointed Oscar S. Straus, the first Jew ever to serve in the cabinet. His message contained a call for greater emphasis on the conservation of natural resources. He asked for a stronger navy and advocated the building of a canal to connect the Atlantic and Pacific Oceans.

Early in his administration, President Roosevelt antagonized many white southerners when he invited the distinguished black educator Booker T. Washington to dine with him at the White House. It was the first time a president had a White House dinner with an African American, leading one southern paper to call the occasion "the most damnable outrage ever."

TR was a high-handed president, moving unilaterally to do things "his way." Without informing his cabinet, he had his attorney general, Philander C. Knox, prepare an antitrust suit against the Northern Securities Company, a giant railroad trust organized by J. P. Morgan. Two years later, the Supreme Court backed Roosevelt and decreed that Morgan's trust should be dissolved. "The corrupt corporations need the knife as much as the corrupt politicians," TR once said.

Despite his often unilateral approach to governing, President Roosevelt surrounded himself with competent people. Among his most notable appointments were his choice of Oliver Wendell Holmes of Massachusetts to sit on the Supreme Court and his selection of Elihu Root to serve as secretary of war as a holdover from McKinley's cabinet and then, beginning in 1905, as secretary of state. (Root in 1912 became the second American to win the Nobel Peace Prize; the first was Roosevelt.)

In May 1902, in the anthracite mines of Pennsylvania more than a hundred thousand members of the United Mine Workers struck for higher wages and better working conditions. When mine owners refused to negotiate, President Roosevelt told them privately he would take over the mines unless they agreed to arbitration. He had no legal basis to make such a threat, but the owners agreed to let him appoint an arbitration commission, which settled the strike by granting the strikers a 10 percent increase from their average yearly wage of $600.

The president considered the Panama Canal his greatest achievement. "I took Panama without consulting the Cabinet," TR boasted later in his autobiography. The Spooner Act had authorized the government to negotiate with Colombia for the construction of a canal across the Isthmus of Panama. For their sovereign rights in the province of Panama, the Colombians demanded more money than Roosevelt was willing to pay. Instead, TR encouraged the Panamanians to revolt against Colombia, then recognized Panama as a new country and sent U.S. warships to dramatize American support. The new government promptly agreed to a treaty, and construction of the canal got under way.

Conservation was a major project of Roosevelt's presidency. In 1903, ornithologists were pressing him to create a federal wildlife refuge to protect endangered birds on Pelican Island, Florida, already owned by the federal government. When he learned that no law prohibited him from declaring it a federal bird reservation, he said, "Very well, then I so declare it." During his first term, he took a number of other strong environmental actions. He sought protection for the few remaining bison (American buffalo) in this country, made Crater Lake in Oregon a national park, added about 126 million acres to the national forests, and by executive order established fifty-one national bird preserves.

America's sensational "yellow journalism" press, which knew a good story when it saw one, covered Roosevelt's active presidency with enthusiasm. Delighted Americans voted overwhelmingly for him for a full term as president in November 1904, electing him with the largest percentage of the popular vote in the history of the United States up to that time. His vice president was Charles W. Fairbanks, a senator from Indiana.

In his first message to Congress following the 1904 election, the president added the Roosevelt Corollary to the Monroe Doctrine, contending that flagrant cases of wrongdoing in the Western Hemisphere might force the United States "to the exercise of an international police power." He used his newly declared power to intervene in the internal affairs of Santo Domingo (now the Dominican Republic). Because the Caribbean island nation was no longer making good on its payment of foreign debts, TR ordered American officials to seize the customs office of Santo Domingo, collect taxes, and then make payments on the country's debts. The arrangement continued for two years.

Despite his generally belligerent attitude, Roosevelt in his second term demonstrated a more conciliatory outlook. Serious friction developed in 1905 between France and Germany over the control of Morocco. President Roosevelt intervened and persuaded the two European powers to attend an international conference in 1906 in Spain, which resolved the dispute peacefully.

In 1905 TR helped negotiate an end to the war between Russia and Japan over control of Manchuria and Korea. He brought representatives of the two nations to Portsmouth, New Hampshire, then served as mediator at peace talks that produced the 1905 Treaty of Portsmouth. For his achievement at Portsmouth, President Roosevelt was awarded the Nobel Peace Prize in 1906, the first American to receive the honor. With the prize money of $36,735, he created a trust fund to promote industrial peace. After the entry of the United States into World War I, he diverted the trust to aid war victims.

In the fall of 1906, Roosevelt issued an order that produced one of the bitterest controversies of his second term. In mid-August, he had received a wire, alleging that black soldiers stationed at Brownsville, Texas, had shot up the community, killing a white bartender and wounding a police lieutenant. An army probe proved inconclusive. Denials by all of the African Americans convinced investigators they were facing a cover-up. The accused soldiers were not accorded the presumption of innocence nor did the government provide them with any legal representation. President Roosevelt ordered all 160 men "discharged without honor" and "forever barred from reenlistment." Six of the men held the Medal of Honor.

Three years later the president accepted a compromise measure establishing a special military court to review the case. Eighty-four of the soldiers testified, and fourteen of these were ruled eligible for reinstatement. The Brownsville affair demonstrated how far TR had moved from the relatively tolerant racial attitudes of his first term. By 1906, he was courting the support of white southerners by speaking about "the Negro problem." He did not mention the Brownsville episode in his autobiography.

In October 1907, Roosevelt was away from Washington on a bear hunt when Wall Street plunged into a "bear market" so severe that it triggered the Panic of 1907. The last days of his administration were plagued with a severely depressed economy.

In his last months in office, Roosevelt used his powers to gain the Republican nomination for his candidate, William Howard Taft, a man who served as his secretary of war and who he believed would continue his progressive policies. Roosevelt worked hard in Taft's successful run for the presidency, then treated himself and his son Kermit to a yearlong big game hunt in Africa. He bagged nearly three hundred animals, including nine lions, five elephants, and thirteen rhinoceroses. A triumphal tour of Europe brought the hospitality of kings and queens and the adulation of the masses.

Back in the United States, he spoke out on issues, convinced that President Taft had strayed from the Roosevelt agenda. In 1912, TR decided to run again for the presidency. The Republican National Convention, ruled by Taft supporters, refused to seat many delegates pledged to Roosevelt. After Taft won the nomination, TR, a lifelong Republican, formed the Progressive Party, better known as the Bull Moose Party, to run against the incumbent Republican president and against Woodrow Wilson, the Democratic nominee.

Wilson won overwhelmingly. Roosevelt finished second, with Taft, the candidate for the party that TR had split apart, running a humiliating third. In 1916, the Progressive Party nominated Roosevelt again, but he declined to run. After the United States entered World War I, he pleaded with President Wilson to let him form a "Roosevelt Division" to fight against Germany. Wilson rejected the offer. A year later, Roosevelt's youngest son, Quentin, was killed in an air battle in France. In 1919, Theodore Roosevelt died of a blood clot at his Oyster Bay home at the age of sixty.

In ranking him America's fifth most effective president, our poll participants are impressed by his boldness and vision in facing up to the challenges of the twentieth-century presidency, calling him "a leader," "a bundle of energy," and "largely effective." His marks are extremely high in every category except one. In the Character and Integrity category, he fell to twelfth out of forty-one, eliciting such comments as "charistmatic warmonger," "the U.S.'s roving gunboat," "a bully with bravado," and "about six years old but lucky and shrewd . . . as well as a dynamo."

President Roosevelt had redefined the American presidency, establishing a more powerful role for the chief executive for the century that lay ahead. He gave an eloquent description of his vision: "While president, I have been president, emphatically; I have used every ounce of power there was in the office and I have not cared a rap for the criticisms of those who spoke of my 'usurpation of power.' . . . I believe in a strong executive; I believe in power."

WILLIAM HOWARD TAFT

1909–1913
27TH PRESIDENT
OVERALL RANKING: 20

Leadership Qualities: 25
Accomplishments and Crisis Management: 21
Political Skill: 30
Appointments: 20
Character and Integrity: 14

My sin is an indisposition to labor as hard as I might; a disposition to procrastinate and a disposition to enjoy the fellowship of others more than I ought.

—William Howard Taft

William Howard Taft often quipped that it would be a "cold day when he got to be president of the United States." He was right. On March 4, 1909, Taft's inauguration was forced inside the Capitol in the Senate chambers to escape a fierce, wintry storm that held Washington in a snowy grip. From that day on, the political climate turned ever chillier for the jovial, warmhearted Republican from Ohio.

Handpicked by President Theodore Roosevelt as his successor, Taft appeared ideal to carry out his progressive platform. Big Bill Taft, who carried 350 pounds on his six-foot frame, had done such an outstanding job as governor of the Philippines that President Theodore Roosevelt named him secretary of war, sending him abroad often to settle diplomatic disputes that required delicate negotiations.

Taft was honest, intelligent, and charming, and wholeheartedly supported Roosevelt's policies. But that was not enough for a nation entertained for more than seven years by the charismatic, freewheeling Teddy Roosevelt. And it was definitely not enough for Roosevelt loyalists and Democratic opponents, who found little to like in Taft's plodding style. Ugly infighting eventually led to a split in the Republican Party, the creation of a third party led by Roosevelt, and the humiliating defeat of Taft.

The irony is that Taft never wanted to be president. His life's ambition was to sit on the Supreme Court. In 1921, President Warren Harding appointed him to the Supreme Court as chief justice of the United States.

William Howard Taft was born September 15, 1857, in Cincinnati, Ohio, into the politically well-connected family of Alphonso and Louise Torrey Taft. His father, a local judge, served in the administration of President Ulysses S. Grant as U.S. attorney general, as secretary of war, and as minister to Russia and the Austro-Hungarian Empire. By all accounts, he was a cheerful youth with a knack for settling disputes.

Active in sports and debating, he graduated from Yale, second in his class, in 1878. At the University of Cincinnati Law School, he graduated with top honors. While studying law, Taft worked as a reporter, covering the courts for the *Cincinnati Commercial* newspaper.

Thanks to his father's prominence and his own ability, Taft benefited from a series of political appointments in Cincinnati. His work caught the eye of President Benjamin Harrison, who called him to Washington to serve as U.S. solicitor general. Next, Taft was appointed a judge on the Sixth U.S. Court of Appeals, a circuit that left him ample time with his ambitious wife Helen "Nellie" Herron and their three children—daughter Helen Herron Taft Manning, who in 1917 became dean of Bryn Mawr College, and two sons—Charles Phelps Taft, who became a politician and lawyer, and Robert Alphonso Taft, who became a prominent U.S. Republican senator.

Appointed by President William McKinley to head a commission to establish civil government in the Philippines, he organized American-style municipal and provincial governments, established a Philippine police force, converted the islands from military to civilian rule, upgraded health standards, and reformed a corrupt judicial system. His commitment to the Filipinos cost him dearly. Not once but twice, Taft was offered appointments to the Supreme Court. And twice, Taft reluctantly rejected the post he wanted above all others because he felt obligated to complete his mission to the Philippines.

In 1904, his friend President Theodore Roosevelt named Taft secretary of war, an odd appointment for a man of peace. But Roosevelt soon found Taft invaluable as an international troubleshooter with a knack for defusing potential crises such as the threat of civil war in Cuba. As secretary of war, Taft supervised preparations for the construction of the Panama Canal and continued to oversee progress in the Philippines. The canal was completed in 1914, during his administration.

Roosevelt, who wanted to return to private life at the end of his second term, urged Taft to follow in his footsteps as president, a job Taft had never wanted. At the Republican National Convention of 1908 in Chicago, Taft won the nomination by acclamation. James S. Sherman, a New York congressman, was chosen as his running mate.

"Hit them hard, old man," Roosevelt urged Taft as he set out on the campaign trail against the Democratic nominee William Jennings Bryan. Taft disliked politics and hated campaigning but swung through the country addressing legitimate issues such as tariff reform. Bryan answered with mudslinging attacks, calling Taft, who was a lifelong Unitarian, an anti-Christian heathen.

"If the American people are so narrow as not to elect a Unitarian, well and good," Taft responded. "I can stand it."

Taft scored an easy victory, winning 7,675,320 popular votes to Bryan's 6,412,294. The electoral vote favored Taft 321 to 162.

On that icy inauguration day, March 4, 1909, Taft promised much: he would lower the tariff, strengthen antitrust laws, save the nation's forests, change banking laws, and stimulate foreign trade. He said farewell to Roosevelt, who planned a yearlong safari in Africa. At the inaugural ball, Taft, ever a graceful waltzer, danced every dance.

The gala evening was a pleasant prelude to the worst period of his life. While his wife turned the White House into a whirl of social events, Taft began the struggle to make good on his campaign promises. His first major legislative defeat came when Congress ignored his call for tariff reform and passed the Payne-Aldrich Tariff Act of 1909, which offered only slight relief from the punishing rates. Since Taft did not veto the act, the public blamed him for the unpopular law.

From then on, it was downhill. Liberal Republicans charged him with abandoning Roosevelt's principles and befriending millionaires and corporate lawyers. And laissez-faire, conservative Republicans were unhappy with his strong antitrust stance.

The next battle was over conservation. Taft's secretary of the interior, Richard A. Ballinger, became involved in a feud with a Roosevelt favorite, Gifford Pinchot, head of the U.S. Forest Service. Pinchot accused Ballinger of selling land concessions too cheaply to water and power companies and of illegal sales of Alaska coal lands. The controversy ballooned with charges and countercharges. Taft called for a special investigation by Congress, which found no evidence to support Pinchot's charges. But the damage to Taft's administration had been done. Instead of issuing a strong response and taking his case to the press, Taft had tried to avoid a fight. He gave out ponderous statements about his careful review of the matter. In the end, Taft had to fire Pinchot, which further irritated the pro-Roosevelt faction and fueled the public's perception of Taft as a political blunderer.

His enemies claimed Taft had turned his back on conservation. Yet it was this president who developed legal procedures for setting aside land for conservation. Under his administration, 71.5 million acres in the United States plus 770,000 more in the territory of Alaska were set aside for preservation. But unlike TR, Taft failed to trumpet his positive record for conservation, which in many ways surpassed Roosevelt's. As one who had climbed the ladder by appointments, Taft had never developed the political skills to match those of the charismatic Roosevelt.

Although Taft still admired his friend and mentor, Roosevelt launched a devious campaign to regain the presidency. The split within the Republican Party and the clash between the two men spilled over into the primary race. Roosevelt called Taft a "puzzlewit" and "fathead." Taft called Roosevelt "a dangerous egotist and demagogue."

When the Republican National Convention met on June 18, 1912, in Chicago, Taft had 63 delegates compared with 60 pledged to Roosevelt. After weeks of wrangling, Taft won the nomination on August 1. Four days later, Roosevelt bolted the Republican Party, announcing he would campaign as the candidate of the newly created Progressive, or Bull Moose, Party. The three-way election guaranteed victory for the Democrats and the election of Woodrow Wilson.

Despite his failure to inspire the public, Taft left behind enough solid accomplishments to secure his place as a good, though not great, president. His administration conducted a vigorous antitrust campaign to rein in corporate excesses, and it undertook tariff reform. Taft created a separate Children's Bureau within the Labor Department and named Julia C. Lathrop as the first woman to head the new federal agency. His administration created parcel post and the postal savings banks. Arizona and New Mexico obtained statehood during his term. He sponsored legislation to regulate corporate campaign contributions and was the first president to submit a federal budget to Congress. And his record on conservation was outstanding.

Taft embarked on a second career, that of a law professor, and taught at Yale for eight years. In 1921, Taft finally realized his dearest ambition when President Warren Harding chose him as chief justice of the United States, the only former president to hold that position on the Supreme Court. During his eight years on the bench, Taft streamlined the Court's procedures to eliminate backlogs of cases.

A series of small heart attacks weakened Taft's health, and in February 1930 he resigned from the Court. He died at age seventy-two on March 8, 1930.

Much maligned in his time, Taft is viewed today as a good, average president, ranking twentieth in our poll, thus placing him in the top 50 percent. Lack of political skills hurt him in the view of poll participants, who balance that rating out with a high ranking for Character and Integrity. Poll participants' comments range from "poor politician" and "more action in his bathtub than in the Oval Office" to "amiable walrus," "350 pounds of progressivism," and "continued the progressive movement, overshadowed by his predecessor and his successor."

William Howard Taft wrote, "The president cannot make clouds to rain and cannot make the corn to grow, he cannot make business good; although when these things occur political parties do claim some credit for good things that have happened this way."

WOODROW WILSON

1913–1921
28TH PRESIDENT

OVERALL RANKING: 6

Leadership Qualities: 7
Accomplishments and Crisis Management: 7
Political Skill: 13
Appointments: 6
Character and Integrity: 8

The world must be made safe for democracy.

—Woodrow Wilson

On April 2, 1917, President Woodrow Wilson asked Congress to declare war against Germany. Less than three weeks earlier German submarines had sunk three unarmed American merchant ships in the war zone. A man of peace, Wilson brought the United States into war reluctantly, then worked zealously to defeat Germany and its allies. In the peace conference that followed, he represented the United States personally in pressing his idealistic Fourteen Points for achieving a just and lasting peace. The fourteenth point was a revolutionary concept, a League of Nations, designed to settle international conflicts without warfare. Though he failed to gain American support for the league, his administration achieved major domestic reforms. In 1920, at the end of his term in office, Wilson was awarded the Nobel Peace Prize for his visionary efforts to bring about international peace.

Thomas Woodrow Wilson was born December 29, 1856, in Staunton, Virginia, the son of a prominent Presbyterian minister. When he was two, the family moved to Augusta, Georgia. Sickly from early childhood, he later lived in Columbia, South Carolina, and Wilmington, North Carolina.

The best educated of all American presidents, he enrolled in 1873 in Davidson College in North Carolina to study for the ministry, then switched to another Presbyterian school, Princeton University in New Jersey. Later he studied law at the University of Virginia, practiced law briefly in Atlanta, then earned a Ph.D. in political science at Johns Hopkins University in Baltimore. His thesis at Johns Hopkins was his first book, *Congressional Government*, a perceptive, critical study of the dominance of Congress when the president is weak, a description no one would apply to him. His book, translated into several languages, went through twenty-nine editions.

In 1885, Wilson married Ellen Louise Axson, of Savannah, and then began his teaching career at Bryn Mawr College near Philadelphia. A few years later, he taught at Wesleyan University and finally at Princeton, where he became its president.

In 1910, the Democratic state convention nominated him for governor of New Jersey on the first ballot. Although the Republicans had controlled the state government for fourteen years, Wilson won by more than 50,000 votes and delivered a Democratic majority in the state legislature. Governor Wilson pushed through significant legislation: electoral reforms, regulation of public utilities, a workmen's compensation law, a pure food law, and regulation of women's and child labor conditions.

When the Democratic National Convention met in late June and early July 1912 in Baltimore, Democrats saw opportunity in the divisive battle between Theodore Roosevelt and the incumbent president Taft, which was splitting the Republicans badly. Although the Democratic favorite was Beauchamp Clark (known as Champ Clark), a conservative senator from Missouri, Wilson won the nomination after six days and forty-six ballots. His running mate was Thomas Riley Marshall, governor of Indiana.

In August, Roosevelt deserted the Republican Party and ran on the Progressive, or Bull Moose, ticket. His defection assured Wilson's election. He won with 435 electoral votes to 88 for Roosevelt and 8 for Taft. To cheering Princeton students, he said, "I myself have no feeling of triumph tonight. I have a feeling of solemn responsibility." The voters had elected a serious man. His witty vice president was less serious. His most famous remark would be, "What this country needs is a good five-cent cigar."

Wilson surrounded himself with strong advisers. Three-time presidential nominee William Jennings Bryan was named secretary of state. For the position of secretary of the treasury, Wilson picked William Gibbs McAdoo, who in 1914 also became Wilson's son-in-law in a White House ceremony. Josephus Daniels, a North Carolina newspaper publisher, was selected as secretary of the navy and a young Franklin D. Roosevelt as assistant secretary of the navy. Wilson's only Supreme Court nominee was James C. McReynolds, of Tennessee, who had been the president's first attorney general.

The new president broke precedent by addressing a special session of Congress in person for the first time since the administration of President John Adams more than a century earlier. Thus began the annual tradition of the State of the Union Address. He decried the custom of sending a message over to be read, preferring to show that he was "a human being trying to cooperate with other human beings in a common service." He spoke eloquently for lower tariffs, and the House quickly passed a tariff reform bill. When the bill bogged down in the Senate, as tariff reform had for many years, President Wilson went directly to the people, asking that they help him defeat the business lobbies working against the measure. So many letters poured in to Washington that the senators voted with Wilson. The new law generally reduced tariffs about 25 percent, while removing tariffs on

wool, sugar, iron, steel, and food. The law also provided for the first constitutionally authorized income tax, as approved that year by ratification of
the Sixteenth Amendment. The law placed a 1 percent tax on incomes
above $3,000 and an additional graduated surtax of 1 to 6 percent on in-
comes above $20,000.

In June, President Wilson was back again before Congress, calling for
reform of outmoded banking and currency laws. The Federal Reserve Act
of 1913 that resulted is regarded by many as the most important piece of
domestic legislation of the Wilson administration. The Act established
twelve regional banks designed to regulate the nation's money supply in
response to such changing economic conditions as inflation and recession.

President Wilson also pushed through the establishment of the Federal
Trade Commission to regulate business, the Clayton Anti-Trust Law of
1914 to strengthen the government's hand in curbing the power of monopolies and to affirm farm labor organizations' and labor unions' right to
exist, and the La Follette Seamen's Act of 1915 to improve safety and working conditions for sailors. During his administration two child labor laws
were passed, but these were ruled unconstitutional by the Supreme Court.
Wilson's social justice agenda did not extend to the plight of black Americans. As more southern Democrats came into power in the administration,
racial segregation restrictions were imposed in many federal departments
and agencies. Wilson did little or nothing to restrain his fellow white southerners.

Foreign affairs wasted little time in bringing major problems right to the
border for the new president. In 1913, Victoriano Huerta overthrew the democratic government of Mexico and murdered its president. Within a year,
relations with Mexico deteriorated sharply after Mexican authorities arrested U.S. sailors in Tampico. The sailors were quickly released, but the
Wilson administration demanded a twenty-one gun salute as an apology.
When none was forthcoming, U.S. Marines bombarded and briefly occupied Vera Cruz. Nineteen Americans were killed in the operation, but it
led to the resignation of Huerta in 1914.

Two years later more trouble erupted with Mexico when followers of
Francisco Villa, known as Pancho Villa, killed eighteen American mining
engineers working in Mexico. A few months later, Villa crossed the border
into the United States and raided the town of Columbus, New Mexico,
killing seventeen Americans. Gen. John J. Pershing led an army of 4,000
into Mexico. Later the expeditionary force was increased to 10,000 men.
Villa was never captured by the Americans as uneasy relations continued
between the two countries.

In August 1914 Europe was plunged into World War I, which pitted the Central Powers—Germany, Austria-Hungary, Bulgaria, and Turkey—against the Allies, principally, Great Britain, France, Italy, Russia, Japan, and Portugal.

That same month Ellen Wilson, Wilson's talented wife of twenty-nine years and mother of his three daughters, died of kidney disease. An artist, the first lady had arranged the White House weddings of two of their daughters and had been active in lobbying Congress on behalf of slum clearance. In December 1915, President Wilson married an attractive Washington widow, forty-three-year-old Edith Galt, a descendent of Pocahontas.

In 1916, a reunited Republican Party nominated Charles Evans Hughes, an associate Supreme Court justice, to run against Wilson. That summer the railroad unions threatened a nationwide strike unless the railroads granted their workers an eight-hour workday. Wilson intervened and convinced the unions to accept arbitration, but the presidents of the railroads refused to cooperate. Before the strike, Wilson convened a joint session of Congress and persuaded it to pass legislation for an eight-hour workday. The Republican candidate attacked Wilson's action as a "surrender to the unions."

The strike, however, was not the main campaign issue. What concerned the voters most was the war in Europe. The Democrats made effective use of the slogan, "He kept us out of war." On election day, Hughes won so heavily in the Northeast that Wilson went to bed convinced he had lost. He awoke the next morning to learn that he had done surprisingly well in the West. Even so, two days elapsed before the winner could be determined. When Wilson carried California by about 4,000 votes, its 13 electoral votes gave him a 277 to 254 edge in the electoral college.

In January 1917, Germany announced that its submarines would without warning sink any ship engaged in trade with the Allies—even those of neutral countries such as the United States. On his own authority, Wilson set about arming American merchant ships and placed U.S. defenses on a wartime footing. He continued to work, however, for a peaceful end to the war until German subs sank three American merchant ships with a loss of thirty-six lives.

At a special session of Congress on April 2, 1917, the president called for a declaration of war. Within four days, both houses of Congress had made it official. The United States was at war with Germany.

President Wilson moved quickly. A Selective Service Act was passed to draft men between the ages of twenty-one and thirty. Factories began operating around the clock to produce food, uniforms, and military equipment. A Republican mining engineer named Herbert Hoover was placed in charge of a nationwide food and fuel rationing program.

The first American troops landed in France on June 26, 1917. On January 8, 1918, President Wilson addressed Congress, setting forth the Fourteen Points on which he insisted a lasting peace could be made. Among the points were a call for "open covenants of peace, openly arrived at," freedom of the seas, free trade, arms reductions, and settlement of a number of territorial disputes. The fourteenth point advanced a revolutionary idea: "A general association of nations must be formed under specific covenants for the purpose of affording mutual guarantees of political independence and territorial integrity to great and small [states] alike."

That spring the German army massed a powerful offensive to capture Paris before the Americans could arrive in full force, but the Germans fell short of their goal. By summer, General Pershing had assembled an army of one million men in France. In September, at the Battle at Saint-Mihiel, air power was launched on a scale never before seen. U.S. Army combat air commander Billy Mitchell directed an aerial assault by 1,481 Allied airplanes. That month the Central Powers began to crumble. Bulgaria surrendered, then the Ottoman Empire, and in early November, Austria-Hungary. Germany saw itself alone against a fresh 2-million-man American army. Germany agreed to an armistice. On November 11, 1918— on the eleventh hour of the eleventh day of the eleventh month—the war stopped, but not before more than a hundred thousand American soldiers had died in a war that claimed the lives of nearly nine million combatants.

Determined that his Fourteen Points would form the basis for the settlement, Wilson headed the American delegation at the Paris Peace Conference. It was the first trip to Europe by an American president while holding office. Unfortunately he neglected to include a representative from the U.S. Senate or from the Republican Party, an oversight that would later haunt him. The president was received triumphantly by the French people. He found resistance, however, at the negotiating table where he sat as a member of the Big Four with Prime Minister David Lloyd George of Great Britain, Premier Vittorio Orlando of Italy, and Premier Georges Clemenceau, who was called the Tiger of France. The American's moral fervor was too much for the worldly-wise Europeans. Lloyd George remarked that he felt as though he were seated between "Jesus Christ and Napoleon Bonaparte." In June 1919, Germany signed the treaty.

When Wilson finally returned to the United States to get the Senate's approval of the Treaty of Versailles, he found powerful opposition, particularly to the League of Nations. Unwilling to compromise, the inflexible president went on an eight-thousand-mile speaking tour to rally public support. On the night of September 25, 1919, he collapsed from exhaustion after speaking in Pueblo, Colorado. Cutting his train trip short, he returned to Washington. On October 3, a stroke paralyzed his left side.

The president was an invalid, but the country was not aware of it. Edith Wilson took control of her husband's schedule and agenda, carefully managing who could see him. Wilson was no longer able to negotiate effectively with the Republican opponents to his treaty. Still, he declined to relinquish his post to the vice president, who in turn did not challenge him for the office. The Senate rejected the treaty and the League of Nations. Not until late 1921, after Wilson left office, did the Senate ratify a separate peace with Germany.

Two amendments to the Constitution were ratified during Wilson's administration. The Volstead Act, prohibiting the use of intoxicating beverages, was passed by Congress in 1919 over the president's veto. It was ratified as the Eighteenth Amendment in October 1919. That same year the Nineteenth Amendment, granting women the right to vote, was passed by Congress and was ratified in August 1920.

One last triumph remained for Woodrow Wilson. For his efforts to negotiate a just and lasting peace in Europe, he received the 1919 Nobel Prize for Peace, awarded to him in December 1920. On February 3, 1924, Woodrow Wilson died quietly in his sleep in his Washington home at age sixty-seven.

Wilson is often called a "near great" president. Our poll participants rank him high in every category except Political Skills, where his rating is thirteenth. Derogatory comments on his presidency usually cite his personal traits. He was described as "self-righteous," "too pure," "too idealistic," "priggish," and "undone by his own stubbornness." Many of the comments, however, praise his "marvelous intellect and great achievements," "great world influence," and "great world vision."

Into the presidency, Woodrow Wilson brought an intellect exceeded only by that of Thomas Jefferson and an intensity exceeded by none. Supported by a deep religious faith, he advanced his programs with uncommon zeal. He pushed through much-needed reforms on the home front and then made the United States the major player on the global scene. In the process, he became a powerful force in creating the modern presidency, thus leading to his ranking as our sixth most effective president.

Warren G. Harding

1921–1923
29th President

Overall Ranking: 41

★

Leadership Qualities: 41
Accomplishments and Crisis Management: 40
Political Skill: 38
Appointments: 41
Character and Integrity: 40

I am not fit for this office and should never have been here.

—Warren G. Harding

Warren G. Harding occupies an unenviable position in the pantheon of United States presidents. He has been voted the worst chief executive in every presidential poll ever conducted.

Weary of World War I, rancorous peace talks, and two terms of moralizing from reform-minded President Woodrow Wilson, voters turned happily in November 1920 to the restful, shallow Harding, who promised "a return to normalcy." They gave the likable Ohio Republican one of the biggest majorities in the popular vote for any president in U.S. history.

"He was not a man with either the experience or the intellectual quality that the position needed," said Harding's own secretary of commerce, Herbert Hoover, one of several honest, honorable, and competent men Harding appointed. Unfortunately, too many of the men he appointed were not honest, honorable, or competent. They betrayed the affable Harding, a man so broken that after only two years in the presidency he said to Nicholas Murray Butler, president of Columbia University, "I am not fit for this office and should never have been here."

The first of eight children, Warren Gamaliel Harding was born on November 2, 1865, on a farm in north-central Ohio. After his father became a part owner of a weekly newspaper, Warren worked as a printer's devil, learning to set type and run the press. At fourteen, he enrolled at Ohio Central College, a high school, and graduated from it in 1883.

In Marion, Ohio, where the family had moved, he worked as a newspaper reporter for a dollar a week, then with two friends raised $300 to buy a bankrupt daily paper. At twenty-five, editor Harding married thirty-year-old Florence Kling DeWolfe, the divorced daughter of Marion's richest resident. The Duchess, as Harding called her, was promptly disowned by her father, who considered Harding beneath her.

Harding was elected to the Ohio State Senate, where he held office from 1899 to 1902. His flamboyant oratory and impressive appearance helped him rise in Republican ranks.

Harding had caught the eye of an Ohio political operator named Harry M. Daugherty. He and the Duchess induced Harding to run in Ohio's first direct primary for U.S. senator. Their candidate won the primary and then the general election, marred by bigoted attacks on Harding's opponent, a Catholic. After his 1914 victory, his career was largely managed by his wife Florence and by Daugherty.

In his undistinguished Senate term, Harding made many friends, too many. Three of these would later destroy his reputation. In Hawaii, he met a fun-loving naval officer named Charles R. Forbes. In the Senate, Harding sat next to Albert B. Fall of New Mexico, who became a close friend. During those years, Harding also established a liaison with Nan Britton, an attractive blonde from Marion, Ohio. She bore him a child.

Daugherty induced Harding to run for the presidency in 1920. A tall, dark, handsome, six-footer, he, as one of his supporters said, "looked like a president." On the tenth ballot, Republican party leaders, meeting in Chicago's Blackstone Hotel, decided to back Harding, largely because there was no single, strong objection to him. The meeting place was the origin of the phrase "smoke-filled room." Harding's running mate was former Massachusetts governor Calvin Coolidge.

Harding and Coolidge ran against James M. Cox, governor of Ohio, and his vice presidential nominee, Franklin D. Roosevelt, former assistant secretary of the navy. The Democratic ticket backed President Woodrow Wilson's League of Nations, but Harding used a low-key approach that played expertly to a voting populace weary of Wilson's evangelical oratory and the restrictions imposed on them by World War I. With soothing, empty speeches, Harding won overwhelmingly with 61 percent of the popular vote. "We're in the big league now, boys," he told his staff.

"Strive for normalcy to reach stability," he told a delighted America, and he set about picking his cabinet and staff. President Harding brought a number of competent men into his administration, most notably Charles Evans Hughes as secretary of state, Andrew W. Mellon as secretary of the treasury, and Herbert C. Hoover as secretary of commerce. To the Supreme Court, he named former president William Howard Taft.

Harding's fatal mistake was placing friends and cronies in too many sensitive positions. He named Daugherty, a provincial political fixer, attorney general. Albert Fall became secretary of the interior. Other important appointments went to relatives and poker-playing buddies, among them Charlie Forbes, who was appointed chief of the Veterans Bureau. Mrs. Harding's doctor, Charles Sawyer, became White House physician, with the rank of brigadier general.

Daugherty and his aide Jesse W. Smith established the "Little Green House" at 1625 K Street as headquarters for the Ohio Gang, a loose confederation of third-rate politicians who plundered the U.S. government. For sale were permits to withdraw liquor from bonded warehouses, appointments to office, immunity from prosecution, pardons and paroles for criminals, and any other government activities that could be sold.

Harding held poker games in the White House library twice a week, playing with cronies as well as senators, military leaders, and visiting captains of industry. Mort Mortimer served as the official White House bootlegger at a time when whiskey was illegal. Harding himself, as a matter of political expediency, had voted for Prohibition.

Author Samuel Hopkins Adams called Harding a "small town sport," an assessment not out of line with the president's own evaluation of himself as "a man of limited talents from a small town. . . . I don't seem to grasp that I am president." His lack of foreign policy knowledge was reflected by his own statement, "I don't know anything about this European stuff," and his financial grasp by his remark, "I can't make a damned thing out of this tax problem."

Though in far over his head, Harding actually accomplished a number of worthwhile acts during his short time in the White House. With little pomp, he came in off a golf course and signed off on the end of World War I. He convened the successful Washington Conference for the Limitation of Armaments and established the Bureau of the Budget. He pardoned Eugene V. Debs, the leader of the Socialist Party, who had been imprisoned for protesting the war. He also became the first president since the Civil War to speak out in the South for the rights of African Americans.

Near the end of 1922, Harding received two severe setbacks. In the November elections, the Republican majority was reduced in both houses. But that jolt was mild in comparison with news from the Veterans Bureau. Serious irregularities there were pointing directly at one of his closest friends, Charlie Forbes, a Medal of Honor war hero. Forbes was directing a bureau with one of the government's largest budgets. Forbes and Charles F. Cramer, a California lawyer and legal adviser to the bureau, had teamed up to defraud the government by taking payoffs to sell surplus medical supplies, including narcotics, at a fraction of their cost. They took kickbacks from inflated bids for the purchase of hospital sites and construction of new veterans' hospitals. Their activities in just two years cost taxpayers some $200 million.

The president permitted Forbes to resign and flee to Europe. Shortly thereafter, Cramer committed suicide. Forbes returned, confident by then that the government would not prosecute. After all, the president had let him leave the country. Early in the spring, Daugherty gave Harding a full report on Forbes. It was more than he could take. "I am heartsick about it," said a shaken president.

Harding sent for Daugherty's aide, Jesse Smith. He had been forced out of his job for talking too much about the easy-money scams in a Justice Department now known in Washington as the Department of Easy Virtue. Smith broke down and told the president the slimy details of the operations of the Ohio Gang. Harding told the grafter he would be arrested the next day. Smith went back to the apartment he shared with Daugherty and shot himself to death. Either before or after the shooting, Smith's papers were burned.

The president's world changed drastically. The White House poker parties stopped. He gave up drinking. He even sent Nan Britton to Europe, apparently fearful that the Duchess had found out about the illicit relationship. For advice he turned not to his backslapping cronies but to the upright Quaker, Herbert Hoover. Harding planned a vacation trip to Alaska. Unfortunately, betrayal and stress were already undermining his none-too-robust health. He slept poorly and began to put on weight.

The Harding entourage set out on June 20, 1923. Though his public appearances exhausted him, he enjoyed his visit to Alaska. Then, in the final week of July, he went to bed complaining of indigestion and cramps. Surgeon General Sawyer diagnosed it as a simple case of food poisoning. Two other physicians traveling on the presidential train disagreed. They examined him and concluded he suffered from coronary thrombosis. Specialists met the train in San Francisco and checked him quietly into the Palace Hotel. On August 1, he developed pneumonia and the following night died peacefully in his sleep, apparently the victim of a blood clot that had reached his brain. The exact cause was never determined since Florence Harding refused to permit an autopsy. That refusal later led to preposterous suspicions. A conman named Gaston B. Means, who had worked as special investigator for the government's Bureau of Investigation, wrote a bestseller, *The Strange Death of President Harding*, claiming that Mrs. Harding and Dr. Sawyer had conspired to poison the president.

After Harding's death, a series of trials and Senate investigations revealed an incredible saga of graft and corruption. Three high officials, all close friends, went to jail: Charlie Forbes; Secretary of the Interior Albert Fall, who had accepted bribes to let oil men tap U.S. Navy oil reserves at Teapot Dome in Wyoming and at Elk Hills in California; and Thomas W. Miller, Alien Property custodian. Even Harding's bootlegger committed suicide, claiming that his wife had been unfaithful with Charlie Forbes. Two hung juries kept Attorney General Daugherty from prison on charges of influence peddling and defrauding the government. Years later, detailed documentation was found, revealing a second adulterous, fifteen-year affair that Harding had, this time with the wife of one of his closest Ohio friends.

Participants in the Ridings-McIver Presidential poll agree overwhelmingly that Harding deserves low marks for his poor performance in every category. His best rating, for the Political Skill category, apparently for his impressive election margin, was only thirty-eighth. He was ranked our worst president in the Leadership and Appointments category and next to last in the Accomplishments and Crisis Management and the Character and Integrity categories. Descriptive comments include such remarks as "out of his depth" and "over his head."

The revelations that surfaced after his death destroyed Harding's reputation, leaving him the most disgraced president in the country's history up to that time. The presidency demands a person versed in and interested in the great domestic and foreign issues of the time. Alas, Harding was interested mainly in poker, bootleg bourbon, and willing women. He was, sadly, just a small-town politician, an average man in a job that demanded far more than an average man could deliver, or as poll participants describe him, "an amiable fool, incompetent, inept, corrupt, immoral."

CALVIN COOLIDGE

1923–1929
30TH PRESIDENT

OVERALL RANKING: 33

★

Leadership Qualities: 37
Accomplishments and Crisis Management: 34
Political Skill: 28
Appointments: 31
Character and Integrity: 21

The chief business of the American people is business.

—Calvin Coolidge

At 2:00 A.M. on August 3, 1923, an automobile drove into the little Vermont village of Plymouth Notch with the news that President Warren Harding had died. At 2:47 A.M., witnesses crowded into the family parlor as John Coolidge by the light of a flickering kerosene lamp read from a typed copy of the presidential oath, taken from the Constitution, and did what no other American father had ever before done. He swore in his son as president of the United States. As his wife Grace wept, President Coolidge put his arm around her and without a word shook the hand of his father. Then he went back upstairs and slept for three hours.

Across the country, Americans found themselves touched by the simple ceremony in a Vermont farmhouse. At a time when the United States was reeling from the dazzling, bewildering world of the Roaring Twenties—Prohibition, bootleg booze, and flappers in short skirts—Calvin Coolidge had stepped forward and reaffirmed traditional American values. Biographer William Allen White called him "a puritan in Babylon." Silent Cal brought a shy, restrained dignity to the presidency and with it a simplistic philosophy, typified by one of his most famous quotations: "The chief business of the American people is business."

Calvin Coolidge was born in the crossroads village of Plymouth Notch, Vermont, on the Fourth of July, 1872, the only president to be born on that national holiday, although three had died on the Fourth. At age six he became the owner of a forty-acre farm left to him by his paternal grandfather. Much of his character was molded on that rocky farm, surrounded by villagers who believed in honesty, hard work, and living within one's means. His father owned a store and had served in the Vermont legislature and other local political offices.

Cal attended Amherst College, then clerked in a law office at Northampton, Massachusetts, and passed the bar examination in 1897. He went into practice there and soon became active in Republican politics, winning elections as a city councilor and as city solicitor.

Coolidge was elected to the Massachusetts House of Representatives, then was elected mayor of Northampton in 1909 and 1910. He served from

1912 to 1915 as state senator and president of the state senate. He was elected lieutenant governor and then governor of Massachusetts. In 1919, a Boston police strike suddenly thrust Coolidge into the national spotlight. When rioting and looting followed the police strike, Coolidge called in the state militia to restore order, declaring, "There is no right to strike against the public safety by anybody, anywhere, anytime." His words caught the fancy of the American people. The Republicans turned to him as their nominee for vice president on the 1920 ticket headed by Warren Harding.

Vice President Coolidge sat in at cabinet meetings, a practice that proved beneficial when he was thrust into the presidency. He was not aware of the corruption that permeated the Harding administration, but he had observed the poker games and the freely flowing bootleg whiskey in the White House. The poker and the whiskey stopped immediately, as the new president moved to restore dignity to the office.

Initially, Coolidge kept Harding's cabinet in place until the scandals began to surface. Then he accepted the resignation of Edwin Denby as secretary of the navy and forced the resignation of Attorney General Harry M. Daugherty, the principal architect of the graft and corruption that poisoned the Harding administration. To restore the integrity of the Department of Justice, he named Harlan Fiske Stone, a classmate of his at Amherst, as attorney general. He continued the terms of such cabinet stalwarts as Secretary of Commerce Herbert Hoover and Secretary of the Treasury Andrew Mellon. Following the return of Charles Evans Hughes to private practice, he named Frank B. Kellogg, ambassador to Great Britain, to succeed Hughes as secretary of state. (For negotiating the 1928 Kellogg-Briand Pact, renouncing war as a means of settling international disputes, Kellogg was awarded the Nobel Peace Prize in 1929.) Coolidge's only appointment to the Supreme Court was a distinguished one. Harlan Stone, who had performed in exemplary fashion in cleaning up the Department of Justice, was named an associate justice. Later President Franklin D. Roosevelt named Stone to the position of chief justice of the United States.

Coolidge's image as a man of few words encouraged the belief that he was a deep thinker. Contrary to his image, he held more press conferences than any of his predecessors and made skillful use of a new means of communication—radio. In fact, the 1924 Republican Party's national convention in Cleveland was the first ever broadcast on radio. Coolidge's nomination on the first ballot was nearly unanimous, a tribute to his considerable skills. In the November election, Coolidge won overwhelmingly with more than 54 percent of the vote in a three-man race.

Coolidge required eleven hours of sleep each day. He regularly napped for two to four hours in the afternoon and retired each night at ten. He brought less energy, and thus less leadership, to the demanding job of president than any other man who ever held the office, a major reason he has always ranked low in presidential polls.

"His chief feat . . . was to sleep more than any other president—to sleep more and say less," said journalist and author H. L. Mencken. "And while he yawned and stretched the United States went slam bang down the hill—and he lived just long enough to see it fetch up with a horrible bump at the bottom."

Though generally an inactive president, Coolidge took pride in reducing the national debt and in cutting taxes twice, in 1924 and 1926, principally for the benefit of the wealthy. Ronald Reagan would later commend him for trimming taxes *four* times. Coolidge's tax reduction, however, cut in an unexpected way. By freeing up excess funds for private investment, he fueled a dizzying splurge of speculation that soon reached alarming proportions. Despite urging from many quarters, Coolidge not only declined to try to rein in the binge, he continued to issue statements that encouraged further speculation.

Wrote author Irving Stone, "On the afternoon of the day that Treasury Department officials laid on Calvin Coolidge's desk the documented case for immediate and drastic control of the investment market, and he turned them away, defeated by his icy silence, he went down into the basement of the White House to count the number of apples in a barrel sent him by a friend in Vermont. While Rome burned, Nero at least made music. But President Coolidge counted apples."

Enormously popular to the end of his term, Coolidge was rated an easy winner in the upcoming 1928 election. As party leaders in 1927 geared up for his campaign, he startled the world with his announcement: "I do not choose to run for President in 1928." The Republicans nominated his secretary of commerce, Herbert Hoover.

In 1929, Coolidge returned to private life and escaped much of the blame for the economic depression that engulfed Hoover. Back in Northampton, he wrote his autobiography and a syndicated newspaper column on politics. He also acknowledged the arrival of the Great Depression with a remarkable quote: "When a great many people are unable to find work, unemployment results."

On January 5, 1933, the sixty-year-old Coolidge died of a heart attack while shaving. The unkindest remark was uttered by the famed author, Dorothy Parker. Told that the former president had died, she said, "How can they tell?"

Our poll participants rank him as the ninth worst president, giving him good marks only for character. "A stable nonentity," one pollster calls him. Unfortunately for America, the night of his swearing-in proved a metaphor for his presidency—few words, lots of sleep.

Kinder words were spoken by Alfred E. Smith, the Democrats' unsuccessful candidate for the presidency in 1928: "His great task was to restore the dignity and prestige of the presidency when it had reached the lowest ebb in our history, and to afford, in a time of extravagance and waste, a shining public example of the simple and homely virtues which came down to him from his New England ancestors."

HERBERT HOOVER

1929–1933
31ST PRESIDENT

OVERALL RANKING: 24

Leadership Qualities: 22
Accomplishments and Crisis Management: 33
Political Skill: 34
Appointments: 21
Character and Integrity: 11

The poorhouse is vanishing among us. We in America today are nearer to the final triumph over poverty than ever before in the history of the land.

—Herbert Hoover

Herbert Hoover assumed the presidency of the United States on March 4, 1929. In accepting the Republican Party's nomination the previous summer, he had cheerily looked ahead to "the final triumph over poverty." Then came October. WALL STREET LAYS AN EGG, read the headline in *Variety* on October 30, 1929. The Great Depression would throw 12 million people out of work, plunge more than five thousand banks and thirty-two thousand businesses into bankruptcy, and tarnish cruelly the reputation of Herbert Hoover.

The new president and his advisers misread the severity of the collapse. His millionaire secretary of the treasury, Andrew Mellon, a laissez-faire conservative, even saw some advantages to the depression: "People will work harder, live a more moral life. Values will be adjusted, and enterprising people will pick up the wrecks from less competent people."

Coming only eight months after he took office, the collapse was hardly President Hoover's fault. Yet the simple fact is he failed to deal with it effectively. Hoover left office one of the most despised of all American presidents. Fortunately, he lived on another three decades, long enough to restore his reputation.

Born on August 10, 1874, in West Branch, Iowa, Herbert Clark Hoover was the first president born west of the Mississippi River. An orphan by the time he was eight, he was sent to Oregon, where he lived with a Quaker aunt and uncle. Herbert worked his way through Stanford University in California, earning a degree in engineering.

A wealthy man by thirty, Hoover planned and supervised engineering projects all over the world. When World War I broke out in 1914, Hoover embarked on a career of public service. He organized massive food distribution and raised relief funds for Belgians and others during the war. Hoover came back to the United States in 1917 to run the U.S. Food Administration, controlling the production and distribution of American food as part of the war effort. In 1918, he went back to Europe to help organize the feeding of starving people there. By the time he returned to the United

States after World War I, Hoover was revered as "the great humanitarian."

Both Republicans and Democrats saw him as a potential presidential candidate in 1920. Hoover quickly made it clear that he was a Republican. He supported Warren Harding for president and was named secretary of commerce in the Harding cabinet. After Harding's death the new president, Calvin Coolidge, kept him on as commerce secretary, although he did not hold the Harding holdover in high regard.

After Coolidge issued his ambiguous "I do not choose to run" statement, Hoover sought the Republican nomination in 1928. He was picked on the first ballot, with Senator Charles Curtis of Kansas as his vice presidential running mate. Against Hoover, the Democrats named Alfred E. Smith, governor of New York. A major issue in the campaign was Prohibition, which Smith opposed and Hoover defended. Another was Smith's religion. He was a Roman Catholic, and this was effectively used against him, especially in the South, which was primarily Protestant. Hoover, competing in his first election, captured 58 percent of the vote.

Hoover's inaugural speech glowed with optimism, but he saw many problems ahead. He wrote later, "Little has been done by the federal government in the fields of reform or progress during the fourteen years before my time. After 1914 the Wilson administration had been absorbed mostly in problems of war. The Harding and Coolidge administrations had been concerned with economic reconstruction after the war. . . . And by 1929 many things were already fourteen years overdue."

One thing that was overdue was a cautionary approach to stock market excesses. Hoover warned about wild speculation, but he was much too late. In the buying frenzy, individuals were borrowing heavily to purchase stock, gambling on a quick run-up of stock prices. Worse yet, banks and trusts were speculating with depositers' funds.

Hoover had looked forward to developing a progressive, reform agenda, aimed at creating a more efficient, better managed government. His dream crumbled in October. The stock market crashed and with it America's rosy optimism. People who had bought stocks with borrowed money were ruined. A quarter of all the nation's banks failed. Layoffs began to spread as factories shut down.

Dreadful though it was, Hoover and his aides believed the depression was simply a normal phase of the business cycle, just more severe than usual. Hoover continued to reassure the American people: "The crisis will be over in sixty days."

Hoover initiated many programs to try to tame the depression. He launched public works programs to provide more jobs and lowered income taxes sharply to stimulate new investment. Still, his steadfast belief in the philosophy of "rugged individualism" led him to oppose federal relief for the unemployed and to veto the Bonus Act, which would have given almost a billion dollars to veterans of World War I. In 1930, against the advice of more than a thousand economists, he signed the Smoot-Hawley Tariff Bill, increasing tariffs, hoping it would help American industry and agriculture. Instead, it quickly led to international trade wars, further exacerbating the problem.

Advising Hoover was a strong cabinet, including such experienced men as Secretary of State Henry L. Stimson, and Mellon, who had already served eight years at Treasury. Hoover's three Supreme Court appointments were Charles Evans Hughes, who became a chief justice, Owen J. Roberts, and Benjamin N. Cardozo.

One of Hoover's greatest weaknesses as a leader was his dry, undramatic speaking style. Maxim E. Armbruster, in his *The Presidents of the United States*, wrote, "The trouble with the Hoover policies was not that they were unworkable but their workability was not communicated to the people: their chief advocate could not communicate them himself."

As the depression worsened, President Hoover was publicly jeered and his name became synonymous with poverty. Hoboes and homeless people huddled in makeshift shanties of cardboard and scrap metal in villages called Hoovervilles. Newspapers were called Hoover blankets, and empty pockets turned inside out were called Hoover flags.

By 1932, the Great Depression had deepened and the hopes of the Democrats had risen. In their June convention in Chicago, they nominated Governor Franklin Delano Roosevelt of New York to run against the incumbent president.

During the spring, veterans, many with their families, had marched on Washington to demonstrate for the passage of a bonus bill in Congress. Although the House passed a bonus bill, the Senate defeated it in June. Congress passed another bill to give the veterans enough money in the form of loans to return home, but many no longer had a home. Several thousand members of the Bonus Army remained behind in a shantytown Hooverville in Anacostia Flats, near downtown Washington, D.C. To disperse them, in late July President Hoover ordered in U.S. Army troops, commanded by Gen. Douglas MacArthur. MacArthur's orders were to remove them peacefully. In full battle regalia, MacArthur sent in six tanks, cavalrymen, and infantry. A seventeen-year-old boy trying to save his pet rabbit was bayoneted in the leg, and an infant died, possibly as a result of tear gas. MacArthur then burned the Hooverville down in defiance of orders.

Hoover's failure to discipline the formidable MacArthur for his insubordination made him seem insensitive to the veterans' misery.

When Roosevelt heard of the Bonus Army fiasco, he turned to Felix Frankfurter, a professor at the Harvard Law School, whom he would later appoint to the Supreme Court, and grinned: "Well, Felix, this will elect me." And he was right. In November, the voters gave Hoover the most resounding defeat ever administered to an incumbent president, just under 40 percent of the votes in contrast to Roosevelt's 57 percent.

Removed from office in disgrace, Hoover did not go quietly into oblivion. In addition to the three books he had already written, he wrote nine more, including one on fishing. In 1945, President Harry Truman said to him, "I have a job for you that nobody else in the country can do." In organizing European war relief for the Truman administration, Hoover traveled to thirty-eight countries. Two years later, Truman called on Hoover's management skills again when he named him chairman of the Commission on Organization of the Executive Branch of the Government. Truman put into effect more than two hundred of Hoover's recommendations for streamlining the government. President Dwight D. Eisenhower also put him to work heading a second commission on government reform.

Participants in the Ridings-McIver Presidential Poll rank Hoover twenty-fourth, balancing his performance against the magnitude of his problems. His marks were high in the Character and Integrity category, average in the Leadership and Appointments categories, and low in the Political Skill and the Accomplishments and Crisis Management categories. Comments depict him as a man of ability and character overmatched by the disaster he faced: "[N]ormally capable but overwhelmed by the Depression," "great talent, wrong time," "a humanitarian caught in the wrong place when the lightning struck," and "overcome by events." One participant calls the principled Hoover "a Quaker in a quagmire."

Hoover died in 1964 at the age of ninety. Before and after his presidency, he earned acclaim as one of the most effective public servants this country has seen. John Nance Garner, Roosevelt's vice president, 1933 to 1941, recognized this with a perceptive tribute: "I have never reflected on the personal character or integrity of Herbert Hoover. I have never doubted his probity or his patriotism. In many ways he was superbly equipped for the presidency. If he had been president in 1921 or 1937 he might have ranked with the great presidents."

Franklin D. Roosevelt

1933–1945
32ND PRESIDENT

Overall Ranking: 2

Leadership Qualities: 1
Accomplishments and Crisis Management: 2
Political Skill: 1
Appointments: 2
Character and Integrity: 15

The only thing we have to fear is fear itself . . .

—Franklin D. Roosevelt

On March 4, 1933, Franklin Delano Roosevelt stood at the microphone to speak his first words as the thirty-second president of the United States. Stricken with polio a dozen years earlier, he could no longer stand without the aid of heavy steel braces on his paralyzed legs. A nation waited, paralyzed by unemployment, bank failures, factory closings, farm foreclosures, hunger. It was a nation without hope.

Then came the voice, resonant, cheerful, confident: "So, first of all, let me assert my firm belief that the only thing we have to fear is fear itself— nameless, unreasoning, unjustified terror which paralyzes needed efforts to convert retreat into advance."

FDR, as he was called, went on to promise public works for the unemployed, programs to increase farm prices, and "strict supervision" of the "money changers." Above all, he promised action.

The next day he launched the Hundred Days, the most far-ranging social and governmental upheaval ever known in peacetime. He declared a bank holiday to buy time to stop the hemorrhaging in the financial institutions. He called a special session of Congress and pushed through major legislation designed to make a sick economy well again, to put people back to work, and to see to it that citizens of a rich country did not starve. Taken together, these actions and innovations became known as the New Deal.

By no means did all of the programs work as planned, and few worked as quickly as hoped. Actually, the country was not truly back on its feet until the wartime economy of World War II.

The most important achievement of FDR that March day was to return to the American people a commodity called hope. On that day Franklin Delano Roosevelt passed into legend, a status accorded to only two other presidents, George Washington and Abraham Lincoln.

Franklin Delano Roosevelt was born on January 30, 1882, on his father's country estate at Hyde Park, New York. Like his idol and fifth cousin, Theodore Roosevelt, he attended Harvard University, where he earned a degree in history in three years.

While attending Harvard, he became engaged to Eleanor Roosevelt, a distant cousin. At their wedding in 1905, she was given away by her uncle, Theodore Roosevelt. In contrast to the handsome, extroverted Franklin, Eleanor was homely and shy. She was also highly intelligent and sympathetic to the lot of those not born to wealth and power. Drawing on these traits, she later emerged as the nation's most powerful first lady, a woman both loved by the downtrodden and despised by members of her own class.

In 1910, Roosevelt was elected to the New York State Senate from Dutchess County as a Democrat in a strongly Republican area. President Woodrow Wilson in 1913 appointed him to serve as assistant secretary of the navy under newspaper publisher Josephus Daniels. In World War I in 1917, Roosevelt was given responsibility for recruiting and training seamen, planning military strategy, and inspecting naval facilities in Europe, experience that later served him well in World War II.

During this period, he engaged in an affair with Lucy Mercer, Eleanor's social secretary. (She was with him again years later at Warm Springs, Georgia, the day he died.)

After the war, the Democrats nominated Governor James M. Cox of Ohio for president and Roosevelt for vice president. The ticket, which strongly supported Wilson's League of Nations, was soundly beaten by Republican Warren G. Harding in the November 1920 election.

The following summer, Roosevelt was vacationing at the family's summer home at Campobello Island in Canada. On the night of August 9, 1921, he suffered a chill, followed by a fever. He had contracted polio, and at thirty-nine, the athletic outdoorsman faced the fact that he would never again walk without crutches or braces.

Ahead lay six years of rehabilitation. During the long period of recovery, Franklin and Eleanor Roosevelt kept up their political contacts. In 1924, he attended his party's convention in New York's Madison Square Garden. He walked to the rostrum on crutches and nominated Governor Alfred E. Smith for president with an electrifying speech, labeling the New York governor the Happy Warrior.

In 1928, he returned to the political wars, capturing the Democratic nomination for governor of New York. It was time to face up to the problem of how to overcome the voters' potential uneasiness with his handicap. With help, he could move to a podium with a cane and stand while speaking. For campaigning, Roosevelt drove a custom-made car with special hand controls.

Roosevelt won the election for governor in a close race. In 1930, after the 1929 stock market crash had ushered in the Great Depression, he was reelected by a wide margin. He established a progressive record as governor. Roosevelt set up a state relief program that became a model for other states, providing for unemployment insurance and conservation-related jobs. As New York governor, he gave his first fireside chat, an informal radio address that he later used with great effectiveness as president.

In January 1932, Roosevelt announced for the presidency. His principal opponents for the nomination were his old friend Al Smith and Congressman John Nance Garner of Texas, who was the Speaker of the House of Representatives. Roosevelt won on the fourth ballot by naming Garner as his choice for vice president, thus picking up the delegates pledged to the Texan. He promptly broke precedent by flying to the Chicago convention to make his acceptance speech in person. "I pledge you, I pledge myself, to a new deal for the American people." The phrase "New Deal" emerged later as the name for his domestic program to fight the Great Depression.

Since the American people held his opponent, President Herbert Hoover, responsible for the terrible plight of the country, Roosevelt looked ahead to a fairly easy trip to the presidency. It was made even easier in late July when Gen. Douglas MacArthur used excessive force to chase the Bonus Army out of Anacostia Flats (see page 196). In a campaign remarkable for few specific promises, Roosevelt won by a landslide, taking the electoral vote by 472 to 59.

Elected on November 8, 1932, Franklin D. Roosevelt did not assume the presidency until March 4, 1933. In mid-February, he visited Miami after a fishing trip in the Bahamas. Just after he finished a short talk, a deranged man shot at the president-elect. He missed, but his round of bullets struck Chicago Mayor Anton Cermak, who shared the podium with Roosevelt. Secret Service men rushed forward to whisk the president-elect to safety. Instead, he countermanded their orders and organized a motorcade to carry all the wounded to the closest hospital where Cermak died. Later that night, Roosevelt was calm after the attempt on his life, unlike his jittery aides and the Secret Service, an indication of a trait that served him well in the years ahead, a calmness in the face of crisis.

Roosevelt was fifty-one when he took the oath of office. His confident voice calmed and uplifted American spirits. America would learn quickly what he had in mind. More than half of the country's national banks either had gone bankrupt or had suspended withdrawal privileges. Roosevelt immediately declared a bank holiday while federal auditors went over the books to determine which banks were sound enough to reopen. Among the programs to put banks back on their feet was the Federal Deposit Insurance Corporation.

In his first year, Roosevelt pushed through Congress an unprecedented series of programs:

- Civilian Conservation Corps. The CCC hired more than 3 million young men from poor families and put them to work building roads, planting trees, and working on flood control and conservation projects.
- Agricultural Adjustment Administration. The AAA sought to reduce farm surpluses and thus boost farm prices by paying farmers to limit production. It proved effective until declared unconstitutional by the Supreme Court in 1936.
- Tennessee Valley Authority. To aid the depressed Tennessee Valley, the TVA sought to control the flood waters of the Tennessee River, improve river navigation, encourage soil and forest conservation, and generate inexpensive electricity for a seven-state area.
- Federal Emergency Relief Administration. The FERA program, run by Harry Hopkins, provided money to states and municipalities for local relief and work projects to assist the poor.
- National Industrial Recovery Act. The huge NIRA program created the Public Works Administration to provide grants-in-aid to states and cities for large construction projects such as highways, dams, sewage systems, and public buildings. The NIRA also set up the National Recovery Administration (NRA) to revitalize business by suspending antitrust laws and encouraging greater cooperation among businesses. Business, labor, and government representatives in major industries met to draw up codes of fair practice that regulated competition, length of the work week, and in some cases wages. The Supreme Court declared the NIRA unconstitutional in 1935.

It was an explosive period, with reforms and new concepts on a scale never before seen. And its results and its reception were mixed. Thurman Arnold, who served as assistant attorney general in the administration, wrote, "The underlying idea of the Roosevelt New Deal was conservative, not radical. The idea was that people had to be fed while industry got going again; that industry would get going as soon as it believed that prices were stable and investment safe."

That first year Roosevelt also established formal diplomatic relations with the Soviet Union. In his second year, the Securities and Exchange Commission was created to correct abuses that had led to the stock market crash of 1929. The National Housing Act of 1934 established the Federal Housing Administration, the Federal National Mortgage Association, and the Federal Savings and Loan Insurance Corporation.

More programs followed in 1935: the Rural Electrification Program; the Wagner Act, setting up the National Labor Relations Board and guaranteeing the right of workers to organize and join unions and to bargain collectively; and the Works Progress Administration. Widely criticized for its "make work" philosophy, WPA nonetheless employed workers who constructed 125,000 public buildings, 650,000 miles of roads, 75,000 bridges, and many other public facilities. The law, however, with the most far-reaching consequences was the Social Security Act, creating the modern Social Security System, providing retirement income to those sixty-five and over, financial assistance for the aged needy, unemployment and disability insurance, and survivors' benefits. Roosevelt signed it into law on August 14, 1935.

Roosevelt surrounded himself with a strong cabinet and competent, bright advisers, among them, Cordell Hull, secretary of state; William H. Wooden and then Henry Morgenthau as his secretaries of the treasury; Homer S. Cummings, a strong attorney general; James A. Farley, postmaster general; Harold L. Ickes, secretary of the interior, and Frances Perkins, secretary of labor and the first woman ever appointed to a cabinet position. The aide closest to Roosevelt was Harry L. Hopkins, who served as secretary of commerce and, prior to that post, director of the FERA and the WPA.

In 1936, the Democratic National Convention in Philadelphia renominated Roosevelt and Garner. In his acceptance speech, Roosevelt delivered one of his most memorable passages: "There is a mysterious cycle in human events. To some generations much is given. Of other generations much is expected. This generation of Americans has a rendezvous with destiny."

To oppose them, the Republicans picked Governor Alfred M. Landon of Kansas, the only incumbent Republican governor to win reelection. The 1936 campaign was a referendum on the New Deal, and Roosevelt won 523 electoral votes to Landon's 8, the greatest electoral vote majority since 1820.

Armed with an overwhelming victory at the polls, Roosevelt, perhaps overly impressed with his own success, momentarily lost his touch. Frustrated by a Supreme Court that ruled many key New Deal programs unconstitutional, he came to see the justices as enemies, too inflexible in their interpretation of the Constitution. He proposed legislation that would increase the number of federal judges, including up to six new Supreme Court justices, thus giving him the opportunity to appoint judges favorable to his programs. Friends and foes alike balked at his plan "to pack the Court." He was finally forced to give up his plan, and the Senate buried the proposed legislation in committee, a resounding defeat for so popular a president. An odd side effect, however, rebounded in his favor. The Supreme Court became more flexible in its interpretation of the new concepts on which it was asked to rule. Eventually, Roosevelt was able to nominate eight justices to serve on the Court. As chief justice, in 1941 he named Harlan F. Stone, a Republican, who had been appointed by President Coolidge.

One of Roosevelt's most significant legislative achievements was the Fair Labor Standards Act of 1939, which established a forty-four-hour work week. It established a minimum wage of twenty-five cents an hour—a 44 percent increase for workers in southern sawmills—to rise to forty cents by 1945. The act also prohibited the use of child labor in interstate commerce.

In his second term, FDR was facing ominous problems overseas. In 1933, Adolf Hitler had taken over Germany and was beginning to loom as a potential threat in Latin America. Roosevelt initiated his Good Neighbor policy to improve relations with the countries to the south. His policy laid the groundwork for the Western Hemisphere's united stance against the Axis powers in a war that Roosevelt saw coming.

After the Germans took Austria and Czechoslovakia without bloodshed, Hitler's invasion of Poland in September 1939 plunged Europe into World War II. Isolationist sentiments blocked FDR's efforts to back the Allies. The fall of France and the start of the Battle of Britain in 1940 shifted American sentiment toward increased support for the Allies.

Although Roosevelt had planned to retire after two terms, the threat of war seemed to make that impossible, even though no president had ever run for a third term. Democrats convening in Chicago in July 1940 had no clear indication of his plans. After leading both Vice President Garner and Postmaster General Farley to believe he would not run again, Roosevelt maneuvered to gain the nomination for himself. For his vice presidential running mate, he ousted Garner and replaced him with his secretary of agriculture, Henry A. Wallace.

The Republicans nominated a dark horse candidate, Wendell L. Willkie, born in Indiana but a longtime New York lawyer and president of a large utility company. Willkie made a strong run, campaigning largely against FDR's violation of the third-term tradition and capturing 45 percent of the popular vote and ten times as many electoral votes as Landon. Still, Roosevelt won, convincingly, and set about preparing the United States for a war he knew was inevitable.

Roosevelt announced plans to deliver fifty old destroyers to Great Britain in return for the right to use certain naval and air bases abroad. Under the 1941 Lend-Lease Act, from 1941 to 1946 the United States provided Britain and other military allies with military equipment and supplies valued at $50 billion. In August 1941, Roosevelt met with Winston Churchill, prime minister of Great Britain, to draft the Atlantic Charter. Meeting alternately aboard an American cruiser and a British battleship in the North Atlantic, they drafted an eight-point agreement on the common principles they believed should be part of any future peace.

Then on December 7, 1941, without warning the Japanese bombed Pearl Harbor, the U.S. Navy base in Hawaii, killing 2,335 American soldiers and sailors and 68 civilians, wounding 1,178, and destroying much of the Pacific fleet anchored there. The next day the president called for, and received, a declaration of war against Japan. Nazi Germany then declared war against the United States, and the nation found itself in a two-ocean, two-continent war. America's principal allies were Great Britain, France, Yugoslavia and the Union of Soviet Socialist Republics.

Within a month, British Prime Minister Winston Churchill had come to Washington to work with Roosevelt and his military staff on a grand strategy for a victory that was by no means assured. The Japanese attack on Pearl Harbor had wreaked terrible damage on the U.S. Pacific Fleet, and in Europe, Nazi Germany was already in control of most of the European continent.

As he had in the fight against the Great Depression, Roosevelt assumed many extraconstitutional powers for the war against the Axis powers, Germany, Japan, and Italy. Rigid controls were placed on prices and wages, hundred of billions of dollars were appropriated, millions of fighting men were drafted. Censorship was imposed, and more than a hundred thousand Japanese Americans were taken from the West Coast homes and interned for the duration of the conflict.

On the home front, Roosevelt demanded what seemed to be impossible production goals—but they were met. In factories and shipyards, women replaced men who had gone to war, and production of war matériel reached incredible heights. Fifty thousand aircraft were built in a single year. In less than three years, the United States was producing more weapons and supplies than all the Axis countries combined.

The president, drawing heavily on his experience in World War I, placed outstanding military leaders at the head of the fighting forces: General George C. Marshall as chief of staff, backed up by Generals Dwight D. Eisenhower and Douglas MacArthur and Admiral Chester W. Nimitz. By 1943, the United States had inducted more than 10 million Americans into a fighting force that was beginning to push back the Axis powers.

In November 1942, General Eisenhower commanded an Allied force that landed on the North African coast to join the British army, which had scored a pivotal victory earlier in the year at El Alamein in Egypt. On the Russian front, USSR forces scored a decisive victory over the Nazi invaders at Stalingrad in February 1943.

It was time, FDR reasoned, to look ahead to postwar America. In a fireside chat, he told Americans he did not want to demobilize "the gallant men and women in the armed services . . . into an environment of inflation and unemployment." The result was the Servicemen's Readjustment Act of 1944, or as the American Legion (which helped write it) called it, the GI Bill of Rights. It provided veterans with billions of dollars for medical treatment, loans for building homes and setting up businesses, and vocational training. Its most important benefit was aid for the higher education of returning servicemen and women. After the war, 20 million Americans went to college under the law.

"It was to prevent the unemployment everybody expected after World War II when the soldiers came home," said George Callcott, a history professor at the University of Maryland. "But what it did was raise the intellectual level of an entire generation. It was—and most economists agree—one of the main forces that stimulated the economic expansion that lasted thirty years after World War II."

In June 1944, Allied troops under General Eisenhower invaded France. That same month the Republicans nominated Thomas E. Dewey, New York governor, for president, and in July the Democrats picked a weary Roosevelt to run for a fourth term. His party, however, concerned that FDR might not last out the term, rebelled against left-leaning Vice President Henry Wallace. The compromise replacement candidate to run for vice president was a Missouri senator named Harry S. Truman. In November, the voters returned Roosevelt to the White House by a large margin, but Dewey, garnering 99 electoral votes, proved the strongest challenger Roosevelt had faced in his four presidential races.

In February, FDR traveled to Yalta in the southwestern part of the Soviet Union to discuss peace plans with Churchill and the Communist dictator Joseph Stalin. When President Roosevelt returned to the United States looking far older than his sixty-three years, he reported to Congress that plans were proceeding for an April 25 organizational meeting of the United Nations, the successor to the League of Nations, for which Wilson had fought so hard twenty-five years earlier.

Worn out, the president went to Warm Springs for a rest in late March. On April 12, 1945, he was in a good mood but was troubled with a headache. He was sitting in his favorite easychair by the fireplace, joking and signing letters and papers on a card table while an artist painted his portrait. At 1:15 P.M., he said, "I have a terrific headache," and slumped over. At 3:35 P.M., he died of a cerebral hemorrhage, like soldiers everywhere, a casualty of the war.

Before the year was over, Germany and Japan had fallen, too late for FDR to rejoice in the final victory. In vanquishing Hitler, he had halted an evil tide of barbarism that had menaced Western civilization. Churchill, tears in his eyes, said to the radio correspondent Edward R. Murrow, "One day the world, and history, will know what it owes to your president."

Participants in the Ridings-McIver Presidential Poll rank Roosevelt second—and far and away the most effective president of the turbulent twentieth century. He is rated America's best in the Leadership and the Political Skill categories and second best in the Accomplishments and Crisis Management category. His ratings plummet only in the Character and Integrity category, for which he is ranked above average but only fifteenth. From participants' comments it is not clear why his Character and Integrity rating drops so far below other categories. He is called "a perfect politician," but to some participants political skills seem to imply "pragmatic," "devious," "slippery," "shrewd," "calculating," and lacking in integrity. Roosevelt is praised most often for his role in preserving the American capitalist system at a time when many countries were opting for fascism. Given the dire crises he was forced to confront, perhaps the highest praise from the poll is "the right man in right place at right time."

Many historians credit Roosevelt with saving the free-enterprise system in the United States at a time when fascism and communism were replacing capitalism all over the Western world. Others praise him for stopping Hitler—and shudder to think what might have been if a less effective president had been at the helm in those dangerous days. Leadership combined with intelligence, experience, and courage made FDR the greatest president of the twentieth century.

Harry S. Truman

1945–1953
33RD PRESIDENT

Overall Ranking: 7

★

Leadership Qualities: 9
Accomplishments and Crisis Management: 6
Political Skill: 8
Appointments: 9
Character and Integrity: 9

I felt like the moon, the stars and all the planets had fallen on me.

—Harry S. Truman

On April 12, 1945, Vice President Harry S. Truman received an urgent call to come to the White House. The first lady, Eleanor Roosevelt, greeted him: "Harry, the President is dead."

And then it hit him. The next day he told reporters, "I felt like the moon, the stars and all the planets had fallen on me."

As commander in chief, he soon faced an awesome decision—whether or not to end World War II by dropping the atomic bomb on Japan. But on April 12, Harry Truman did not even know of the bomb's existence.

To many people, he seemed too ordinary a man to step into the shoes of a titan, Franklin D. Roosevelt. Ahead of him would be the task of leading a nation worn out from almost sixteen long years of depression and war.

Truman paid heavily for the mood of the people and the troubles of the times. Contemporary opinion polls gave him terrible ratings. He was reviled, the endless butt of unkind jokes like "to err is Truman."

In later, calmer years historians and political scientists assessing his standing consistently ranked him among America's ten best presidents. Our poll participants give him high ratings in all categories, never dropping him lower than ninth and in the Accomplishments and Crisis Management category ranking him sixth. Among their comments are such remarks as "an average man" or "truly the people's president." One participant writes, "faced with unprecedented problems, did good job."

Harry S. Truman was born on May 8, 1884, the son of a mule trader. Harry grew up in Independence, Missouri. During World War I, Truman, who advanced to the rank of major, saw action in France.

In June 1919, he married his childhood sweetheart, Elizabeth Wallace, known as Bess. Their only child, Margaret, was born in 1924. When a clothing store Truman ran with a partner went broke, he refused to hide behind bankruptcy, paying off $30,000 in debts over a period of fifteen years.

In the 1920s and early 1930s, he won election to various political posts in Jackson County, Missouri, amassing a record as an honest, competent county executive. In 1934, Thomas Pendergast, the region's Democratic

Party leader known as Boss Tom or Big Tom Pendergast, picked Truman as his candidate for the U.S. Senate. Truman won with an impressive plurality. He was not well received, however, by some senators who called him "the Senator from Pendergast." A staunch supporter of Roosevelt's New Deal policies, Truman gradually built a reputation as an effective senator.

As the armies of Adolf Hitler overran much of Europe, huge amounts of money had to be poured into rapid U.S. defense buildup. Senator Truman, experienced in overseeing the use of taxpayers' dollars in Missouri, suggested a special Senate committee to monitor defense spending. The Senate named Truman chairman with a budget of $15,000. The committee, later expanded, was so effective that production was speeded up and savings on defense spending totaled $15 billion.

By the time the Democratic National Convention met in 1944, left-leaning Vice President Henry A. Wallace had become too controversial for renomination. To replace Wallace, FDR wanted the chairman of the Truman Committee. Against the Republican nominee, Thomas E. Dewey, Roosevelt and Truman won by a wide margin.

On January 20, 1945, Truman was sworn in as vice president. Eighty-two days later he became the country's thirty-third president. Truman's first official act was to give the go-ahead for the organizational meeting of the United Nations in San Francisco.

At noon on Truman's twelfth day on the job, Henry L. Stimson, secretary of war, whose public service dated back to the cabinet of President William Howard Taft, came to the White House. He handed President Truman a typewritten memo: "Within four months we shall in all probability have completed the most terrible weapon ever known in human history, one bomb of which could destroy a whole city."

After the atomic bomb's first test in July, it was Truman's responsibility to decide when, where, and if the bomb would be dropped on Japan. The first president in a half century to reach the White House without a college education, Truman had educated himself by reading exhaustively about the country's history, including the lives of its presidents. He knew that every president's job was to make tough decisions. "The buck stops here," said a plaque on his desk.

On Truman's sixty-first birthday and his twenty-fifth day in office, Germany surrendered. But the war with Japan went on. Ahead lay the probability that invading Japan could mean a quarter of a million U.S. casualties. A bomb that could destroy a city might force Japan to surrender without an American invasion.

In July, he sailed to Europe for the Potsdam Conference with Prime Minister Winston Churchill of Great Britain and dictator Joseph Stalin of the Soviet Union. On July 16, Stimson brought a telegram to the president that read: "Operated on this morning. Diagnosis not yet complete but results seem satisfactory and already exceed expectations."

The message was coded. It meant that the first test of the atomic bomb in the New Mexico desert had been a success. Events were moving fast. On July 25, Churchill's Conservative Party was defeated in the British elections, and his place was taken by Clement R. Attlee.

Then, on July 30, came the word that the bomb was ready. Truman's decision was to drop the atomic weapon on Hiroshima, Japan. The results were devastating, but Japan fought on. The second bomb was dropped on Nagasaki. Five days later, Japan surrendered. For days after the bombings, Truman suffered terrible headaches. He was sickened at the thought of killing "all those kids."

That summer the president's approval rating, according to the Gallup Poll, sailed to a lofty 87 percent. It would not stay there as he presented his postwar domestic program to a country tired of new initiatives.

Truman proposed controls on prices, wages, profits, and rents to temper the economic dislocation expected from the pent-up postwar demand and the shortages that would quickly follow. As part of his Fair Deal, he also proposed new laws to protect the civil rights of minorities, a national health plan, and federal aid to local schools. Many of these ideas were not popular with the voters. By the end of his first year in office, his approval rating had dropped to 50 percent. In the November congressional elections, the Republicans won control of both houses for the first time since the Hoover administration.

The Eightieth Congress made life difficult for Truman, harassing him and trying to embarrass him by digging for scandals in the government. Over his veto Congress passed the Taft-Hartley Act of 1947, restricting many rights gained by labor during the previous Roosevelt administration. The act outlawed the closed shop, thus sustaining a worker's right not to join a union; empowered the attorney general to secure an eighty-day injunction in strikes affecting the national health or safety; and barred unions from contributing to political campaigns.

Rough on Truman in domestic affairs, the Congress supported many of his foreign policy objectives. Since the end of the war, the Communist-run Soviet Union, repeatedly reneging on Yalta and Potsdam agreements, had heated up the cold war, seeking to gain control of more countries in Europe and Asia. The president responded with the Truman Doctrine, a containment policy of supporting "free peoples who are resisting attempted subjugation by armed minorities or by outside pressures." He sent the fleet to Turkey to discourage attack by the Soviet Union and followed with economic and military aid to Turkey and Greece, the latter being threatened by Communist insurgents.

In June 1947, Secretary of State George C. Marshall announced an extension of the Truman Doctrine, which became known as the Marshall Plan. Its purpose was to rebuild war-torn Europe with the cooperation of European countries and with massive American foreign aid. The Soviet Union and other Communist countries in Europe refused to cooperate. With bipartisan support from Congress, the plan pumped $13 billion into reconstruction programs that strengthened the anti-Communist countries of Europe. For this achievement, Secretary Marshall was awarded the 1953 Nobel Peace Prize. The Truman Doctrine was used to support such measures as the 1948–49 Berlin Airlift to supply West Berlin against a Soviet blockade and, even more important, the 1949 creation of the North Atlantic Treaty Organization (NATO), a military alliance of countries pledged to check the Communist aggression. The United States had for the first time joined a European military alliance during peacetime.

Participants in the Ridings-McIver Presidential Poll gave Truman high marks for his strong stance against communism. "Faced Soviet down," writes one participant. Writes another, "He won the Cold War."

Support for a Jewish homeland in Palestine had accelerated following World War II and the Holocaust in Europe. When the British mandate over Palestine expired on May 14, 1948, the Jewish state of Israel was declared that same day at 6:00 P.M. Washington time. Eleven minutes later, the United States became the first nation to recognize Israel. In July of that year Truman issued an executive order putting an end to segregation and discrimination in the U.S. armed forces.

In general, Truman surrounded himself with competent people, including such cabinet members as George C. Marshall and then Dean Acheson, secretaries of state, and W. Averill Harriman, secretary of commerce. Several cabinet members, however, resigned to protest various Truman policies, creating the appearance of disarray.

Truman's image as the 1948 election approached was hurt by his loud shirts and by his salty language, sprinkled with far too many expletives to fit America's concept of a president. By spring, Truman's standing in his own party had dropped so low that Democrats began to talk of drafting the popular war hero Gen. Dwight D. Eisenhower to run for president. Ultraliberals were planning a third-party headed by former vice president

Henry Wallace, who had been fired by Truman as secretary of commerce. To make matters even more complicated, white southern Democrats angered at Truman's civil rights initiatives formed the States' Rights Party, often referred to as the Dixiecrat Party, with Governor J. Strom Thurmond of South Carolina as their candidate. Confident of victory, the Republicans nominated Thomas E. Dewey, governor of New York. His run against Roosevelt in 1944 had made him a well-known figure around the country. Lacking a plausible alternative, the Democrats, resigned to the probability of defeat, nominated Truman.

The president struck quickly with a dazzling piece of strategy. The Republican platform, trying to play safe for the upcoming campaign, had approved many of Truman's goals, such as a national health program, civil rights laws, and an increased minimum wage and more social security benefits. Knowing the Republican Party did not really favor them, Truman called a special session of the Eightieth Congress and in effect dared it to take fifteen days and pass these measures. After eleven days, Congress adjourned without having passed any legislation. Daring strokes such as this led our poll participants to give Truman a high ranking in the Political Skill category.

Polls in 1948 showed Dewey a heavy favorite. The president embarked on a 30,000-mile whistle-stop campaign in which he delivered more than three hundred speeches to some 6 million people, many of them shouting back to him, "Give 'em hell, Harry." Dewey, confident of victory, campaigned cautiously, stirring up few controversies and very little enthusiasm. At election time, pollsters were predicting a Dewey victory by anywhere from five to fifteen percentage points.

On election night, election returns for Truman ran strongly from the start, but political commentators were so sure the results would begin to turn in Dewey's favor they held to their original predictions. The *Chicago Daily Tribune*, a staunchly Republican paper, released its early edition with the headline DEWEY DEFEATS TRUMAN. Truman went to bed at 9:00 P.M. and slept until 6:00 A.M., when he learned he was still leading but had not yet clinched the election. Jerome Walsh, a Kansas City attorney who had been barnstorming for Truman, wrote down his surprised reaction to the president's calm manner: "The serenity of the President . . . suggested to all of us, I think, that his years of crisis in office have equipped him with a very large reserve of inner strength to draw upon."

At 8:30 A.M., it was clear that Truman had won Ohio, thus clinching the victory. An hour later, it was certain that the Democrats had also carried both houses of Congress. In scoring the biggest upset in American presidential history, Truman outpolled Dewey by more than 2 million votes and won in the electoral college by 303 to 189.

Truman's second term was a difficult one. A coalition of conservative Republicans and southern Democrats blocked his domestic programs. The cold war gave him severe problems both at home and abroad. In 1949, the Communist forces of Mao Zedong were victorious in China. The following January, Alger Hiss, a former State Department official under Roosevelt and Truman, was convicted of perjury, the result primarily of effective investigative work by a young California congressman named Richard Nixon. The following month, Senator Joseph R. McCarthy of Wisconsin announced that he had a list of more than 200 Communists working in the State Department. He failed to come up with his list or to present any proof, yet the issues raised by Nixon and McCarthy led to repeated calls for the ouster of Truman's secretary of state, Dean Acheson. McCarthy labeled the Roosevelt-Truman administrations "twenty years of treason." Severe headaches returned as the president battled unrelenting criticism from conservatives and a hostile press.

In June 1950, the Communist North Korean army crossed the thirty-eighth parallel and invaded South Korea, a direct challenge to Truman's doctrine of containing the Communists. Within hours, the president had ordered American ships and planes to South Korea to stop the Communist invasion. After the United Nations called on its members to join the United States in sending troops, a powerful, mostly American and South Korean force was assembled, led by Gen. Douglas MacArthur, the hero of the war against Japan. Under his leadership, the North Koreans were pushed back north across the border, the thirty-eighth parallel, in October 1950.

Almost from the start of the war there had been friction between MacArthur and Truman. Communist China and the Soviet Union had remained out of the fighting in the early stages, and Truman wanted to keep them out by restricting the fighting to South and North Korea. Truman did agree with MacArthur that UN troops should pursue the North Korean army into North Korea. Soon the UN army had occupied almost all of North Korea and was getting close to North Korea's border with China. At that point, in late 1950, Chinese Communist troops entered the war and inflicted a severe defeat on MacArthur, pushing the UN troops southward, back into South Korea.

Encouraging anti-Communist Chinese on Taiwan to invade mainland China and bombing China could widen the conflict and bring the Soviet Union into the war, Truman reasoned. Truman wanted to confine the war to Korea. MacArthur disagreed. He wanted an all-out war against Communist China. He defied the orders of his commander in chief not to make any public policy statements. For violating his orders, Truman relieved the popular general of his command in April 1951, prompting calls for the impeachment of the president. Meanwhile UN forces pushed the Communist Chinese and the North Koreans back into North Korea.

Although Communist and UN negotiators began truce talks in July 1951, the war dragged on for two more years, creating serious inflation on the home front. Congress voted Truman powers to reestablish price and wage controls. In April 1952, strikes broke out in many of the nation's steel mills, a severe blow to the war effort. Truman ordered the steel mills seized. But in June, his action was declared unconstitutional by the Supreme Court.

Earlier that spring, worn out by two hard terms, Truman, sixty-eight, announced he would not seek reelection. When he left office in January 1953 and returned to Independence, Missouri, he was reviled and repudiated by most Americans—a view still held by some poll participants. "An overrated hack," one of our poll participants calls him, while another labels him "small-minded and mean-spirited."

At home again, Truman wrote his two-volume memoirs of his presidency. In 1965, he welcomed Lyndon B. Johnson to Independence where President Johnson signed the Medicare Act, which was based on providing medical insurance for older Americans, a concept first proposed by Truman two decades earlier.

On December 26, 1972, Harry Truman died at age eighty-eight. Columnist Mary McGrory wrote, "He was not a hero or a magician or a chess player, or an obsession. He was a certifiable member of the human race, direct, fallible, and unexpectedly wise when it counted. . . . [H]e proved that the ordinary American is capable of grandeur. And that a President can be a human being."

McGrory's assessment is echoed by many of our poll participants who balance his performance against the troubles of his time and rank him America's seventh best president.

DWIGHT D. EISENHOWER

1953–1961
34TH PRESIDENT

OVERALL RANKING: 9

★

Leadership Qualities: 10
Accomplishments and Crisis Management: 10
Political Skill: 14
Appointments: 16
Character and Integrity: 10

The United States never lost a soldier or a foot of ground in my admin-
istration. We kept the peace. People asked how it happened—by God, it
didn't just happen, I'll tell you that.

—Dwight D. Eisenhower

His name was Dwight David Eisenhower but Americans called him Ike. They elected him to the presidency twice, chanting the best political slogan a president was ever blessed with—"I like Ike."

To a nation weary of twenty years of depression, war and rebuilding, the hero of World War II served as a calm, dignified father figure. For the 1950s, Dwight Eisenhower was just what the doctor ordered for America's jangled nervous system.

A moderate Republican, he appealed to his own party with his conservative fiscal and domestic philosophy and to the Democrats with his internationalist approach, which was at odds with the GOP's isolationist wing. Even more important, he appealed to voters disillusioned with both parties and hungry for a hero.

Eisenhower served in dangerous times. He inherited the cold war and the already hot Korean War. On his watch America and Russia both entered the Space Age, and in Cuba communism gained a foothold in the Western Hemisphere. One of the warrior-president's proudest claims was that he kept the peace, that the country "never lost a soldier or a foot of ground in my administration."

On October 14, 1890, Dwight David Eisenhower was born in Denison, Texas. Two years later, the Eisenhowers moved to Abilene, Kansas, where Dwight's father worked in a creamery to support a large family that included his six sons. Though his father could not afford to send him to college, Ike earned an appointment to the U.S. Military Academy at West Point. In the graduating class of 1915, he ranked 61st in a class of 164.

Eisenhower served first as a second lieutenant at Fort Sam Houston near San Antonio, Texas. In 1916, he married Mamie Geneva Doud, of Denver. They had two sons. One died in infancy; the other, John, became an army officer and diplomat. The marriage lasted fifty-three years, until Ike's death, but during World War II, Eisenhower developed a close relationship with Kay Summersby, a pretty, young Irish woman who served as his personal secretary and military aide with the rank of captain. Later, she wrote *Past Forgetting: My Love Affair With Dwight Eisenhower,* published in 1975. After the war, Eisenhower broke off the relationship and never saw Summersby again.

During World War I, Eisenhower worked as a training instructor at U.S. military camps. After the war, he served in the Panama Canal Zone and was then assigned to duty at the army's Command and General Staff School in Fort Leavenworth, Kansas. There he graduated first in his class of 275 officers and moved on to the Army War College in Washington, D.C. In the 1930s, he served as a military aide and assistant to Gen. Douglas MacArthur in the Philippines. By the time the Japanese attacked Pearl Harbor on December 7, 1941, Eisenhower had advanced to the rank of colonel and chief of staff of the Third Army in San Antonio.

Five days after the Japanese attack on Pearl Harbor, Gen. George C. Marshall, the chief of staff, summoned him to the War Department in Washington to help plan American strategy in the Pacific. Eisenhower was named commanding general of the European Theater of Operations with the rank of major general. He commanded the Allied invasions of French North Africa, Sicily, and Italy. In December 1943, President Roosevelt appointed him Supreme Commander of all Allied forces in Europe. His mission was to direct nearly 3 million troops in the invasion of France.

On June 6, 1944—D-Day—he ordered the cross-Channel assault on Normandy, the greatest amphibious invasion in history. In less than a year, Adolf Hitler's Nazi Germany had surrendered and the war in Europe was over.

Eisenhower, hailed now as the country's greatest hero, returned to the United States, where he supervised the demobilization of the army and the unification of the armed forces under a single command. In 1948, he also wrote a bestseller, *Crusade in Europe,* his account of the war in Europe, and served as president of Columbia University, then returned briefly to military duty in 1951 to establish a unified military force as Supreme Commander of NATO, the North Atlantic Treaty Organization.

As early as 1948, both political parties made overtures to Eisenhower. Early in 1952, he disclosed he was a Republican. As a moderate, he defeated Senator Robert A. Taft of Ohio, the conservative Republicans' standard-bearer, at the first televised presidential convention.

Next came a decision that had enormous consequences for decades to come. Party leaders urged him to balance the ticket by picking as his running mate Senator Richard M. Nixon of California. Since Ike at sixty-two was one of the oldest men ever to run for president, Nixon, thirty-nine, could offset the age difference. Nixon's impressive credentials in fighting communism were an asset to the ticket.

The Democratic candidate was Illinois governor Adlai E. Stevenson, the grandson of Grover Cleveland's vice president. Little known outside of Illinois, Stevenson was never in a close race against the hero of World War II, a warm, genial candidate whose supporters proudly proclaimed, "I like Ike." The Democrats were particularly vulnerable on the issue of the Korean War, which had dragged on into its third year.

Nixon, who had been attacking the Democrats' "shady and shoddy government operations," caused Ike his only real problem. In September, the *New York Post* exposed Nixon's $18,000 slush fund. Some major newspapers called for his resignation, as did many on Ike's campaign staff. In a television speech punctuated by occasional tears, Nixon declared he would never return his dog Checkers, given to him by an admirer. Nixon received a warm outpouring of support after his Checkers speech.

In November, Eisenhower won 55 percent of the popular vote and captured the electoral vote, 442 to 89 to become the first Republican president since 1933.

During his first year in office, President Eisenhower made a dramatic appearance before the United Nations General Assembly to call for a world organization to plan for peaceful uses of atomic energy. This led four years later to the formation of the International Atomic Energy Agency.

As he had promised in his election campaign, President-elect Eisenhower made a dramatic trip to Korea in December 1952. Once in office, he proceeded to revive the stalled peace talks. By the following July, he had gained an armistice, separating the two Koreas by a demilitarized zone at the thirty-eighth parallel. While many were dismayed by the war's stalemated conclusion, it was seen by others as proof that the Communist aggression could be contained without resort to nuclear weapons. It also proved that the newly organized UN could be effective in resisting aggression.

President Eisenhower's cabinet has sometimes been called by his detractors "nine millionaires and a plumber." The plumber, Martin Durkin, president of the Plumbers Union, resigned in less than a year in protest against the president's labor policies. Among the so-called millionaires, Ike called on the services of a number of strong cabinet members, including Secretary of State John Foster Dulles; Secretary of the Treasury George M. Humphrey, and Secretary of Defense Charles E. Wilson, the president of General Motors.

President Eisenhower showed a sure touch in dealing with foreign and military affairs, but domestic events gave him many problems. In 1950, a Wisconsin senator, Joseph McCarthy, had startled the Senate and the country by claiming he had a list of 205 known Communists in the State Department. The number changed from speech to speech, and he failed to provide names. Still, in a United States obsessed with communism and the cold war, his charges of treason in the government played skillfully on the fears of many Americans. One who came under attack was Gen. George C. Marshall. In campaigning for the presidency in 1952, Ike had planned to defend his friend and mentor from the senator's wild charges in a speech in McCarthy's home state. Under pressure from his staff and the Wisconsin governor, Eisenhower reluctantly deleted his defense of Marshall.

Privately, Eisenhower despised McCarthy, whom he compared with Hitler. As president, he soon felt the sting of McCarthy's attacks. The Wisconsin Republican, who had described the Roosevelt-Truman administrations as "twenty years of treason," now extended the number to twenty-one. Ike, too, was labeled as "soft on Communism." Unlike Truman, who had confronted McCarthy directly—and ineffectively—President Eisenhower worked behind the scenes to bring down the Wisconsin senator. At the same time, the army filed countercharges against McCarthy, and the Senate held special televised hearings where McCarthy's unsupported charges against the army angered millions of TV viewers. The Senate voted, 67 to 22, to censure McCarthy at the end of 1954.

Earlier that year, the Supreme Court made one of the twentieth century's most momentous decisions. In *Brown* v. *Board of Education of Topeka, Kansas*, the Court voted unanimously that racial segregation in education was unconstitutional because it violated people's right to "equal protection of the laws" as protected by the Fourteenth Amendment. "Separate but equal" schools, it contended, were not really equal. Ike had told his attorney general, Herbert Brownell, Jr., whose office had pressed the case that he hoped the Court would defer its decision until it became the problem of the next administration. No such luck. Eisenhower was plagued with the problems, tensions, and violence of desegregation for the rest of his years in office. The 1954 congressional elections revealed that Eisenhower's high approval ratings could not keep the Republicans from losing control of both houses of Congress.

In September 1955, Eisenhower suffered a heart attack while vacationing in Colorado. Three months later, he was back on the job. Still, his heart attack loomed as a possible problem in the 1956 presidential race. It did not develop, however, as an obstacle, for the enormously popular president again defeated Adlai Stevenson, this time capturing more than 57 percent of the popular vote for a 457 to 73 electoral college edge. Despite winning by more than 9 million votes, Ike was unable to carry with him a majority of Republicans in either house, the first time this had occurred since the election of Zachary Taylor in 1848.

The Soviet Union continued to be a problem for Eisenhower. In October 1956, the people of Hungary revolted against their Communist rulers and appealed to the United States for help. Soviet tanks quickly crushed the rebellion, and the United States was widely criticized for not backing the Hungarians against the Soviet Union. Then, in 1957, the Soviet Union successfully launched Sputnik, the first satellite sent by rocket into orbit around the earth.

In the summer of 1957, Ike signed a civil rights bill, the first in eighty-two years, giving the federal government increased power to protect minority voters' rights. Then, in September, Governor Orval Faubus of Arkansas defied a federal court order to admit nine black students to a Little Rock high school. Eisenhower was reluctant to intervene. Only after the confrontation grew uglier did Eisenhower take action, putting the Arkansas National Guard under federal control and dispatching a thousand U.S. paratroopers to Little Rock to halt rioting that was denying the constitutional rights of African-American students.

In 1957, Congress approved the Eisenhower Doctrine, which authorized the president to provide military and economic aid or to use armed force if necessary to help any Middle Eastern nation "requesting assistance against armed aggression from any country controlled by international communism." The Eisenhower Doctrine was used the following year, when he sent in U.S. Marines to protect Lebanon.

When Communist China began shelling offshore islands controlled by the Chinese Nationalist government on Taiwan, Eisenhower ordered the U.S. Navy to provide protection for Chinese Nationalist supply ships from Taiwan. The Chinese Communists backed down and stopped their attacks.

One of Eisenhower's most visible and lasting legacies is the Interstate Highway System. In 1956, he signed into law the bill that authorized the building of a 42,000-mile nationwide network of high-speed expressways. The idea for the system was said to have originated with Gen. John Pershing in 1918.

For all of its popularity, the Eisenhower administration had a rather lackluster finish. During 1957 and 1958, the economy soured and the Democrats increased their majorities in both houses of Congress in the 1958 elections. In 1959, Cuba was rocked by a revolution that brought Fidel Castro to power; he soon allied himself with the Soviet Union. John Foster

Dulles, Eisenhower's secretary of state, died, and Eisenhower's trusted aide Sherman Adams was implicated in a number of embarrassing corruption scandals. Perhaps most disappointing for Ike was the scuttling of a four-power Summit conference in Paris in May 1960 when the USSR shot down an American U-2 spy plane over its airspace. After initially denying the spy flights, the president was publicly embarrassed when Soviet premier Nikita Khrushchev produced the downed American airman, Francis Gary Powers, and put him on trial.

In his *Presidential Greatness*, Thomas Bailey wrote, "Eisenhower restored dignity to his exalted office, while often appearing to be above the battle, as though politics were too dirty for a clean old soldier. He was a conciliator and accommodator, an apostle of the middle way, rather than a critic and crusader; a tranquilizer rather than a stimulant. American soldiers are trained to defend things, not uproot them; the Army does not ordinarily produce flaming liberals."

In stepping down as then the country's oldest president—he was seventy when he left office—Eisenhower delivered a surprising farewell address over television and radio, surprising because it came from a president who was both a military man and a strong advocate of big business. Said Ike, "In the councils of government, we must guard against the acquisition of unwarranted influence, whether sought or unsought, by the military-industrial complex. The potential for the disastrous rise of misplaced power exists and will persist."

Participants in our presidential poll like Ike. In fact, one writes, " 'I like Ike' says it all." Eisenhower is praised for keeping the peace and for conducting his presidency with restraint. Some, however, fault him for his insensitive view of the emerging issue of civil rights. Ranked ninth overall, President Eisenhower draws rankings of ten in the categories of Leadership, Accomplishments and Crisis Management, and Character and Integrity. Poll participants give him lower marks in the Political Skill and the Political Appointments categories.

After leaving office, Ike and Mamie Eisenhower retired to their farm at Gettysburg, Pennsylvania. There he wrote his two-volume memoirs and two other books. On March 28, 1969, former president Dwight Eisenhower died from a series of heart attacks. The hero of World War II was seventy-eight and still one of the most beloved of all American presidents.

JOHN F. KENNEDY

1961–1963
35TH PRESIDENT

OVERALL RANKING: 15

★

Leadership Qualities: 8
Accomplishments and Crisis Management: 16
Political Skill: 10
Appointments: 7
Character and Integrity: 34

Let the word go forth from this time and place, to friend and foe alike, that the torch has been passed to a new generation of Americans. . . .

—John F. Kennedy

At dawn the snow began to slow. By midday the skies above Washington were blue and cloudless and the temperature stood at twenty degrees above zero, a bitterly cold and windy day in Washington. At 12:51 P.M., the president-elect, wearing neither hat nor coat, took the oath of office from Chief Justice Earl Warren to become at forty-three the youngest man ever elected to hold the highest office in the land. The first U.S. president born in the twentieth century, he spoke eloquently that day as he told the nation that the "torch has been passed to a new generation of Americans." He spoke of the challenges that lay ahead. "Together let us explore the stars, conquer the deserts, eradicate disease, tap the ocean depths, and encourage the arts and commerce." Then prophetically he said, "All this will not be finished in the first one hundred days. Nor will it be finished in the first one thousand days. . . ."

A thousand days would be all that remained for Jack Kennedy. He should have been able to look ahead that day to a long career in politics, as president and then later as an elder statesman, speaking and writing about contemporary affairs. His personal magnetism projected hope and excitement, particularly to a younger generation of Americans. But a thousand days—1,037 to be exact—was only long enough for a start.

John F. Kennedy—JFK as he would be known—was born on May 29, 1917, in Brookline, Massachusetts, the second of nine children of wealthy parents, Joseph and Rose Kennedy. He was born into a politically charged family. Joe and Rose Kennedy drilled into their sons the importance of public service.

Jack Kennedy was educated at Harvard University. A thesis he wrote on the British appeasement of Hitler at Munich won such high praise from the Harvard faculty that it was expanded into a book published as *Why England Slept* (1940).

After rejection by the army because of a back injury, he completed a strenuous course of exercises and passed a navy physical just two months before Pearl Harbor was attacked. Assigned to PT-boat training, Lieutenant (jg) Kennedy assumed command of a torpedo boat in the South Pacific in March 1943.

On August 2, 1943, a Japanese destroyer sliced through Kennedy's boat near New Georgia Island in the early morning darkness. Two of his crew were killed. For towing an injured crewman four miles by a life jacket strap in his teeth, Kennedy received the U.S. Navy and U.S. Marine Corps Medal. Malaria and worsening problems with his back sent Kennedy home to the United States. A year later in a navy hospital he learned that his older brother Joe, groomed for a political career, had been killed in action in western Europe.

"Because Joe died" was the reason Jack gave for entering politics. He worked briefly after the war as a journalist, covering the organizational meeting of the United Nations and the Potsdam Conference following the fall of the Nazis in 1945.

In January 1946, Kennedy began his political career at twenty-eight by running for a Massachusetts seat in the U.S. House of Representatives. Kennedy won in a crowded primary against nine other candidates and easily defeated his Republican opponent in November. Voters reelected him in 1948 and 1950.

In 1952, he ran for the U.S. Senate against a powerful incumbent Republican, Henry Cabot Lodge. In the year of Gen. Dwight Eisenhower's Republican landslide victory in the presidential race, Kennedy defeated Senator Lodge by 70,000 votes.

A year after his Senate victory, the thirty-six-year-old Kennedy married Jacqueline Bouvier, twenty-four, at St. Mary's Church in Newport, Rhode Island. Kennedy's best man was his brother Bobby (Robert F. Kennedy). The couple had three children, Caroline, John, Jr., and Patrick, who died within a couple days of birth.

Their marriage was troubled by Jack's infidelities. After his death, his name was linked to many women, among them the famous stripper Blaze Starr; Judith Campbell Exner, reportedly linked to a Mob figure; and Marilyn Monroe.

While Kennedy pursued an active role on Senate committees, he was criticized by his fellow Democrats for his hands-off treatment of the demagogic Wisconsin senator, Joseph R. McCarthy, a personal friend of his father's.

Kennedy underwent spinal surgery so serious that at one point he was given the last rites of the Catholic Church. His recovery was complicated by Addison's disease, a malfunctioning of the adrenal glands aggravated by his wartime experiences. While hospitalized, he helped write *Profiles in*

Courage, a collection of short biographies of politicians who stood up for unpopular principles, a course he had not taken in the case of the Wisconsin fearmonger. His book was awarded the Pulitzer Prize in 1957.

In the 1956 Democratic National Convention, JFK lost his bid for the vice presidential nomination to Senator Estes Kefauver of Tennessee but emerged as a man with a future. He won reelection to the Senate with 74 percent of the vote, then on January 2, 1960, announced he would seek the presidency. Youth and lack of experience were potential problems. And then there was the matter of religion. Kennedy was a Catholic in a nation where the majority of people are Protestant. Only one other Catholic, New York governor Alfred E. Smith, had ever been nominated by a major party, and his Catholicism was used effectively to defeat him.

Kennedy also had strengths. He had impressed viewers watching the 1956 Democratic National Convention on television. He had prepared diligently for the race, and he had access to his father's money and support from a large and active political family. Kennedy named his brother Bobby campaign manager.

Though the front-runner, JFK faced strong opposition at the Democratic National Convention in Los Angeles in July 1960, particularly from Senator Lyndon Baines Johnson of Texas. Still, Kennedy won handily on the first ballot. To balance the ticket, Kennedy picked Johnson, who surprised him by accepting a position that was actually less powerful than his post as Senate majority leader. Though they made a strong ticket, Kennedy and Johnson were never close.

Later in July, the Republicans meeting in Chicago nominated Vice President Richard M. Nixon, who chose as his running mate UN Ambassador Henry Cabot Lodge, Jr.

On many issues the two candidates were not all that far apart. Polls showed the lead seesawing during the race. "Let's get America moving again," said Kennedy, decrying a "missile gap," which turned out to be nonexistent, and attacking the Eisenhower-Nixon administration for permitting the Communists to take over a country only ninety miles from the United States. Pointing to Kennedy's spotty Senate record, Nixon touted his own experience.

Many feel that the race was decided by a series of four nationally televised debates between September 26 and October 21. The first debate, which drew the largest audience, 70 million viewers, was pivotal in fixing voters' perceptions of the two men. Nixon appeared haggard and pale from a stay in a hospital battling a knee infection. He also looked jowly and menacing. Kennedy appeared tan, fit, composed, handsome. Many, listening to the debates on radio, thought Nixon had won on debating points. Many of those who saw the two men on TV were swayed by Kennedy.

On election night, the vote was so close that Kennedy turned in at 3:00 A.M., still eight electoral votes short of victory. At 6:00 A.M., aides woke him to tell him he had won by the closest margin in history, only .2 percent out of more than 68.3 million votes cast. His electoral margin was 303 to 219.

From inauguration day, it was clear that the young president was ushering in a new era. There could be no doubt from his call to his generation that a new energy and a new style were taking over at the White House. The vigorous, handsome president and his glamorous first lady brought youth, excitement, and culture to the scene. Writers, artists, musicians, and Nobel Prize winners were welcome again in the Executive Mansion. Some later called the Kennedy White House Camelot.

To help him push forward his ambitious New Frontier program, Kennedy surrounded himself with a strong cabinet: Dean Rusk, secretary of state; C. Douglas Dillon, secretary of the treasury; Arthur J. Goldberg, secretary of labor, and Robert S. McNamara (president of the Ford Motor Company), secretary of defense. The most controversial appointment was his choice for attorney general. He picked his closest confidant, his brother Bobby. The appointment was widely criticized as outright nepotism. Later critics claimed the family was trying to take over Washington when the president named his brother-in-law Sargent Shriver head of the Peace Corps and his brother Ted (Edward M. Kennedy) came to the Capitol as a Massachusetts senator.

President Kennedy barely had his team in place before a major crisis struck. During the Eisenhower administration the U.S. Central Intelligence Agency had trained and armed 1,500 Cuban exiles in Guatemala for an invasion of Cuba in early spring of 1961. Their mission was to establish a beachhead that, it was hoped, would spawn a popular uprising.

On April 17, 1961, the attack was launched against Cuba at the Bay of Pigs, but without the air support originally planned. Cuba's forces, far stronger than expected, easily stopped the invaders. After three days of fighting, eleven hundred exiles surrendered. In late 1962 Cuba was paid $53 million, privately raised, in food and medical supplies for the release of the prisoners. It was a humiliating defeat for the United States and its young, inexperienced president. He publicly assumed responsibility for the botched raid. Americans overlooked the blunder, admiring his courage in acknowledging failure.

That same year President Kennedy launched the Alliance for Progress, a ten-year plan to develop the resources of Latin America. He also created the Peace Corps. In his inaugural speech, JFK had said, "[M]y fellow Americans, ask not what your country can do for you; ask what you can do for your country." With the Peace Corps, he set up a vehicle for tapping the idealism of Americans who wanted to do something for their country. The goal of the Peace Corps was to enlist volunteers to teach and provide technical services to people in developing nations.

The Soviet Union had put the first satellite in orbit in 1957 and the first man in space in 1961. Determined that the United States would not be outdone, in May 1961, President Kennedy made a pledge: "I believe that this nation should commit itself to achieving the goal, before this decade is out, of landing a man on the moon and returning him safely to earth." During that year, he also launched a massive military arms buildup and an extensive civil defense plan designed to protect the country against a nuclear attack.

That same busy year President Kennedy sent federal marshals to Montgomery, Alabama, when a white mob attacked a bus carrying white and black passengers. The integrated bus had been traveling through the South, its Freedom Riders testing to see whether or not accommodation facilities at bus terminals could be desegregated using a strategy of nonviolent resistance. Growing up in Brookline, JFK had had little contact with African Americans and little grasp of the depth of their anger at the cruelty of segregation. He would learn. When James H. Meredith attempted to become the first black to enroll at the University of Mississippi, Governor Ross Barnett defied federal court orders and blocked him. The president, pursuing a moderate course, tried to reason with Barnett and work out a compromise to minimize the dangers of a confrontation. Barnett double-crossed him by withdrawing the protection of the state highway patrol. Then protesting white students rioted and two people were killed and many injured. At that point, JFK realized he had no choice but to take stronger measures. He sent in federal troops, and the next day Meredith enrolled in Ole Miss.

In Alabama in 1963, Kennedy had to call in the National Guard when Governor George Wallace, defying a federal court order on integration, tried unsuccessfully to block the admission of two black students to the University of Alabama. In Birmingham, police turned dogs loose on nonviolent marchers led by Dr. Martin Luther King, Jr., who was heading an effort to desegregate lunch counters and public facilities and to end job discrimination. Angry reactions erupted around the country. As protests and violence continued in 1963, Kennedy proposed the boldest civil rights program in a century, introducing a bill designed to protect the right of blacks to vote, to ban discrimination in hotels and restaurants, and to give the attorney general real power to challenge segregation in tax-supported schools.

In 1961, East Germany increased international tensions by building the Berlin Wall, an ugly symbol of Communist determination to keep even its dissident citizens from leaving. For many months, it seemed that war could break out any day.

Closer to home, the Soviet Union had begun supplying military aid to Communist Cuba. The president ordered the CIA to double its high-altitude U-2 reconnaissance flights over the island. On October 16, 1962, an adviser showed him aerial photographs of Soviet missile sites and silos for offensive missiles, capable of delivering nuclear warheads to any East Coast city.

On October 22, the president announced he was ordering a blockade of Cuba. He called for "the prompt dismantling and withdrawal of all offensive weapons in Cuba." He warned Moscow: "[I]t shall be the policy of this nation to regard any nuclear missile launched from Cuba against any nation in the Western Hemisphere as an attack by the Soviet Union on the United States, requiring a full retaliatory response upon the Soviet Union."

For days the United States and the Soviet Union hovered on the brink of war. Soviet ships continued to steam toward Cuba as U.S. troops massed in Florida. Then the Soviet ships turned back. Russia agreed to remove the weapons from the island in exchange for a U.S. pledge not to invade Cuba. Said Secretary of State Dean Rusk, "We're eyeball to eyeball, and I think the other fellow just blinked." By the end of 1962, the missiles were gone.

In 1963, President Kennedy initiated talks with the Soviet Union and Great Britain that led to the Limited Nuclear Test Ban Treaty, the first arms control agreement in the nuclear age. Eventually, the treaty, restricting the testing of atomic weapons in the atmosphere, was ratified by more than a hundred nations.

Meanwhile, Vietnam continued to demand Kennedy's attention. Divided since 1954 into a Communist North and a pro-West South, Vietnam had the potential to become another proxy war between the United States and the Communist powers, China and the USSR. To shore up the government of South Vietnam, President Eisenhower had sent American military advisers to Southeast Asia. Two thousand advisers were in place in Vietnam when JFK took office. By November 1963 there were 16,000. At the time of his assassination in Dallas, Texas, on November 22, 1963, it was not clear what Kennedy's policy would be toward the escalating troubles in Southeast Asia.

Kennedy was assassinated in Dallas while on a political trip. He was trying to reconcile differences between quarreling Texas Democrats. It is not the purpose of this book to speculate about who shot John F. Kennedy or why. The fact that this has been the subject of fervent and at times morbid speculation for more than thirty years is evidence enough that something very drastic happened to the nation's psyche on the day Kennedy was shot. Some think it is a wound from which our society has yet to recover.

Our poll reflects both the promise and the unfulfilled expectations of Kennedy's presidency. "Inspiring, learned but given insufficient time," writes one poll participant. Many feel his time was too short to evaluate his effectiveness. Still, he earns an overall ranking of fifteenth, with particularly high rankings for the Appointments category, seventh, and the Leadership Qualities category, eighth. His combined standing was hurt somewhat by a thirty-fourth ranking for the Character and Integrity category. "Camelot fantasy voided by reality and sex life," writes one participant. "All style, little substance," writes another, and others criticized his Bay of Pigs and Vietnam policies but credit him with trying "to infuse government with youthful vigor."

In his book *In Search of History: A Personal History*, Theodore H. White wrote the following:

> So the epitaph on the Kennedy Administration became Camelot—a magic moment in American history, when gallant men danced with beautiful women, when great deeds were done, when artists, writers and poets met at the White House, and the barbarians beyond the walls held back.
>
> Which is, of course, a misreading of history. The magic Camelot of John F. Kennedy never existed. . . . The knights of his round table were able, tough, ambitious men, capable of kindness, also capable of error. . . . What made them a group and established their companionship was their leader. Of them all Kennedy was the toughest, the most intelligent, the most attractive—and inside, the least romantic. He was a realistic dealer in men, a master of games who understood the importance of ideas. He assumed his responsibilities fully. He advanced the cause of America at home and abroad. But he posed for the first time the great question of the sixties and the seventies: What kind of people are we Americans? What do we want to become?

LYNDON B. JOHNSON

1963–1969
36TH PRESIDENT

OVERALL RANKING: 12

★

Leadership Qualities: 11
Accomplishments and Crisis Management: 12
Political Skill: 3
Appointments: 10
Character and Integrity: 37

The kids were right. I blew it.

—Lyndon B. Johnson

Lyndon Baines Johnson came so close to greatness. He assumed the presidency after the assassination of President John F. Kennedy and, like the cowboy he was, rode the country's shocked and grieving goodwill into the passage of a vast and far-reaching domestic program.

And then the man from the bleak Texas hill country lost his way in the jungles of Southeast Asia. The war in Vietnam undid the country, and it undid Lyndon Johnson.

At six-foot-three, he was the twentieth century's tallest president—second overall only to Abraham Lincoln. Johnson was also the most contradictory and possibly the most complex man ever to occupy the White House.

Lyndon Baines Johnson was born on a ranch west of Austin, Texas, on August 27, 1907, the first of five children of Samuel and Rebekah Johnson, both of whom were teachers. Education and politics ran in the family. His father and both his grandfathers had been elected to the state legislature. As a child, he traveled with his father on the campaign trail.

At five, Lyndon moved with his family to Johnson City, named for his grandfather. He graduated from high school at fifteen. After a year on the road as a hobo, he enrolled in Southwest Texas State Teachers College, where he worked as a janitor. He dropped out of school for a year to earn extra money by teaching Mexican American children in a small-town school. Out of his meager salary he bought playground equipment for his impoverished students. Then he returned to college and graduated in 1930 at twenty-one.

Johnson wasted little time in moving into politics. After eighteen months teaching in a Houston high school, he accepted a job as secretary to U.S. Representative Richard M. Kleberg, a Democrat and one of the owners of the King Ranch, the world's largest ranch with an acreage twice the size of Rhode Island. In his three years in Washington, D.C., with the the congressman, he learned how the U.S. Congress worked.

On one of his trips back to Texas, he met Claudia Taylor, better known as Lady Bird. At twenty, she already held two degrees from the University of Texas. He asked her to have breakfast with him the next morning. She found him, she said, "a little bit scary. . . . He came on strong." In fact, before the day was over, he asked her to marry him. Two months later they were married at St. Mark's Episcopal Church in San Antonio. The Johnsons had two daughters, Lynda Bird and Luci Baines. Everyone in the family had the same initials—LBJ. Some years after their marriage, Lady Bird bought a small radio station in Austin and parlayed her investment into a television and radio empire valued at $20 million.

In 1935, Johnson was named head of the National Youth Administration in Texas, a program to help colleges provide part-time jobs for needy students. When he ran for Congress in 1937, many of the young people he had helped worked to elect him. He won by a wide margin and was reelected to the U.S. House of Representatives six straight times. The young congressman was befriended by Sam Rayburn, the House of Representatives majority leader, who had served in the Texas state legislature with Lyndon's father. When a Texas senator died, Johnson ran in the special 1941 election to fill the remainder of the term. Out of nearly 600,000 cast, he lost by just 1,311 to Texas's conservative Governor Lee O'Daniel, then returned to the House.

A few months after the Japanese bombed Pearl Harbor, Johnson, a lieutenant commander in the Naval Reserve, volunteered to become the first member of Congress to go on active military duty. On a special fact-finding mission for President Roosevelt, he flew aboard a plane that was shot up by Japanese. Another time he was in a plane that crash-landed in Australia. Gen. Douglas MacArthur decorated him with the Silver Star for gallantry under enemy fire. In July 1942 the president ordered all members of Congress to return to their legislative posts in Washington.

After the war, Johnson decided to try again for the Senate. In 1948, he ran against ten other candidates, qualifying for a second primary runoff with former Texas governor Coke Stevenson. Out of nearly a million votes cast, Johnson won by just eighty-seven ballots. The victory earned him the nickname Landslide Lyndon. Nine years later, at forty-six, he became the youngest senator ever to serve as majority leader. He established a policy of never permitting his party to indulge in obstruction for obstruction's sake. Republican measures were to be evaluated on the grounds of merit, not partisanship. Much of President Eisenhower's second-term program, opposed by his party's conservative wing, was passed because Johnson marshalled it through the Senate with the support of moderate Democrats.

As the most powerful member of the Democratic Party, Johnson sought the party's nomination for president in 1960. Senator John F. Kennedy of Massachusetts, who had won every primary, was the convention's overwhelming choice on the first ballot. Kennedy then asked Johnson to be his running mate, reasoning that he would bring strength to the ticket in the South and West. In the closest presidential election in U.S. history, the Kennedy-Johnson ticket won.

President Kennedy gave Johnson the most active role of any vice president up to that time. He became a regular member of the cabinet and the National Security Council and served as chairman of the National Aeronautics and Space Council and the President's Committee on Equal Employment Opportunities.

When President Kennedy went to Texas on November 22, 1963, Johnson rode two cars back in the motorcade through Dallas. Two hours after the president's assassination, at 2:39 P.M., Lyndon Johnson was sworn in aboard the presidential plane as the nation's thirty-sixth president. The oath was administered by Federal Judge Sarah T. Hughes, the first woman ever to swear in a president.

Johnson stayed in the background during the funeral ceremonies, then came forward to address Congress five days after the assassination. He called on its members to honor Kennedy's memory by passing his New Frontier program.

The new president retained the members of the Kennedy cabinet, most of whom he regarded highly. There was, however, friction between Johnson and Bobby Kennedy, who left the cabinet in 1964 to run successfully for the office of U.S. senator from New York. Among the new Johnson cabinet appointees was Attorney General Nicholas Katzenbach, who played an active role in the civil rights battles.

On January 8, 1964, President Johnson introduced his Great Society program. In his first State of the Union address to Congress he said the following:

> Let this session of Congress be known as the session which did more for civil rights than the last hundred sessions combined; as the session which enacted the most far-reaching tax cut of our time; as the session which declared all-out war on human poverty and unemployment in these United States; as the session which finally recognized the health needs of all our older citizens . . . and as the session which helped to build more homes and more schools and more libraries and more hospitals than any single session of Congress in the history of our Republic.

President Johnson was able to convince Congress to pass all of his program except medical care for the aged. His cornerstone War on Poverty program included the Job Corps, which provided vocational training for disadvantaged youths, and Head Start, preschool instruction for the disadvantaged.

From his years as Senate majority leader, LBJ had developed extraordinary skills in persuading people to do his bidding. He made it a point to know the strengths and weaknesses of the people he dealt with, what they most wanted, what they feared. Trading heavily on this knowledge, he pushed through not only his programs but also those of Eisenhower and Kennedy. It was said that Kennedy inspired and Johnson delivered.

There was about Johnson an earthiness, bordering at times on the crude. After a gallbladder operation, he pulled up his shirt and posed for news photographs with an ugly scar across his stomach. He dismayed humane societies by lifting his dogs up by their ears and frightened his own Secret Service agents and newspaper correspondents by racing along Texas highways at eighty miles an hour while drinking Pearl beer out of a cup.

In *Lyndon*, Washington journalists Richard Harwood and Haynes Johnson wrote the following: "Lyndon Johnson floated in and out of our consciousness under many labels—New Dealer, Wheeler Dealer, Crude Texan, Friend of the Poor and the Black, Warmonger, Tyrant, Fool, Imperialist. . . . [O]ld Wright Patman of Texas, who knew him and his father, saw in him the qualities of a 'folk hero out of a saga from our frontier days—larger than life, like Davy Crockett or one of the storied martyrs who died at the Alamo.' "

In the summer of 1964, the Republicans nominated for president conservative senator Barry M. Goldwater of Arizona, who declared in his acceptance speech, "I would remind you that extremism in the defense of liberty is no vice. And let me remind you also that moderation in the pursuit of justice is no virtue."

A month later, the Democrats nominated Johnson for president by acclamation and named Senator Hubert H. Humphrey of Minnesota as his vice presidential running mate. Senator Goldwater's extreme positions made the campaign easy for them. Goldwater had voted against the civil rights bill, called for the end of a mandatory Social Security program, and had frightened Americans by proposing that field commanders in Vietnam be authorized to use tactical nuclear weapons at their discretion. Perhaps haunted by the memory of the eighty-seven vote margin that had earned him his nickname Landslide Lyndon, Johnson campaigned at a furious rate, seeking the largest landslide in history. He was widely criticized for a TV commercial in which a tranquil scene of a little girl picking a daisy was suddenly overpowered by a mushroom cloud—a brutally effective device associating Goldwater with nuclear war.

With a margin of 16 million votes, Johnson achieved the largest popular majority in American history. In the electoral vote, his edge was exceeded only by Roosevelt's 1936 victory. "For the first time in all my life I truly felt loved by the American people," he said, revealing the immense insecurity that still haunted him.

Johnson made two Supreme Court nominations. In 1965, he named Abe Fortas, his personal attorney, an associate justice. Two years later, he sought to elevate him to chief justice but was forced to withdraw the nomination by overwhelming conservative Senate opposition. After Johnson had left office, Fortas resigned from the Court in 1969 after it was learned he had accepted $20,000—later returned—from a foundation established by an industrialist under investigation by the Securities and Exchange Commission.

Johnson's second appointment to the Court was Thurgood Marshall, of Baltimore, Maryland. The first African-American justice to serve on the Supreme Court, Marshall, legal counsel for the National Association for the Advancement of Colored People, had argued the case for the desegregation of public schools before the Court in the landmark *Brown* v. *Board of Education of Topeka, Kansas* in 1954.

Buoyed by his landslide, President Johnson and Congress moved his Great Society plan ahead with a federal aid-to-education program to improve schools and libraries. To the Social Security system were added Medicare to provide federal hospital and medical insurance for those sixty-five and over and Medicaid with hospital and medical benefits for the poor and the disabled of any age.

President Johnson followed up his success with the Civil Rights Act of 1964, which barred discrimination in employment and in the use of public facilities, with the Voting Rights Act of 1965, outlawing discriminatory literacy tests and empowering the federal government to promote voter registration. The Civil Rights Act of 1968 barred discrimination in the sale and rental of housing and stiffened federal criminal penalties for civil rights violations. These legislative actions vastly expanded the rights of minorities. Unfortunately these strides were accompanied by a surge in black radicalism and violence. In 1967, riots erupted in more than a hundred cities. When civil rights leader Martin Luther King, Jr., was assassinated on April 4, 1968, cities all over the country, most notably Washington, D.C., were plunged into violence.

Against this backdrop of domestic violence, Vietnam spiraled out of control.

In August 1964, North Vietnamese gunboats reportedly attacked two U.S. ships in the Gulf of Tonkin. Within two days Johnson requested and received open-ended congressional authority to "take all necessary measures to repel any armed attack against the forces of the United States and to prevent further aggression." The Gulf of Tonkin Resolution passed both houses of Congress with just two dissenting votes. President Johnson escalated the war, but as he did, he kept pressing North Vietnam to negotiate. By 1968 more than half a million American soldiers were fighting in Vietnam and peace seemed as elusive as ever.

Americans were divided over the Vietnam War as they had not been since the Civil War a century earlier. Some critics called for total war against North Vietnam. Others demanded that the United States unconditionally end its bombing. In 1967, an antiwar rally in New York drew 125,000 demonstrators.

Johnson, struggling to find an answer, continued to send messages to North Vietnam calling for negotiations. The Communists held the line, insisting that the United States halt the bombing and withdraw its troops before any negotiations could be held. In January 1968, the North Vietnamese launched a powerful attack against South Vietnam. The Tet Offensive made a disturbing fact abundantly clear to the administration. America's limited warfare approach was nowhere near to winning the war.

Johnson's credibility continued to plunge. In the New Hampshire presidential primary, Minnesota senator Eugene McCarthy, who opposed the war, won a surprising 42 percent of the vote. Next, New York senator Robert Kennedy decided he, too, would run on an antiwar ticket.

On March 31, 1968, the president made two stunning announcements. He declared the United States would unconditionally halt its bombing attacks in the North—and that he would not run for reelection. Hanoi agreed to negotiate, but talks bogged down on such trivia as the shape of the bargaining table.

Bobby Kennedy's antiwar candidacy was gathering momentum. Then, in June 1968, following his victory in the California primary, he was killed, like his brother, by an assassin's bullet. Vice President Hubert Humphrey with help from Johnson won the Democratic nomination as five thousand antiwar protesters clashed in the Chicago streets outside the convention hall. The Republicans nominated Richard Nixon with Spiro Agnew, governor of Maryland, as his running mate for vice president. Governor George Wallace of Alabama, appealing for votes from disaffected white southerners as well as working-class northerners, ran on an American Independent Party ticket and received 13.5 percent of the popular vote. Nixon won a narrow victory by less than one percentage point, but surprisingly the Democrats maintained control of both houses of Congress.

Lyndon Johnson's presidency, so successful in its early years, had collapsed at the end. LBJ received some satisfaction from the final week of his administration. In late December 1968, three American astronauts in the Apollo 8 spaceship orbited the moon ten times before returning to earth.

After his term, Johnson went back to the LBJ Ranch in Texas. There he wrote his memoirs and went about the job of running a ranch. On January 22, 1973, Johnson, troubled for years by arteriosclerosis, died at sixty-four. Buried at the Johnson family plot in Johnson City, Texas, he left behind an estate valued at $20 million.

Poll participants see him as a "tragic figure," "a man of noble sentiments," and "a great political talent who overreached himself and his country." In ranking him in the top third of American presidents, they give him high praise for his domestic achievements, low marks for his Southeast Asia failure. "Great Society torpedoed by Vietnam," writes one participant. In the Political Skill category, Johnson is outranked only by Franklin Roosevelt and Lincoln. In all other categories he holds high positions—except for the Character and Integrity category, where he is placed thirty-seventh. Or as one poll participant sums it up, "Conniving but good at it."

In a book about President Johnson, published in 1982, his press secretary George Reedy wrote the following:

> He may have been a son of a bitch but he was a colossal son of a bitch. . . . He also possessed the finest quality of a politician. It was a sense of the direction of political power—the forces that were sweeping the masses. He did not merely content himself by getting ahead of those forces. He mastered the art of directing them. . . .
>
> Of all his qualities, however, the most important was that he knew how to make our form of government work. That is an art that has been lost since his passing and we are suffering heavily as a result.

RICHARD M. NIXON

1969–1974
37TH PRESIDENT

OVERALL RANKING: 32

Leadership Qualities: 21
Accomplishments and Crisis Management: 19
Political Skill: 18
Appointments: 34
Character and Integrity: 41

I'm not a crook.

—Richard M. Nixon

The president that Richard Nixon, a Republican, admired most was a Democrat—Woodrow Wilson. Both were dedicated to world peace. Shortly after Nixon's inauguration, he had Wilson's huge desk moved into the Oval Office. Since he liked to sit with his feet on the desk, his heels left scars. Once, while he was abroad, someone had the mahogany surface refinished. Nixon was not pleased: "Dammit, I didn't order that. I want to leave my mark on this place just like other Presidents."

Richard Milhous Nixon left his mark, but it was more than scuff marks on a desktop. The mark he left behind was a scar on a nation he betrayed. In the cause of peace he achieved an enviable record in foreign affairs, proving himself a highly effective president. Then he threw it all away.

On June 17, 1972, Washington police arrested five men in the act of burglarizing the Democratic National Headquarters, located in the Watergate complex. Dismissed by the White House as "a third-rate burglary," the break-in refused to go away. Despite a massive cover-up, tainting both the White House and the Justice Department, the biggest government scandal in United States history finally came to light.

As Congress set in motion impeachment proceedings, Nixon protested, "I'm not a crook." It was clear by the following summer that very few in Congress believed him. At noon on August 9, 1974, Nixon became the first American president to resign from his office under threat of impeachment.

Wrote Frank Kessler in *Popular Images of American Presidents*, "For a man burdened with such a need to achieve and such a sense of history, how unfortunate it is that the abuses of presidential power and the tarnishing of the public perceptions of the presidency stand to be the principal legacy he leaves the nation."

Richard Nixon was born January 9, 1913, on his family's lemon farm in Yorba Linda, California. Nixon attended Whittier College, where he graduated second in his class in 1934 and was elected president of the student body. At Duke University Law School at Durham, North Carolina, he finished second in his class, but an odd event occurred that foreshadowed Watergate. He was so anxious to learn his grades, he and a classmate broke into a professor's office to look at the grade book.

After graduation, he joined a Whittier law firm. One of his hobbies, theater, brought him together with Thelma Catherine Ryan, known as Pat, a red-haired high school teacher. He proposed to her the night they met. The Nixons had two children, Patricia and Julie.

After World War II service as a naval lieutenant commander in the South Pacific, Nixon ran for Congress as a Republican against a liberal Democratic congressman, Jerry Voorhis, a former Socialist. Nixon attacked Voorhis savagely as a tool of the Communists, which he was not, and went on to win a seat in the U.S. House of Representatives in the 1946 election.

From the start, Nixon brought a powerful anti-Communist voice to Congress just as the cold war was accelerating. The key to his meteoric rise was his relentless probing of Alger Hiss, president of the Carnegie Endowment for International Peace and a former State Department official who had organized the UN charter meeting. His skillful interrogation led to Hiss's conviction on a perjury charge and a five-year prison sentence.

In 1950, Congressman Nixon ran for the U.S. Senate against Congresswoman Helen Gahagan Douglas, a former opera and Broadway star and wife of movie actor Melvyn Douglas. Nixon flooded the state with "pink sheets," seeking to link Mrs. Douglas, whom he always called the "pink lady," with the Communist Party. His tactics earned him the nickname Tricky Dick but also won for him a smashing victory.

In the summer of 1952, the Republicans nominated General Dwight D. Eisenhower for president. As his running mate, the party picked Nixon, thirty-seven, a man who could bring to the ticket geographical balance, an impressive anti-Communist record, and youth to offset Eisenhower's advancing years. Nixon's future, never brighter, suddenly became shaky as a *New York Post* story revealed that he had been using an $18,000 slush fund collected by a "millionaires club." Five days after the story broke, Nixon with his wife Pat at his side went on national television to defend himself before 60 million viewers—the largest audience ever to watch a TV program up to that time. The response was overwhelmingly in his favor. In November, the Republican ticket swept to a decisive victory and carried with it Republican majorities in both the Senate and the House.

Nixon was an active vice president. President Eisenhower sent him on goodwill tours to fifty-four nations, vastly increasing his knowledge of foreign affairs. In addition, he had to assume many presidential duties since Eisenhower was troubled by serious health problems.

In 1960, Nixon was his party's overwhelming choice for president. He chose as his running mate Henry Cabot Lodge, Jr., the U.S. ambassador to the UN. Nixon's Democratic opponents were a formidable ticket of Senator John F. Kennedy of Massachusetts and Senate Majority Leader Lyndon B. Johnson of Texas. Polls showed the race would be close.

In 1960, television, which Nixon had used skillfully in 1952, backfired against him. In the first of a series of four televised debates with Kennedy, Nixon, recovering from a stay in the hospital from a serious infection, appeared gaunt and menacing. A lack of makeup contributed to his unappealing appearance, a sharp contrast to the image projected by the handsome Kennedy to an audience of seventy million viewers.

Kennedy won one of the closest presidential races in U.S. history, but reports of fraud in two key states, Illinois and Texas, justified a recount. Nixon declined to challenge the results. To drag out the decision would do, he said, "incalculable and lasting damage throughout the country." He conceded the election, congratulated Kennedy, and went back to California.

In 1962, he returned to politics, running for governor against a popular incumbent, Edmund Brown, known as Pat Brown, whose son Jerry later became a California governor. Nixon waged a strong campaign but was beaten badly.

After his California defeat, Nixon joined a New York law firm that also listed John N. Mitchell among its partners. By late 1967, Nixon had emerged as a leading contender for the presidency. Badly split over the Vietnam War, the Democrats nominated a ticket headed by Senator Hubert Humphrey of Minnesota for president and Senator Edmund Muskie of Maine for vice president.

Nixon won his party's nomination on the first ballot, defeating two formidable opponents, Governors Nelson Rockefeller of New York and Ronald Reagan of California. He chose as his vice presidential candidate Spiro Agnew, the little-known governor of Maryland. In the campaign, Agnew played the role of the heavy, freeing Nixon to upgrade his image to the electorate.

The election of 1968 was complicated by the entrance of a third party—the American Independent Party—formed by the segregationist governor of Alabama, George Wallace. Avoiding debates, Nixon waged a bland, low-key campaign.

On election night, Humphrey took an early lead, but Nixon's strength showed itself in the South and the Far West. Although his electoral vote margin was substantial, Nixon won the popular vote by only .7 percent out of more than 72 million votes cast. The Democrats retained control of both houses of Congress. For the first time in 120 years the party of a new president had failed to carry either house.

Nixon's cabinet included his old friend and former attorney general, William P. Rogers as secretary of state; Melvin R. Laird as secretary of defense; and John N. Mitchell as attorney general. Overshadowing all his other appointments was his national security adviser, Henry Kissinger. Early in his administration, Nixon appointed Warren E. Burger to the Supreme Court as chief justice, succeeding Earl Warren.

Nixon depended heavily on his White House staff, headed by H. R. Haldeman, known as Bob Haldeman, an advertising executive. His staff was described by author Frank Kessler as an " 'old buddies' staffing system with its excessive emphasis on loyalty, team players, and isolation at the top created by hierarchical staffing patterns." Haldeman, chief of staff, ruled imperiously, a gatekeeper who severely limited access to the president.

The new president faced the difficult task of calming down the country's seething dissent over Vietnam. Two days before he took office, expanded peace talks resumed in Paris but moved slowly. Then, in March 1969, the Communists accelerated the fighting with a new offensive into South Vietnam.

On July 20, 1969, astronaut Neil Armstrong, commander of Apollo 11, became the first man to set foot on the moon, fulfilling the pledge made by President Kennedy in 1961. "That's one small step for a man, one giant leap for mankind," said Armstrong.

In 1970, Nixon signed into law the National Environmental Policy Act of 1969, establishing the Council on Environmental Quality. The Environmental Protection Agency (EPA) was created in 1970 by consolidating a number of existing departments. Congress passed other important environmental laws during his administration, among them acts to provide cleaner water and air and to encourage recycling. The Water Pollution Act of 1972 to curtail the discharge of industrial waste into the nation's waterways was passed by Congress over Nixon's veto.

Nixon began a Vietnamization program to withdraw American troops from Vietnam and train local troops to replace them. From a 543,000-person contingent in 1969, he brought the number down to 344,000 in 1970, to 177,000 in 1971, and to 25,000 in 1972. As he was withdrawing Americans, he also engaged in widening the conflict by striking at North Vietnam forces from neighboring Cambodia and Laos. His raid into Cambodia on April 30, 1970, brought out antiwar protesters all over the country. On the campus at Kent State University, Ohio National Guardsmen fired into a crowd of two thousand antiwar demonstrators, killing four and wounding nine. At Jackson State College in Mississippi, two students were killed by state police. By the end of 1970, Congress repealed the Gulf of Tonkin Resolution, which had legalized the war in Vietnam, and Nixon signed the bill containing the repeal. A peace agreement between the United States and North Vietnam was not signed until January 1973. For his role in the negotiations Henry Kissinger was awarded the Nobel Peace Prize.

To combat inflation, Nixon imposed a freeze on wages and prices in 1971, then replaced them with a complex system of wage-price controls. These controversial controls were removed two years later.

On June 13, 1971, the *New York Times* began the publication of the Pentagon Papers—a secret Pentagon study of how the Vietnam War came about. The papers had been leaked to the press by Daniel Ellsberg, a Pentagon bureaucrat, although charges against him were dismissed in 1973. The Pentagon Papers revealed that Congress had not been fully informed about the Gulf of Tonkin incident of 1964 that had led to greater U.S. involvement in the war, that President Johnson had been making plans to enter the war even as he was telling voters in 1964 that he wasn't, and that the United States had no plan to end the war as long as the North Vietnamese wanted to continue fighting. The incident left Nixon obsessed with leaks within his administration.

In October 1971, Nixon reversed himself to support Communist China's admission to the UN. The following February, Nixon became the first American president to visit China, leading to broader scientific, cultural, and trade contacts. In May, his record of international achievements was enhanced further by the successful conclusion of the Strategic Arms Limitation Talks (SALT) with the Soviet Union.

The president had positioned himself effectively for the election year of 1972. The Democrats were struggling. Governor George Wallace of Alabama won impressively in southern primaries, then was shot while campaigning in Laurel, Maryland, and paralyzed from the waist down. Senator Edmund Muskie of Maine, the man the Nixon forces feared most, started strongly but his campaign to win the Democratic nomination ran into many problems and he dropped out. By summer, George McGovern, a liberal senator from South Dakota, with strong ties to the antiwar movement, was well on the way to winning the Democratic Party's nomination.

What voters didn't know was that some fifty well-financed saboteurs had used the powers of government to manipulate the operations of the opposition party's selection process. And they may never have discovered this if five burglars had not been caught breaking into the Democratic National Headquarters at the Watergate complex in Washington on June 17, 1972. Yet the break-in attracted little attention during the campaign.

Even though the race between Nixon and McGovern was never a close contest, the Nixon camp went all out to win. Mitchell stepped down from his post as attorney general to manage the campaign. For his services to Nixon, he later went to prison and four other members of the Committee to Reelect the President (CREEP) would also be convicted of felonies. Ironically, the president needed little campaigning to win forty-nine of the fifty states in one of the biggest landslides in history.

Three days after he was sworn in on January 20, 1973, President Nixon announced the end of U.S. involvement in the war in Vietnam. In less than three weeks, the first group of American prisoners of war returned to the United States.

Watergate surfaced slowly. When the five burglars had been arrested in June 1972, ties to Nixon were discovered early through an address book with names, phone numbers, and checks traced to CREEP. When the men were brought to trial in late 1972, few questions were asked, few answers were given. Even after perpetrators of the burglary were found guilty, the public knew little about the case. That changed after the Senate voted, 77 to 0, in February 1973, to empower a select committee to investigate Watergate, chaired by Senator Sam Ervin, a North Carolina Democrat generally regarded as the Senate's authority on constitutional law.

A parade of staff and campaign people testified before the committee, grudgingly revealing a pattern of "dirty tricks," lies, perjury, "high crimes and misdemeanors"—and on July 13, 1973, the existence of an elaborate system for taping all conversations in the Oval Office. Nixon had the system installed to serve him when he wrote the memoirs that he hoped would secure his place in history. They secured it but not in the way he wanted.

Special Watergate prosecutor Archibald Cox subpoenaed taped records of nine presidential conversations. Nixon refused to turn over subpoenaed tapes, citing executive privilege. A year of appeals and infighting passed before the Supreme Court ruled unanimously in favor of the prosecutor.

As Watergate captured the public's attention, federal prosecutors revealed that Vice President Agnew was the target of an investigation into a kickback scheme conducted when he was county executive of Baltimore County and later governor of Maryland. A forty-page indictment revealed he was still taking bribes in the White House. Faced with forty-six felony indictments, he struck a deal with federal prosecutors, agreeing to resign on October 10 and to plead no contest to one count of income tax evasion. He was fined $10,000 and placed on three years' probation. Nixon named Congressman Gerald Ford of Michigan, the House minority leader, as his new vice president. Ford was the first person to attain that office by appointment of the president and confirmation by both houses of Congress under the provisions of the Twenty-fifth Amendment, ratified in 1967.

On October 20, 1973, the roof fell in on Nixon. When special prosecutor Cox, a Harvard law professor, persisted in seeking the tapes, Nixon ordered the prosecutor fired. Attorney General Elliot Richardson resigned rather than fire Cox. He was replaced by William Ruckelshaus, who in turn resigned rather than follow the president's order. Solicitor General Robert H. Bork then became acting attorney general and agreed to fire Cox. General Alexander Haig called the event "the day of the firestorm." To most of the country it became known as "the Saturday Night Massacre."

Three days after the "massacre," twenty-two resolutions of impeachment were introduced in the House of Representatives. As chairman of the House Judiciary Committee, Peter Rodino, a congressman from New Jersey, headed the impeachment investigation. Articles of impeachment could be voted by the House for acts of "Treason, Bribery, or other high Crimes and Misdemeanors." It would then become the task of the Senate to hold a trial and vote on whether or not to convict. To remove a president from office the margin to convict had to be two-thirds of senators present.

On July 24, 1974, the Supreme Court ruled, eight to nothing, that Nixon had to relinquish the tapes to Leon Jaworski, who had succeeded Cox as special prosecutor. On that same day, the House Judiciary Committee began public debate on three articles of impeachment against Nixon: One: Obstruction of justice, making false or misleading statements, withholding evidence, counseling perjury, misusing the CIA, misusing confidential FBI information, and other crimes; Two: Abuse of Power, misusing the Internal Revenue Service, FBI, Secret Service, and other executive personnel, maintaining an unlawful secret investigative unit, and interfering with the Watergate investigation; Three: Failure to comply with congressional subpoenas. By wide margins the thirty-eight members of the House Judiciary Committee voted to recommend to the full House the impeachment of the president on all three counts.

The impeachment never came to a vote in the House or a subsequent impeachment trial in the Senate. One of the recently released tapes dated June 23, 1972, revealed that the president had directed the CIA to halt the FBI's investigation of Watergate, which would be embarrassing to his reelection. After the smoking gun revelations, it quickly became apparent that he would not survive the impeachment process. Calls for his resignation came from even the most staunch Nixon loyalists.

On the evening of August 8, 1974, Richard Nixon spoke on television in the Oval Office, declaring he no longer had "a strong enough political base" to continue the fight. His resignation, he said, would become effective the following day at noon.

Nixon was not invited to attend the swearing in of Gerald Ford as the thirty-eighth president on August 9, 1974. When his presidency formally expired at noon, Nixon was flying in Air Force One over Missouri enroute to his home in California.

A month after his resignation President Ford issued his predecessor a full pardon. Other members of his team did not fare so well. Three cabinet members were convicted, one of whom served time in prison. Nixon's top staff members and his top campaign officials went to jail. Close to fifty people were convicted of felonies or misdemeanors, spun out from the Watergate case.

Poll participants rank Nixon as one of America's ten worst presidents. The key, of course, is the Character and Integrity category, one in which he was given the lowest rating of any president. Nixon gained low marks, too, for the Appointments category, understandable since many of his appointees went to jail. Better ratings for the Political Skill, the Achievements and Crisis Management, and the Leadership categories are not enough to overcome what to many has become the defining word for him—"Watergate." It shows up often as a one-word evaluation in our poll's "comments" column.

The words used to describe Nixon are devastating: "corrupt and corrupting," "slimy," "warped," "pathological," "sick, disturbed, and repulsive," and "an enemy of his country." Many sadly observe that he "could have been great," and one writes, "near great in foreign policy but a great threat to the Constitution." Poll participants generally acknowledge his achievements in foreign policy but as one person puts it, "criminal behavior ruined everything else."

After his fall from power, Nixon wrote extensively in an attempt to rehabilitate his image, producing seven books including his memoirs. To some extent he regained some of his old stature but the Ridings-McIver Presidential Poll reveals that to many the word that defines him is still "Watergate."

GERALD R. FORD

1974–1977
38TH PRESIDENT
OVERALL RANKING: 27

★

Leadership Qualities: 34
Accomplishments and Crisis Management: 28
Political Skill: 24
Appointments: 23
Character and Integrity: 17

I'm a Ford, not a Lincoln.

—Gerald R. Ford

When Gerald R. Ford took the oath of office on August 9, 1974, he became the first American to reach the presidency without ever having campaigned for votes in a national election. He was, as his wife Betty put it, "an accidental President."

Accidental or not, Jerry Ford faced the awesome task of restoring dignity and trust to the office of the presidency after the scandal of Watergate.

"I believe that truth is the glue that holds government together, not only our Government but civilization itself," said Ford upon taking office. ". . . I expect to follow my instincts of openness and candor with full confidence that honesty is always the best policy in the end. My fellow Americans, our long national nightmare is over."

Gerald Rudolph Ford, Jr., was born July 14, 1913, in Omaha, Nebraska, as Leslie Lynch King, Jr. He was renamed three years later after his mother's second husband, who adopted him. Jerry grew up in Grand Rapids, Michigan, in a happy, caring family.

He received a football scholarship to the University of Michigan, where he played center. The Wolverines' most valuable player as a senior, he rejected offers to play pro football, deciding instead to take a coaching job at Yale University, where he could pursue his law studies. He graduated in the upper third of his class in June 1941.

During World War II, Ford saw combat duty with the navy in the Pacific Ocean. When he was discharged in January 1946, his victory ribbon featured ten battle stars.

In October 1948, he married Betty Bloomer Warren, an attractive divorcee who had been a Powers model and a professional dancer. Two weeks later, he was elected to the U.S. House of Representatives from Michigan's heavily Republican Fifth District, then reelected to Congress twelve times in a row.

In Washington, Ford moved steadily up the GOP ladder. His party named him chairman of the House Republican Conference in 1963 and minority leader in 1965. Early in his career he set his sights on becoming Speaker of the House. The presidency was never one of Ford's goals.

Early in 1973, Ford decided that the congressional election of 1974 would be his last. Not even Nixon's landslide victory in 1972 had been enough to give the Republicans control of the House, which would have made Ford the Speaker of the House. Ford decided to retire in 1976 at sixty-three.

After Vice President Agnew's resignation in October 1973, Nixon considered many candidates for his replacement, including Secretary of the Treasury John Connally of Texas, Nelson Rockefeller, and Ronald Reagan before picking Ford. Both well liked and respected by most Republicans, he could also withstand the intensive FBI investigation that preceded congressional hearings. The Senate confirmed Ford, 92 to 3, and the House approved him, 387 to 35. Ford took the oath of office on December 6, 1973.

The new vice president soon found himself in a difficult position. As the Watergate probe expanded, Ford continued to defend the president, but he became increasingly aware that he too was being lied to.

As vice president, Ford had brought his old law partner, Phil Buchen, to Washington as his personal adviser. Without Ford's knowledge, Buchen organized a transition team—just in case. By August 1974, this contingency had become a reality. Buchen's team helped Ford through his first few days. On August 20, President Ford announced his nomination for vice president, Nelson Rockefeller. As leader of the party's liberal wing, Rockefeller had many enemies but also a strong staff, a commodity Ford had never had to develop. Congress confirmed the appointment, and Rockefeller became the vice president in December 1974.

In August, Ford enjoyed an approval rating of 71 percent in the Gallup Poll. On September 8, exactly one month after assuming the office of president, he made an announcement that sent his rating plunging instantly to 50 percent. At eleven o'clock on a Sunday morning, television carried nationwide a stunning message: ". . . I, Gerald R. Ford, President of the United States . . . do grant a full, free, and absolute pardon unto Richard Nixon for all offenses against the United States which he, Richard Nixon, has committed or may have committed or taken part in during the period from July 20, 1969 through August 9, 1974." President Ford then headed to the exclusive Burning Tree Club for a round of golf.

The storm broke immediately. Neither the new president nor his advisers had anticipated the fury of the response. Calls and wires pouring into the White House ran eight to one against Ford's decision. Newspapers, TV commentators, and private citizens across the country expressed outrage. Dozens of Nixon's people would be severely punished with prison sentences or heavy fines while a disgraced president would go freely into a retirement paid for by the taxpayers he had betrayed. To many it seemed like a prearranged deal.

Gerald T. terHorst, President Ford's press secretary and one of his oldest friends, resigned in protest. He had been the new president's first appointment, named to the post of press secretary the day Ford learned of Nixon's resignation. In his book *Gerald Ford and the Future of the Presidency*, he wrote: "The Nixon pardon . . . revealed that he could change his mind within ten days of his original public position, which was that he would not consider a Nixon pardon until it was before him as a result of an indictment, a conviction or an admission of guilt."

Determined to heal the country's rifts, Ford followed the pardon with an offer of amnesty to all draft dodgers and deserters of the Vietnam War. Unlike the pardon of Nixon the offer was not unconditional; it required an oath of allegiance and two years of public service. The program was not successful. It angered veterans groups as too lenient while offering little appeal for exiles convinced they had done no wrong.

Despite his personal friendship with many congressmen, Ford had little luck in overcoming the problem of Democratic majorities in both houses. Gerald Ford was also president when the United States suffered its final blow from its experience in Vietnam. In April 1975, in defiance of the peace treaty Nixon and Kissinger had negotiated only two years earlier, the North Vietnamese invaded the South and routed its American-trained army. After fifteen years and at a cost of more than fifty thousand American lives, the war in Vietnam was over.

Ford's other ventures in foreign affairs were closely associated with Secretary of State Henry Kissinger, perhaps the most notable member of the Nixon cabinet not destroyed by Watergate. In 1974, Ford became the first U.S. president to visit Japan while in office. In 1975, the Helsinki Agreement brought together thirty-five nations to ease East-West tensions, including improved communications and a relaxing of travel restrictions.

In September 1975 Ford had two close encounters with assassins. In Sacramento, Lynette Fromme, known as Squeaky Fromm, a disciple of mass murderer Charles Manson, tried to shoot President Ford with a Colt .45. The gun failed to fire. Less than three weeks later, in San Francisco, Sara Jane Moore, a former FBI informant, fired at the president with a .38 caliber revolver. An alert bystander spoiled her shot. Both women were sentenced to life in prison.

Betty Ford proved an active and popular first lady. She spoke out in favor of liberalized abortion laws and the Equal Rights Amendment. She spoke openly about her bout with breast cancer and helped increase public awareness of an affliction that kills thousands of women every year. After her husband left the White House, she was candid in revealing her struggle against dependency on alcohol and pain-killing drugs, the result of her efforts to find relief from an inoperable pinched nerve. After her recovery, she established the Betty Ford Clinic, a chemical-dependency recovery center.

When he sought a full term as president, Ford faced many problems. For most of his term, his approval ratings had hovered just below 50 percent. One of his worst difficulties arose from the Nixon "hangover" effect. Perhaps even more serious was the new climate within the media, now extremely distrustful of any president.

Ford's path to the Republican nomination in 1976 was not an easy one. Running against him was a formidable foe, former governor Ronald Reagan of California, who rallied many conservatives distrustful of Ford and Kissinger's policy of détente with the Soviet Union. At the party's Kansas City convention, Reagan came within a few delegates of denying Ford the nomination. As his vice presidential running mate Ford chose Senator Robert Dole of Kansas over the incumbent vice president Rockefeller, felt by many Republicans to be too liberal.

His Democratic opponent was former Georgia governor Jimmy Carter. Early polls showed Carter leading by as much as 30 percent, but President Ford cut steadily into that lead. It appeared the outcome would be determined by the televised debates. In the second debate, Ford made a serious foreign policy gaffe when he said the people of Poland and Eastern Europe were not under Soviet domination. Pressed on the point, he repeated his error. The White House was forced to issue a clarification. Ford's running mate did not help matters. In a televised debate, Senator Dole came across as bitter and angry, blaming Democrats for all of the wars of the twentieth century. Carter's running mate, Sen. Walter Mondale, seemed statesmanlike by comparison. Carter prevailed in the election, winning the popular vote by more than 1.5 million votes and the electoral edge by 297 to 240. It was Ford's first loss in twenty-five years of campaigning. A vigorous and athletic man, Ford retired to Rancho Mirage, California, a resort where he could play golf year-round.

In ranking Ford twenty-seventh, poll participants give him low marks in Leadership Qualities but high grades in Character and Integrity. One calls him "a steadying influence," but most comments express dismay over his pardon of Nixon. Many reflect unkindly on his competency with comments such as "a good small town mayor" and "an amiable muffin."

Watergate weighted Ford down too much for him to achieve a distinguished presidency. It is to his credit that he saw clearly what his true mission was. One of the finest tributes to Ford came from the new president, Jimmy Carter. He said, "For myself and for our nation, I want to thank my predecessor for all he has done to heal our land."

Carter's remark in 1977 went to the heart of what Ford saw as his mission. His presidential memoir, published in 1979, was titled *A Time to Heal*.

Jimmy Carter

1977–1981
39TH PRESIDENT

Overall Ranking: 19

Leadership Qualities: 28
Accomplishments and Crisis Management: 22
Political Skill: 32
Appointments: 14
Character and Integrity: 5

Jimmy Who?

—Numerous U.S. Citizens in 1974–75

"JIMMY CARTER'S RUNNING FOR WHAT?" read a headline over a Reg Murphy column in the *Atlanta Constitution:* "Governor Jimmy Carter's timing was just right. The state needed a good belly laugh, and Carter obliged by announcing he would run for President."

From 1971 to 1975 Jimmy Carter had served as governor of Georgia. Still, he was so little known outside of Georgia that he stumped four celebrity contestants, without blindfolds, who failed to identify him on the TV game show *What's My Line?*

In 1974, two years into the governorship, Carter made his announcement: "Hello, I'm Jimmy Carter, and I'm running for president of the United States. I need your help." The response, all too often, was "Jimmy Who?"

As he campaigned across a country still reeling from Vietnam and Watergate, Carter stressed character rather than issues. He was an "outsider," free of the corrupting entanglements of the Beltway. Historian David Halberstam wrote in *Newsweek* that the deeply religious Carter had "skillfully applied . . . the South's traditional sense of place, family and community to national politics," thus reassuring people "deeply threatened" by the rapid changes that were occurring in the country.

Somehow the message reached enough people to earn him the Democratic nomination and then victory over the incumbent president, Gerald Ford. Once in office, Carter was beset by economic crises and foreign policy challenges that seemed impervious to his calls for human rights and moral rectitude.

The oldest of four children, James Earl Carter, Jr., was born October 1, 1924, in Plains, Georgia, the first president to be born in a hospital. His father was a peanut broker who founded the Carter peanut warehouse business. A conservative Democrat, the elder Carter served in the Georgia state legislature. Jimmy's mother Lillian was a liberal who advocated racial equality long before it became acceptable in the South.

Jimmy Carter attended Georgia Southwestern College and Georgia Tech before entering the U.S. Naval Academy in Annapolis, Maryland, in 1943. In 1951, he joined the nuclear submarine program. A month after he graduated from the U.S. Naval Academy, he married Rosalynn Smith in the Plains Methodist Church. They had three sons and a daughter, Amy, their youngest child and the only one of their children who lived with them in the White House.

Carter resigned from the navy after his father's death in 1959, returning to Plains to run the family business. In his first race for the state senate in 1962 he appeared to have lost the Democratic primary in a close race. Carter, however, was able to prove fraud and thus have the outcome reversed in his favor. In 1966, he ran for governor as a moderate but finished third behind the archsegregationist Lester Maddox.

Four years later, Carter ran again, this time as a conservative and won convincingly. As governor he presented a progressive agenda, stressing education, environment, fiscal responsibility, and improved race relations. In 1974, he headed the Democratic National Campaign Committee and became the first Democrat to declare that he would seek the party's nomination in the 1976 presidential race.

After Watergate, Carter believed America wanted an outsider with no ties to the Washington establishment. In a field of six, Carter captured the moderate center and at the Democratic National Convention in New York won overwhelmingly on the first ballot. To balance his ticket, Carter picked the liberal Minnesota senator, Walter Mondale, to challenge Gerald Ford and Robert Dole.

Way behind in the polls, Ford aggressively attacked Carter as a man without national experience and "fuzzy on the issues." He rapidly closed the gap. But when Gerald Ford stumbled in his second debate and said there was "no Soviet domination of Eastern Europe," Carter regained his momentum. On election day, a 1.5 million-vote edge in the popular vote gave Carter an electoral margin of 297 to 240.

On inauguration day, January 20, 1977, Jimmy Carter told the American people: "You have given me a great responsibility—to stay close to you, to be worthy of you, and to exemplify what you are. Let us create together a new national spirit of unity and trust."

In his first full day in office, President Carter redeemed his campaign pledge to pardon the roughly ten thousand draft evaders of the Vietnam War—but not the deserters. The new president moved quickly to push for legislation deregulating airlines, natural gas prices, and the trucking industry. He signed into law a ban on the dumping of raw sewage into the ocean and an act to control strip mining. In his first year, he began to speak out for human rights as a cornerstone for his administration's foreign policy.

In foreign affairs, Carter expended a great deal of political energy and capital to pass a treaty that would return the Panama Canal Zone and the Panama Canal within it to the Republic of Panama, effective December 31, 1999. While the treaty provided plenty of fodder for his conservative critics, particularly Ronald Reagan, Carter considered it one of his administration's most important achievements.

The top positions on Carter's White House staff were filled by Georgians whom he trusted and with whom he had worked before. Hamilton Jordan became his chief of staff and Jody Powell his press secretary. For many of his cabinet appointments, he turned to more traditional Establishment sources by naming Cyrus R. Vance as his secretary of state and Zbigniew Brzezinski as his national security adviser. Carter named two women to his cabinet: Juanita M. Kreps (vice president of Duke University) as secretary of commerce and Patricia Roberts Harris (a former dean of Howard University's law school) as secretary of housing and urban development. Atlanta Congressman Andrew Young became the first African American appointed UN ambassador.

To head the Office of Management and Budget, President Carter picked an old Georgia friend, banker Bert Lance. During the summer of 1977, media reports revealed that Lance was suspected of illegal banking practices in Georgia. Lance was forced to resign.

On February 2, 1977, Carter in his first fireside chat focused on energy conservation as he announced the creation of the Department of Energy. Its first secretary was James R. Schlesinger, a bipartisan choice; he had served in the two previous Republican administrations.

Energy was Carter's number one domestic priority. The Arab oil-producing nations controlled two-thirds of the world's petroleum reserves. During the 1973–74 Yom Kippur War between Israel and three Arab countries, the United States' dependency on Middle East oil produced severe shortages and long lines at U.S. gas stations. President Carter sought to enact an energy program to encourage domestic production of oil and natural gas, promote energy conservation, and develop alternative energy sources such as solar heating. The battle between the president and Congress stretched out over eighteen months before five energy bills passed in October 1978. These bills included fuel-conservation provisions that by 1980 had produced an 11 percent drop in oil consumption and an 8 percent decline in oil imports.

Carter's greatest achievement came at the Camp David presidential retreat in the Catoctin Mountains of Maryland. With his historic visit to Jerusalem, Egyptian president Anwar Sadat had launched a promising

Middle East peace process in 1977. After the process stalled, President Carter restarted it by inviting Sadat and Israeli prime minister Menachem Begin to Camp David. Secluded for thirteen days, the three heads of state hammered out the Camp David Accords. These led to a formal peace treaty in 1979, ending a thirty-one-year state of war between Egypt and Israel. Begin and Sadat received Nobel Peace Prizes for this agreement.

The year 1979 had started well with the United States formally recognizing the People's Republic of China and the establishing full diplomatic relations with China.

In June, the Organization of Petroleum Exporting Countries (OPEC) announced its largest price increase—and its fourth in five months. Frustration at galloping inflation and soaring interest rates persuaded President Carter to hold an eleven-day retreat at Camp David, meeting with many American leaders. When he came down from the mountains, he spoke of the nation's "crisis of the spirit," a phrase the news media called "malaise," denoting a mood of despair for the future. His speech was well received, but its power was undercut shortly when he accepted the resignations from five cabinet members. The shakeup underscored what many Americans were feeling. Wrote Carter's biographer Burton I. Kaufman: "But what distressed Americans almost as much as the economy was their perception of presidential ineptitude."

All of Carter's problems were soon dwarfed by the events of November 4, 1979. Iranian militants seized the U.S. embassy in Teheran, trapping ninety hostages. The militants demanded the return of the deposed Shah Reza Pahlavi, undergoing treatment in New York for a cancer that would kill him within a year. The Ayatollah Khomeini, leader of the Iranians, released roughly half of the hostages, but held fifty-two Americans to use as pawns to force the return of the Shah to stand trial. In the Middle East, hostages were usually released within a few days, but not this time. Carter started negotiations through a mediator, the North African country of Algeria. Diplomatic and economic pressures were exerted. On and on the ordeal dragged. President Carter authorized a small military strike force to attempt a secret rescue. A sudden April dust storm caused two helicopters to collide, and eight servicemen were killed. Many blamed Carter for the fiasco.

As 1979 ended, the Soviet Union invaded Afghanistan. President Carter suspended sales of high-technology equipment and grain to the Soviet Union, won passage of a UN resolution calling for the withdrawal of Soviet troops, and joined sixty-three other nations in boycotting the 1980 Olympic Games in Moscow.

Failure to bring home the hostages dropped Carter's approval rating to 20 percent. Senator Ted Kennedy decided to seek his party's presidential nomination. Carter beat back Kennedy's challenge, but the Massachusetts senator refused to concede, carrying his divisive campaign all the way to the Democratic National Convention in New York. Carter won the nomination convincingly on the first ballot, but he faced the November election as head of a badly divided party.

By contrast, the Republicans had united behind a formidable ticket, Governor Ronald Reagan of California and George Bush, former director of the CIA. In the fall campaign, Carter fought a gasoline shortage, runaway inflation, and an Iranian hostage crisis that refused to go away. Carter based his hopes for reelection on the televised debates. What he found was that the medium was made to order for his handsome, telegenic opponent, a former movie actor and broadcaster. Three years later it was learned that the Reagan camp had obtained Carter's "game plan" for the debates, thus giving the actor an unexpected and unethical edge. A third candidate, independent John Anderson, an Illinois congressman, further complicated Carter's campaign. Reagan won overwhelmingly, 489 electoral votes to Carter's 49.

In the few weeks remaining for his presidency, Carter pushed through Congress additional energy legislation and two important environmental laws, one to clean up toxic wastes and one to protect 150 million acres of Alaska wilderness. He also continued to work for the release of the hostages. Iran finally agreed to release the hostages, too late to save the reelection candidacy of the president. The hostages were released just as Reagan was being sworn in.

As an outsider, Carter had proven ineffective in dealing with a Congress steeped in traditions and customs—and unable to lead or inspire either the legislators or the people. His tendency to micromanage the office further diminished his effectiveness.

Erwin C. Hargrove in *Jimmy Carter As President* argued that one of Carter's problems was that he did not calculate the political consequences of his actions. Other authors have pointed out that he was damaged by his willingness to face up squarely to difficult, unpopular, and politically damaging decisions. For example, he called for higher taxes on petroleum to force Americans to cut back on energy conservation.

Participants in the poll make Carter the highest-ranking president since Lincoln in the Character and Integrity category. Character, however, was not enough, as low marks in the Political Skill and Leadership Qualities categories result in an overall ranking of nineteenth. "Honesty is not necessarily a political virtue," comments one poll participant. Others recognize the difficulties of the troubled time in which he served. One calls him "not a great president but the best we've had in the past quarter century."

Defeated and dejected, Carter returned home to Plains, Georgia, to learn that his family agricultural business, which had made him a wealthy man, had fallen deeply into debt while he was away in Washington. He sold the warehouse business, signed lucrative book contracts, and established the Jimmy Carter Library, Museum and Presidential Center in Atlanta. From the Presidential Center he embarked on an active role in global peacekeeping missions. In addition, he became active in Habitat for Humanity, working with hammer and nails to build homes in slum areas around the country.

In *The Presidency of James Earl Carter, Jr.*, Burton I. Kaufman wrote the following:

> Ironically, one issue that has contributed to Carter's rising reputation has been his management of the 1979/80 hostage crisis. Even though this was a crucial factor in his defeat, political commentators have favorably compared the way he handled this situation with Ronald Reagan's handling of a similar crisis in 1984 involving Americans kidnapped in Lebanon. In nationally televised congressional hearings in 1987, Americans learned how the Reagan administration tried to barter arms for Iran in return for the release of the hostages. Its backroom approach appeared in sharp contrast to the former president's refusal to make such deals during the 1979/80 hostage crisis. Carter himself has condemned the Reagan arms deal. "To me, the bribery of kidnappers is unconscionable," he remarked in an interview in April 1987. "What we did in Iran, in the most recent scandal, has not only encouraged additional takings of hostages but it rewarded those who did kidnap Americans."

In the years since he left the White House, Jimmy Carter became what *Newsweek* called "the modern model of a successful ex-President of the United States."

RONALD REAGAN

1981–1989
40TH PRESIDENT

OVERALL RANKING: 26

★

Leadership Qualities: 16
Accomplishments and Crisis Management: 27
Political Skill: 9
Appointments: 39
Character and Integrity: 39

Honey, I forgot to duck.

—Ronald Reagan

Seventy days into his administration, President Ronald Reagan addressed a luncheon of labor leaders at the Washington Hilton Hotel. At 2:30 P.M. on March 30, 1981, he left the hotel. As he walked to his waiting limousine, he waved to a crowd that was friendly—except for one crazed drifter.

John Hinckley, Jr., began firing a .22 caliber revolver. Bullets hit Reagan's press secretary, James Brady, a Secret Service agent, a policeman, and the president himself. The president's bodyguards shoved him into the limo. At George Washington University Hospital, doctors found the bullet had penetrated his left lung and lodged an inch from his heart.

To First Lady Nancy Reagan his first words were, "Honey, I forgot to duck." As he was wheeled into the operating room, perilously near death, he grinned at the surgeons and said, "Please assure me you are all good Republicans."

With the eyes of America on him, Ronald Reagan called on some deep inner resources to reassure family and country. What Americans saw was a courageous, cheerful, confident president. Writer Ernest Hemingway would have described it as "grace under pressure."

Journalist and biographer Lou Cannon said, "[H]is resonant performance" following the shooting "endowed him with a mythic quality" that became an underestimated ingredient of his political success.

Ronald Wilson Reagan was born February 6, 1911, in Tampico, Illinois. Raised in a lower-middle-class family environment, he attended Eureka College (in Illinois), where he led a student strike to protest against curriculum cutbacks, leading to the resignation of the college president. In college, he was president of the student council.

After graduation in 1932, he entered radio broadcasting, working primarily as a sportscaster. In 1937, a successful screen test led to a seven-year movie contract with Warner Brothers. He appeared in roughly fifty pictures during his screen career.

During the 1938 filming of *Brother Rat* he met actress Jane Wyman, who became his first wife. They had two children, Maureen and Michael.

During World War II, Reagan served as a U.S. Army captain, narrating preflight training films for the Army Air Force First Motion Picture Unit.

After the war, he became president of the Screen Actors Guild. Alarmed at what he saw as Communist influences in the movie colony, he became an informant for the FBI. Along the way he changed from "a near hopeless hemophiliac liberal," as he described himself, to a conservative Republican.

After World War II, Reagan's screen career began to flounder just as his wife's was blossoming. In 1948 she earned a Best Actress Oscar nomination for her performance in *Johnny Belinda*. That year she divorced Reagan, blaming the breakup of their marriage on his heavy political involvement in the Screen Actors Guild. He later became the first divorcé elected president of the country.

His second marriage in 1952 was to the young film actress Nancy Davis. She emerged as a powerful influence in her husband's future career. They had two children, Patti and Ronald.

During the 1950s, Reagan became an increasingly conservative Republican. In 1960, he deliver two hundred speeches for the Republican presidential nominee, Richard Nixon. Reagan's address to the 1964 Republican National Convention was one of the highlights of that ill-fated affair.

In 1966, Reagan ran successfully for governor of California, decisively defeating the incumbent governor, Pat Brown, who had vanquished Richard Nixon four years earlier. Reagan was sworn in at one minute past midnight on January 1, 1967, the exact timing selected by Nancy Reagan's astrologer.

The new governor, who had inherited a budget deficit from Brown, immediately imposed a 10 percent across-the-board cut for all state agencies. That coupled with an income tax increase brought the deficit under control. Reelected in 1970, Reagan continued his conservative policies aimed at restricting the size and cost of state government.

In his two terms as governor, Reagan became a major figure in the Republican Party. By the 1980 Republican National Convention, he was far and away his party's most popular candidate, winning on the first ballot with 1,939 votes to 37 for Congressman John Anderson of Illinois and 13 for George Bush. As his vice presidential running mate, Reagan chose Bush, a former congressman, UN ambassador, and director of the CIA.

Running against incumbent president Jimmy Carter and against Anderson, who declared as an independent, Reagan hammered hard at Carter's problems—principally runaway inflation, the gasoline shortage, and the Iran hostage crisis. In televised debates, the polished actor scored well against the president, turning aside many of his points with a smile and a catchy phrase, "There you go again." Three years later, it was learned that the Reagan election team had obtained private Carter campaign strategy documents that it used to prepare for the debates. Reagan won overwhelmingly both in popular and electoral votes.

On January 20, 1981, the Iranians released their fifty-two American hostages after 444 days of imprisonment, and Ronald Reagan, at sixty-nine, became the oldest man ever to take the oath of president of the United States. Americans believed Reagan's pledge to make government work again. "I believe that you surround yourself with the best people you can find, delegate authority, and don't interfere," said Reagan. Unfortunately, his "best people" should have been interfered with, as he painfully discovered years later. "The aides in close contact with President Reagan today are the least distinguished such group to serve any President in the postwar period," wrote Columnist George Will, a staunch Reagan conservative.

His aides presented Reagan with a list of proposed goals to accomplish during his first hundred days. He accepted the entire plan without asking a question. But before his administration could get under way, the deluded Hinckley fired a bullet into the president's chest. Recovering with remarkable speed for a man his age, Reagan left the hospital after only twelve days.

When he returned to office, he was a national hero. The public loved him so much Congress felt it not expedient to challenge him on his supply-side economic philosophy. His goal was to slash the cost of government, then couple the cost reduction with a lower income tax that would free up more money for investment. The inevitable economic boom, supply-siders reasoned, would cut the deficit and produce a balanced budget. The previous year, rival presidential candidate George Bush had criticized this theory as "voodoo economics." By the end of 1981, Reagan's own budget director, David Stockman, was beginning to agree with Bush. Projected economic models were just not showing the results the administration wanted, particularly after military spending was increased sharply.

Still, Reaganomics, as the White House package came to be called, passed a Democratic-controlled Congress. It produced mixed results. Inflation, which was the great economic problem of the 1970s, was tamed and had not returned as of the end of 1996. The economic expansion that began in November 1982 was the longest in peacetime since World War II. During the Reagan years, a record 20 million new jobs were created.

Unfortunately this success was not without severe pain. In 1982 unemployment, bank failures, bankruptcies, and farm foreclosures reached levels that made some fear a return of conditions similar to those of the Great Depression. During the Reagan years, the United States went from the world's largest creditor nation to the world's largest debtor nation. The biggest problem, however, has been the effect of Reaganomics on the budget deficit. When Reagan took office, the national debt stood at $907 billion. By the end of Reagan's first year in office, the national debt passed a trillion dollars for the first time in history, then more than doubled before he left office. Under Reagan, interest on the national debt became the third largest item in the budget, exceeded only by entitlements and defense spending. As an answer, President Reagan called repeatedly for a constitutional amendment mandating a balanced budget, but critics responded by asking why he never submitted a balanced budget in his eight years in office.

In 1983 U.S. troops were dispatched to help bring peace to Lebanon, which had been ravaged by civil war since 1975. On October 23, 1983, Iranian terrorists drove trucks packed with explosives into the U.S. Marine headquarters at Beirut airport, killing 241 American servicemen. By early 1984 U.S. troops were withdrawn without having had any effect on the situation. Two days after the tragedy in Beirut U.S. forces invaded the Caribbean island of Grenada to rescue hundreds of Americans, many of them medical students, who were endangered by a leftist military coup. Eighteen American soldiers were killed.

The election of 1984 could be considered a referendum on Reagan and his policies. The Democrats nominated former vice president Walter Mondale, who chose Geraldine Ferraro, a New York congresswoman, to become the first woman to run on the presidential ticket of a major party. Reagan's popularity was so immense that he carried the election with the highest electoral total in history, 525 votes to 13. Mondale barely carried his native Minnesota.

Nonetheless, even an overwhelming election victory could not change the difficult reality that President Reagan faced. An October explosion at the U.S. embassy in Beirut killed sixteen Americans. In 1985, Shiite Muslims hijacked a TWA jetliner, and Palestine Liberation Front terrorists hijacked an Italian cruise ship in the Mediterranean. In each hijacking, an American was killed.

As these acts continued, the Reagan administration charged that five nations—Iran, Libya, North Korea, Cuba, and Nicaragua—were sponsoring terrorist acts around the world. Reagan identified Muammar Qaddafi of Libya as the world's principal terrorist. On April 14, 1986, the president ordered the bombing of two Libyan cities.

Closer to home, President Reagan was wrestling with problems in the jungles of Nicaragua. Rebel soldiers, the Contras, were fighting the Communist troops of the country's Sandinista government. Reagan repeatedly asked Congress to authorize military aid for the Contras. With the memory of Vietnam too fresh, Congress refused the president's request, instead passing the Boland Amendment, banning military aid to the Contras.

At roughly the same time, Reagan found himself deeply troubled by a continuing hostage problem in the Middle East. Muslim terrorists were holding seven American hostages in Lebanon. Although it was against U.S. law to provide arms to terrorist nations, the White House sold Hawk missiles and spare missile parts to Iran, the same nation that had held fifty-two Americans hostage for 444 days. In return, Iran was to use its influence to persuade the terrorists to release the hostages.

Robert McFarlane, national security adviser, ran the program for Reagan at first, before assigning it to his aide, Col. Oliver North. Under North's leadership, the Reagan administration began overcharging Iran for missiles, then using the inflated profits to fund the Contras secretly. Fleecing Iran to help the anti-Communists in Central America was, North said, a "neat idea."

In November 1986, a Lebanese publication broke the story of America's secret arms deal with Iran. Within a week, American newspapers were uncovering more details about the mission. The president found himself forced to appoint a commission to investigate the charges. Chaired by former Republican senator John Tower of Texas, the commission produced a report condemning the Reagan administration for secretly trading arms for hostages, placed primary blame on the president's staff, and blamed the president for failing to oversee the operations of his staff and monitor the consequences of his own policies.

The investigations did not stop with the probe by the Tower Commission. A special joint congressional committee, chaired by Democrats Senator Daniel Inouye of Hawaii and Representative Lee Hamilton of Indiana, probed the developing scandal further from May to July 1987. In televised hearings, members of Congress questioned many witnesses, among them National Security Adviser John Poindexter and his subordinate Colonel North. The charismatic North's compelling testimony made him a national hero, even though he freely admitted he had lied, falsified documents, and destroyed evidence to conceal the Reagan administration's involvement in the illegal venture.

The committee's 690-page report concluded that the president was probably unaware of the illegal diversion of the arms-sales profits to the

Contras but agreed with the Tower Commission that the president's "hands-off" style of management was to blame. "The Iran initiative," the report charged, "succeeded only in replacing three American hostages with another three, arming Iran . . . and engulfing the President in one of the worst credibility crises of any administration in U.S. history."

Lawrence Walsh, the special prosecutor appointed by Reagan, secured indictments against McFarlane, Poindexter, and North. McFarlane pleaded guilty. Verdicts against Poindexter and North were later overturned when an appeals court concluded their convictions had been obtained through their testimony before Congress for which they had immunity. Chief of Staff Donald Regan was also forced to resign.

Particularly painful for Reagan were the difficulties that swirled around Attorney General Edwin Meese, one of the president's oldest and most trusted advisers. A special prosecutor was appointed to investigate Meese's possible role in an influence-peddling and bribery scandal involving Wedtech Corporation, a defense contractor. Prosecutor James McKay concluded the evidence against Meese was insufficient to indict him, even though he believed the attorney general had probably violated the law. Meese resigned but came under fire again following a final review of the McKay report by the Justice Department's Office of Professional Responsibility. The review condemned Meese for "conduct which should not be tolerated of any government employee, especially not the attorney general."

For years Ronald Reagan had attacked the Soviet Union as an "evil empire." To counter a continuing Soviet buildup of medium-range missiles, Reagan likewise embarked on a costly national defense program, which included his Strategic Defense Initiative (SDI), better known as Star Wars, involving a space-based missile defense system designed to destroy incoming missiles in outer space. Keeping pace with the U.S. buildup placed a severe strain on the Soviet economy. Many believe this was a factor in the development of a friendlier relationship between the two countries, beginning in 1985 after Mikhail Gorbachev assumed the office of premier.

Reagan pressed for a summit meeting with the new premier, who seemed more amenable to accommodation with the West than his country's previous hard-liners had. Although progress was slow and difficult, the cold war was clearly beginning to thaw, replaced at last by *glasnost*, the Russian word for openness.

In December 1987 the leaders of the United States and the Soviet

Union signed the Intermediate-Range Nuclear Forces Treaty (INF). The two countries agreed to destroy hundreds of medium- and short-range missiles capable of striking targets as far away as 3,400 miles. The INF also permitted inspections by each side on the other's soil until the end of the century.

In the final month of Reagan's administration, Gorbachev declared a unilateral reduction in Soviet armed forces and agreed to withdraw large numbers of tanks and troops from Eastern Europe and Afghanistan. The "evil empire," which Reagan had battled so vigorously throughout his administration, was beginning to crumble. Some regard this as his finest achievement.

In the 1988 presidential election, Reagan's vice president, George Bush, was elected president. Reagan stepped down as the oldest man ever to hold the office, as the first president to serve out two full terms since Dwight Eisenhower, and also as the most popular American president since Franklin Roosevelt.

Reagan's enormous popularity stemmed from many things, starting with his skill in communicating effectively with the American people. Americans, weary of the disillusionment left by the Vietnam War and Watergate, responded enthusiastically to his genial optimism, his patriotism, and the strong leadership he projected. And few forgot his "grace under pressure" after the 1981 assassination attempt.

Soon, however, events seriously impacted his popularity. For a two-day visit to Japan the former president was paid $2 million by a Japanese media company for two twenty-minute talks, raising his critics' eyebrows as they wondered just what he was paid for. Investigations revealed that under Reagan the Department of Housing and Urban Development had been deeply involved in fraud, theft, patronage, and favoritism, which cost taxpayers hundreds of millions of dollars. Still worse was the collapse of the savings and loan industry, the result of CIA manipulation, organized crime infiltration, and inadequate supervision during the Reagan years. Early estimates were that taxpayers would have to contribute $500 billion to bail out what had, before Reagan, been a viable industry.

The year after he left the White House, Reagan became the first American president required to testify in criminal proceedings involving his administration. He spent eight hours answering questions in the trial of John Poindexter. One hundred and thirty times he answered, "I don't know" or "I don't remember." At one point, he failed to identify a photograph of his chairman of the Joint Chiefs of Staff. Did he fail to recall because he was trying to protect his former national security adviser or could it have been a kind of early warning of a dread disease that deprives its victims of their memories? In 1994, Ronald Reagan was diagnosed with Alzheimer's disease, a discovery that saddened Americans everywhere.

Poll participants are less kind to Reagan than the American electorate, ranking him twenty-sixth out of forty-one presidents. "A truly mixed bag," one participant writes, and that seems to sum it up well. In the Political Skill category he ranks ninth, and in the Leadership Qualities category sixteenth; then in the Appointments and the Character and Integrity categories, he ranks near the bottom. Some love him, some hate him. "Why isn't he on Mount Rushmore yet?" asks one while others call him "a con man," "a popular sleepyhead," and "an emperor with no clothes." The most recurrent condemnations of Reagan refer not to Iran-Contra but to the deficit he left as his legacy with such harsh evaluations as "we may not survive the fiscal damage."

Reagan's achievement was summed up well by his former secretary of state, Alexander Haig: "He has contributed greatly to the revival of America's confidence and pride in itself." As Ronald Reagan himself stated so eloquently, "What I'd really like to do is go down in history as the president who made Americans believe in themselves again."

GEORGE BUSH

1989–1993
41ST PRESIDENT

OVERALL RANKING: 22

Leadership Qualities: 24
Accomplishments and Crisis Management: 18
Political Skill: 27
Appointments: 25
Character and Integrity: 24

Read my lips—no new taxes.

—George Bush

For just eight hours on July 13, 1985, Vice President George Bush became the country's first *acting president*. President Ronald Reagan went to Bethesda Naval Medical Center in Maryland for surgery to remove a two-foot cancerous section of his large intestine. Just before anesthesia, President Reagan, under the terms of the Twenty-fifth Amendment, ratified in 1967, signed a document transferring presidential power to Bush. It read: "I have determined and it is my . . . direction that Vice-president George Bush shall discharge powers and duties in my stead, commencing with the administration of anesthesia to me."

George Bush became acting president of the United States at 11:28 A.M., the moment when Ronald Reagan slipped into unconsciousness. Acting President Bush, who did not wish to appear "pushy" in assuming Reagan's job, performed only routine duties. He spent part of the day playing tennis.

After successful surgery, Reagan emerged, clear-headed enough by 7:22 that evening, to sign a second letter, reclaiming his power and duties. Bush, however, continued to run the office until President Reagan regained his strength.

In less than four years, Bush would become president—without the word "acting" in front of his title. He would also become the first sitting vice president in 150 years to be elected to the highest office in the land.

In winning the election of 1988, Bush scored heavily with voters with the oft-repeated phrase: "Read my lips—no new taxes." Once elected, he found that pledge a heavy burden to carry. It brutally drove home to him the fact that governing the United States in these difficult times was no game of tennis.

George Herbert Walker Bush was born June 12, 1924, at his family's Victorian home in Milton, Massachusetts. His father was Prescott Bush, a wealthy Wall Street investment banker, who was elected to the U.S. Senate from Connecticut in 1952. Both of George's parents worked to instill in their children their belief that people of wealth and privilege have an obligation to give something back to society.

On his eighteenth birthday in 1942, Bush enlisted in the U.S. Navy as a seaman second class. In June 1943, he earned his wings as the youngest pilot in the U.S. Navy. He served in the Pacific, earning the Distinguished Flying Cross.

In his final year in the navy, Bush, twenty at the time, married Barbara Pierce, nineteen, the daughter of the publisher of *Redbook* and *McCall's* magazines, at the First Presbyterian Church in Rye, New York. They had five children: four sons and a daughter who died of leukemia at the age of four. Barbara Bush later became one of the most beloved of all first ladies, active in promoting adult literacy.

After the war, Bush entered Yale, where he majored in economics, graduating with honors and a Phi Beta Kappa key. For nearly two decades he worked successfully in the oil business in Texas. He lost a bid for the U.S. Senate in 1964, but two years later he was elected to Congress from a strong Republican district in Houston and then reelected without opposition for a second term. In 1970, he ran again for the Senate, losing to Democrat Lloyd Bentsen.

President Richard Nixon appointed Bush ambassador to the UN (1971–73), then chairman of the Republican National Committee, chief U.S. liaison in China, and director of the Central Intelligence Agency.

After emerging as Reagan's most viable challenger in the 1980 Republican primaries, he was chosen by Reagan to be his running mate. During Bush's eight years as vice president, he served as chairman of presidential task forces on regulatory reform, terrorism, and the drug problem.

After a brief challenge from Sen. Bob Dole, Vice President Bush went on to earn the 1988 Republican nomination on the first ballot. At the August convention in New Orleans, the Republican nominee selected a young, little-known senator from Indiana, Dan Quayle, as his running mate. Criticized in some party circles as a "wimp," Bush mounted a hard-hitting, negative campaign that overcame the early lead staked out by his Democratic opponent, Massachusetts governor Michael Dukakis. Bush won with 54 percent of the popular vote, giving him a 426 to 111 edge in the electoral vote.

Bush was sworn in as president on January 20, 1989, a cold, clear day, marking the two-hundredth anniversary of George Washington's inauguration. "The American people await action," he said, "and tomorrow the work begins. And I do not mistrust the future; I do not fear what is ahead."

The new president's cabinet appointments included James Baker, his campaign manager, as secretary of state; Richard Cheney, of Wyoming, as secretary of defense; Elizabeth H. Dole, as secretary of labor, and Jack Kemp, as secretary of housing and urban development.

What was ahead was a deficit crisis. "If it weren't for this deficit looming over everything," Bush said "I'd feel like a spring colt. We have to sit down with Congress and hammer out a budget-deficit agreement."

The Bush administration was effective in lowering both inflation and interest rates, but other problems were more intractable. Unemployment rose, and more businesses failed during his term than during any presidency since the Great Depression. A record 10 percent of all Americans qualified for food stamps. And behind it all loomed the inherited budget deficit. With Bush, the annual budget deficit doubled to about $350 billion, which was more than ten times as large as the figure he had promised to deliver by the last year of his four-year term.

In 1990, the president was forced to share with Congress the responsibility for a 1991 budget that included tax increases. In the 1992 election year, Bush apologized for the increases, calling his switch a mistake.

President Bush had to contend, too, with the collapse of the savings and loan industry. The year before he took office, more than two hundred bankrupt savings and loan institutions closed or had to be sold off. These S&Ls had failed because of mismanagement, corruption, or inability to compete in a changed banking environment brought on by deregulation. The bankruptcies depleted insurance funds that guaranteed depositors' savings. To close and sell off the assets of failed institutions the Resolution Trust Corporation was created. Nicholas Brady, secretary of the treasury, estimated the crisis might wipe out as much as 40 percent of the thrift industry. In 1990, the General Accounting Office estimated that the ultimate cost of cleaning up the mess could reach $500 billion.

Well seasoned in international affairs, President Bush showed a firm grasp of foreign policy. In December 1989, Bush ordered the invasion of Panama to capture General Manuel Noriega, who had illegally taken over the leadership of the country. Wanted in Florida on drug trafficking charges, Noriega was brought back to the United States, tried, convicted, and sentenced to forty years in prison. Some five hundred Panamanians were killed in the attack and roughly two thousand civilians were wounded. The invasion was criticized vigorously by both the UN and the Organization of American States.

As Eastern Bloc countries began forsaking communism, Bush enjoyed the highest popularity ratings of any post–World War II president. Bush moved quickly to support the new regimes seeking independence. In July 1991, he and Soviet premier Mikhail Gorbachev declared an end to the arms race by signing the first nuclear arms reduction pact.

On August 2, 1990, Iraq invaded the oil-rich emirate of Kuwait. Six days later, Iraqi president Saddam Hussein's troops had annexed Kuwait as a province of Iraq. President Bush immediately established Operation Desert Shield designed to persuade Hussein to withdraw. Capitalizing on his UN experience and contacts, Bush marshaled the support of most of the world's powers to demand Iraq's retreat. Allied troops and ships took up positions in Saudi Arabia. Bush gained overwhelming support from the American people, determined to back his actions in the Middle East.

When Hussein refused to wilt under the pressure, Operation Desert Shield became Operation Desert Storm. On January 17, 1991, the military offensive began under the leadership of General Norman Schwarzkopf. In the first wave of air strikes, Stealth jets knocked out Iraq's radar defenses, leaving the Allies in control of the skies. Around-the-clock television coverage gave Americans a spectacular view of the enormous technological superiority of the U.S. fighting forces and made instant heroes of General Schwarzkopf and America's chief of staff, General Colin Powell.

General Schwarzkopf launched a powerful ground offensive, involving eight hundred U.S. tanks. Four days later, with Iraqi troops in full flight, President Bush called for a suspension of hostilities. On April 3, the UN Security Council imposed a formal cease-fire, demanding that Iraq pay war reparations, accept the prewar boundary of Kuwait, and permit the elimination of its weapons of mass destruction.

In the aftermath of the quick and stunning Allied victory, President Bush's public approval rating soared to 89 percent, the highest ever recorded by a Gallup Poll. The only problem was that soon grumblings began to spread. Hussein, despite an overwhelming defeat, was still in power.

That year, President Bush, who had previously nominated David Souter of New Hampshire to the Supreme Court, picked a conservative black judge to succeed the retiring Thurgood Marshall, a major leader in the civil rights movement. Both for his political views, unpopular with many of his fellow African Americans, and his personal life, he encountered heavy opposition. Charges of sexual harassment were brought by Anita Hill, a former employee. Nevertheless, after a bitter confirmation battle, Thomas was confirmed by the U.S. Senate, 52 to 48.

In the 1992 election, President Bush faced a surprising challenge within his own party from the conservative columnist and television commentator Patrick Buchanan. Damaged by the attacks, Bush entered his party's nominating convention with his renomination clinched but trailing the Democratic presidential candidate Bill Clinton, governor of Arkansas, and his running mate, Senator Albert Gore of Tennessee. Bush's quest for reelection was further complicated by the feisty Texas billionaire Ross Perot, who was running as an independent.

President Bush's greatest problem in the election proved to be the continuing weakness in the economy, coupled with the breaking of his "read-my-lips" pledge and his failure to remove from power Saddam Hussein, a man he had characterized as a contemporary Hitler. Bush's constant attacks on Clinton's character antagonized many voters who wanted a discussion of the issues. On November 3, 1992, President Bush received only 37 percent of the popular vote, as Perot surprised many by garnering nearly 20 percent. Clinton, with nearly a 5-million-vote edge over the incumbent president, won the electoral vote, 370 to 168.

In ranking Bush twenty-second, poll participants play it safe, placing him in the middle third of American presidents, possibly an admission that they think it too early to evaluate effectively the performance of recent chief executives. His highest mark comes in the Accomplishments and Crisis Management category, probably a tribute to his skillful handling of the international complexities of the Gulf War.

President Bush retired to Houston, Texas, a state where his oldest son, George, was then governor. In his final year in the presidency, Bush could look back on a monumental achievement. "Communism died this year," he said. "By the grace of God, America won the Cold War."

BILL CLINTON

1993–
42ND PRESIDENT

OVERALL RANKING: 23

★

Leadership Qualities: 26
Accomplishments and Crisis Management: 23
Political Skill: 20
Appointments: 24
Character and Integrity: 38

Bill Clinton . . . knows adversity. . . . And with each new challenge he has grown wiser and stronger, as he demonstrated with his remarkable resiliency. . . .

—Mario Cuomo

At the 1988 Democratic National Convention, Arkansas governor Bill Clinton was picked to place in nomination the man who had already clinched the honor. In his nationally televised introduction of Governor Michael Dukakis of Massachusetts Clinton rambled on for thirty-three minutes. His speech was so poorly received that his biggest cheer from weary delegates came when he spoke the magic words, "In conclusion. . . ."

For a man who would run for president four years later, it was a terrible introduction to the American public. But he made a quick adjustment. The next night, Bill Clinton appeared on *The Tonight Show* and good-naturedly kidded himself about his performance. He was back on track again. Over the years he showed so amazing an ability to bounce back from adversity that he was labeled the Comeback Kid.

In early 1992, leading Democratic contenders decided against challenging George Bush, whose approval ratings had soared following the Gulf War. Adversity plagued Governor Clinton's campaign both for the Democratic nomination and then for the presidency, but when the votes were counted in November 1992, he had proved again to be the Comeback Kid. As Governor Cuomo said, he "knows adversity."

America's forty-second president was born William Jefferson Blythe, 4th, on August 19, 1946, in Hope, Arkansas. Before Bill was born, his father, a traveling salesman, was killed in an automobile accident in Sikeston, Missouri. After his mother, Virginia, married Roger Clinton, her son's name became Bill Clinton.

That marriage was a stormy one. During alcoholic rages Roger Clinton beat his wife, Bill, and Bill's smaller half-brother, Roger. By the time he was fourteen, Bill was bigger than his stepfather. One night he delivered an ultimatum to the elder Clinton, demanding he stop the abuse of his mother and Roger. From that day on, there was no more physical violence in the Clinton household.

Bill Clinton attended Georgetown University, which offered a strong curriculum in foreign relations. He was elected class president in both his freshman and sophomore years. In 1968, Clinton graduated from Georgetown with a degree in international affairs and then went to graduate school at Oxford University in England on a prestigious Rhodes scholarship.

At Oxford, Clinton joined with Americans in England in peace demonstrations against the Vietnam War. After a U.S. Army draft examination in London, he was classified 1-A. Clinton signed a letter of intent to join the Army Reserve Officers Training Corps at the University of Arkansas, which removed him from the draft pool. After second thoughts, he decided to return instead to Oxford and take his chances with the draft. He drew a high number in the draft lottery, thus minimizing his chances of being called for military service.

In 1970, Clinton accepted a scholarship to Yale University Law School, where he met a fellow law student named Hillary Rodham. The daughter of wealthy Chicago parents, she was raised in a staunchly Republican family and had in 1964 supported the conservative GOP candidacy of Barry Goldwater. By the time she met Clinton, she had become a Democrat and was vehemently against the war in Vietnam. In 1975, they were married in Fayetteville, Arkansas. The Clintons had one child, Chelsea, named after one of her parents' favorite songs, "Chelsea Morning."

Clinton ran for Congress in 1974 in a heavily Republican district. He lost a close race to a four-term congressman, but in 1976, he was elected state attorney general. He established a reputation as a consumer advocate and a strong supporter of environmental protection. In 1978, the United States Junior Chamber of Commerce named him one of the Ten Outstanding Young Men in the country.

Clinton followed his success as attorney general with a successful run for governor in 1978. At thirty-two, he had become the youngest governor in the United States. Surrounded by other energetic, bright, and inexperienced young people, he tried to push through a large agenda that included tax increases to pay for improved education and better roads. Criticism followed, too, because his wife continued to use her maiden name in her law career. He was defeated in the November election by a little-known savings and loan executive.

For the next two years he practiced law in Little Rock, analyzing the reasons for his defeat and planning his comeback. In 1982, he asked the people of Arkansas to give him another chance. "I made a young man's mistake," he said. "I had an agenda a mile long that you couldn't achieve in a four-year term, let alone a two-year term." The people of his home state gave him another chance, electing him governor in 1982, 1984, 1986, and 1990.

He had learned from his errors, but there was one mistake he forgot when he became president—the problems an ambitious agenda can create.

As governor, Clinton's top priority was education. Job growth outpaced the national average and modest gains were made in health care. More women and African Americans were moved into higher state offices. In a 1986 *Newsweek* poll of governors he was ranked the fifth most effective governor in the United States. By 1991, his fellow governors ranked him first.

Clinton was active in the Democratic Leadership Council, a group of moderate Democrats striving to move the party toward the center of the political spectrum. On October 3, 1991, Clinton announced he would run for president.

His road to the nomination was a rocky one, complicated by attacks on his Vietnam War stance and by the sudden appearance of a woman named Gennifer Flowers, an Arkansas state employee and a nightclub singer, who claimed to have had a twelve-year affair with the governor. To try to lessen the political damage, both Bill and Hillary Clinton appeared on the television news show *Sixty Minutes*. Admitting they had had marital problems that had been resolved, they asked the nation to respect their privacy.

Clinton survived the attacks to win the Democratic nomination by a huge margin on the first ballot. He selected as his running mate Senator Albert Gore from the neighboring southern state of Tennessee. As expected, the Republicans renominated the incumbent team of President Bush and Vice President Quayle. Meanwhile, the Texas billionaire Ross Perot announced he would run as an independent.

Bush struggled against a weak economy, and both other candidates hammered Bush hard on the problems the huge Reaganomics deficit had created. Clinton advocated a public works program to stimulate the economy and a small tax decrease for the middle class balanced against an increase in the tax for the richest 2 percent of all Americans. He also called for welfare reform, a cut in defense spending, and reform in the nation's health-care system. Bush depended heavily on negative campaigning as he had against Dukakis in 1988. This approach backfired during the second of the three televised debates when the audience insisted the candidates stick to issues. In November, Clinton, who captured 43 percent of the popular vote, won the electoral vote by a large margin, 370 to 168.

President Clinton had campaigned as a Washington outsider. He brought new faces into his cabinet, among them Janet Reno of Miami, Florida, the first woman attorney general; former Arizona governor Bruce Babbitt as secretary of the interior; and Robert Reich as secretary of labor. Reich, a Harvard professor of political economy, was an advocate of training and education programs for the American workforce, an important element in the new president's economic plan. More familiar names included Senator Lloyd Bentsen as secretary of the treasury; Les Aspin, chairman of the House Armed Services Committee, as secretary of defense; and Warren Christopher, who had served in both the Johnson and Carter administrations, as secretary of state. In his first year in office his Supreme Court nominee, Judge Ruth Bader Ginsburg, of the U.S. Court of Appeals for the District of Columbia, was approved by the Senate, 96 to 3.

The new president got off to a slow start. One of his first acts was to announce his intention to lift the ban on homosexuals in the military. The firestorm that erupted took the administration's attention away from the economy. It was not until July that a compromise was reached, which became known as the "don't ask, don't tell, don't pursue" policy.

Once Clinton took office he discovered just how serious the federal budget deficit was. His goal was to create a budget that would reduce the deficit by $500 billion. Republicans voted as a bloc against his budget, and there was difficulty balancing the demands of the liberal and moderate wings of the Democratic party. The final budget combined $255 billion in spending cuts and $241 billion in new taxes for a total reduction of $496 billion— just short of the $500 billion cut the president had wanted. The vote was extremely close, 218 to 216 in the House, and 51 to 50 in the Senate, with the vice president casting the deciding vote.

President Clinton won another close vote when he persuaded Congress to approve the North American Free Trade Agreement (NAFTA) negotiated with the governments of Mexico and Canada during the Bush administration. Unfortunately for the president, he had used up much political capital in his first year, leaving him weakened for the medical care battle that lay ahead. He named his wife head of a task force to develop a less costly and more broadly based health-care system. The Democrats were divided in their approach to health care; the Republicans simply wanted to block any reforms. The public was further confused by the Health Insurance Industry Association's multimillion-dollar "Harry and Louise" television advertising campaign's attack on the Clinton plan. At the end of his second year in office the president had still not managed to create a workable new health-care program.

Clinton, however, enjoyed success with his crime bill, which funded more police officers, more prison cells, banned assault weapons, and placed controls over handgun purchases. He scored impressive victories, too, in foreign affairs in Haiti and North Korea. The Rev. Jean Bertrand Aristide, Haiti's duly elected president, had been ousted in a military coup followed by continuing political violence. After Clinton announced he was sending an invasion force backed by the UN to Haiti, a negotiating team headed by former president Jimmy Carter and former chairman of the Joint Chiefs of Staff Gen. Colin Powell negotiated a peaceful settlement. Next, President Clinton called on Carter to diffuse a potentially dangerous situation in North Korea where the Communist government was refusing to allow international nuclear inspections.

Clinton has been plagued throughout his term by continuing personal attacks upon himself and his wife. In 1979, long before he became president, Bill and Hillary Clinton had been involved in a failed Arkansas land development called Whitewater. In 1993, Vince Foster, a longtime Clinton friend and White House aide, committed suicide. Shortly after his death, a Whitewater file in his office was removed. This led to the appointment of a special prosecutor to investigate possible involvement by the Clintons in the Whitewater case.

The Whitewater matter and continuing character attacks, many political analysts believe, led to an impressive victory by the Republicans in the congressional elections in the fall of 1994. In gaining control of both houses of Congress for the first time since 1953, the Republicans were led by Georgia representative Newt Gingrich, who gained widespread support for his party with his Contract with America, a pledge from candidates to introduce specific conservative legislation into Congress. Senator Robert Dole became the Senate majority leader and Gingrich Speaker of the House.

Excesses by the new Republican majorities began to alarm many Americans, who were particularly appalled by the arrogance of Gingrich. As the president moved to the center of the political spectrum, his popularity began to recover. A healthy economy strengthened him further by the time the November 1996 presidential election was held. The Comeback Kid won again, garnering 379 electoral votes to 159 for the Republican candidate, the now-retired senator Dole. Clinton became the first Democrat elected to a second term in six decades.

Like Bush, Clinton is placed in the middle range, as poll participants feel the time is just too short for a true historical judgment. Clinton's highest mark comes in the Political Skill category, his lowest in the Character and Integrity category. At thirty-eighth, he finished just ahead of Reagan, Harding, and Nixon.

In the fall of 1995, when President Clinton's approval ratings began to rise again, Sen. Harris Wofford of Pennsylvania said, "He has been through the hottest fire American politics has ever had to test somebody. And he's come out like fine-tempered Pennsylvania steel."

PICTURE ACKNOWLEDGMENTS

——— ★ ———

Dwight D. Eisenhower Library: Dwight D. Eisenhower
Florida State Archives: Andrew Jackson
Herbert Hoover Presidential Library: Herbert Hoover
John F. Kennedy Library: John F. Kennedy
Library of Congress: George Washington, James
Madison, Benjamin Harrison,
Warren G. Harding, Calvin
Coolidge, Lyndon B. Johnson,
Richard M. Nixon, Gerald R.
Ford, James Earl Carter,
George Bush, Bill Clinton.

Ronald Reagan Library: Ronald Reagan
U.S. Army Signal Corps: Franklin D. Roosevelt
U.S. Army/Courtesy
Harry S. Truman Library: Harry S. Truman

APPENDIX

—— ★ ——

PARTICIPANTS IN PRESIDENTIAL POLL

Historians, political scientists and other informed people who participated in the Ridings-McIver Presidential Poll are listed alphabetically with their university or other affiliation.

Abbott, Frank W., Sul Ross State University, Texas
Abrahamson, James L., Campbell University, North Carolina
Achenbaum, W. Andrew, University of Michigan
Alexander, Thomas G., Brigham Young University, Utah
Allen, Howard W., Southern Illinois University at Carbondale
Allitt, Patrick, Emory University, Georgia
Allured, Janet, McNeese State University, Louisiana
Anbinder, Tyler, University of Wyoming
Andrew, John, Franklin & Marshall College, Pennsylvania
Appleton, Thomas H., Kentucky Historical Society
Aurand, Harold W., Jr., University of Minnesota
Bailey, Jackson H., Earlham College, Indiana
Baker, James F., Central State University, Oklahoma
Bakken, Gordon Morris, California State University at Fullerton
Baldrige, Edwin R., Muhlenberg College, Pennsylvania
Bannan, Helen, Florida Atlantic University
Banner-Haley, Charles Pete T., Colgate University, New York
Barnhart, Michael A., State University of New York at Stony Brook
Barrett, Glen, Boise State University, Idaho
Batman, Richard, San Francisco State University, California
Baum, Dale, Texas A & M University
Baur, John E., California State University at Northridge
Baxter, Maurice, Indiana University
Baylen, J. O., Regents' Professor Emeritus, United Kingdom
Beach, Frank L., University of San Francisco, California
Bearss, Sara B., Virginia Historical Society
Becker, Carl M., Wright State University, Ohio
Becker, Robert A., Louisiana State University
Bellesiles, Michael, Emory University, Georgia
Bennett, Edward M., Washington State University
Bensel, Richard F., New School For Social Research, New York
Berg, S. Carol, St. John's University-College of St. Benedict, Minnesota

Berger, Henry W., Washington University, Missouri
Bergquist, James M., Villanova University, Pennsylvania
Bernard, Richard M., Bethany College, West Virginia
Bernard, William, retired engineer, Delray Beach, Florida
Bernhard, Jim, arts management consultant, Houston, Texas
Bernstein, Irving, University of California at Los Angeles
Berwanger, Eugene H., Colorado State University
Bias, Charles, Marshall University, West Virginia
Bigelow, Bruce, Butler University, Indiana
Bilhartz, Terry, Sam Houston State University, Texas
Billias, George A., Clark University, Massachusetts
Billington, Monroe, New Mexico State University
Bindas, Kenneth J., West Georgia College
Bingham, Edwin R., University of Oregon
Bingham, Marjorie, St. Louis Park Senior High School, Minnesota
Birdsall, Richard D., Connecticut College
Birkner, Michael, Gettysburg College, Pennsylvania
Birnbaum, Lucia Chiavola, Stanford University, California
Biskupski, Mieczyslaw B., St. John Fisher College, New York
Blackburn, Charles B., Appalachian State University, North Carolina
Blantz, Thomas, University of Notre Dame, Indiana
Blaser, Kent, Wayne State College, Nebraska
Blayney, Michael, Wayne State College, Nebraska
Bloom, Alexander, Wheaton College, Massachusetts
Blumberg, Barbara, Pace University, New York
Bodnar, John, Indiana University
Bolt, Robert, Calvin College, Michigan
Bolton, Charles C., University of Southern Mississippi
Born, John D., Jr., Wichita State University, Kansas
Borne, Lawrence R., Northern Kentucky University
Boyd, Steven R., University of Texas at San Antonio
Brandes, Ray, University of San Diego, California
Broadwater, Jeff, Mississippi State University
Brown, Jeffrey P., New Mexico State University
Brown, Katherine L., Mary Baldwin College, Virginia
Brown, Norman D., University of Texas at Austin
Brown, Richard D., University of Connecticut at Storrs
Brown, Ronald C., Southwest Texas State University
Browne, Blaine T., Broward Community College North, Florida
Bruce, Robert V., Boston University, Massachusetts
Bruchey, Stuart, University of Maine
Bryan, Charles F., Jr., Virginia Historical Society
Buckley, Thomas H., University of Tulsa, Oklahoma
Buenger, Walter L., Texas A & M University, Texas
Buenker, John D., University of Wisconsin at Parkside
Buice, David, Louisiana Tech University
Burdick, Walter, Elmhurst College, Illinois
Burg, B. Richard, Arizona State University
Burner, David, State University of New York at Stony Brook
Burns, Helen M., retired professor, Baltimore, Maryland
Burns, Michael M., Bishop McDevitt High School, Pennsylvania

Burton, David H., Saint Joseph's University, Pennsylvania
Buzanski, Peter M., San Jose State University, California
Byrne, Frank L., Kent State University, Ohio
Cady, Darrel, Western Illinois University
Callcott, George H., University of Maryland
Camfield, Thomas, Sam Houston State University, Texas
Campbell, Randolph B., University of North Texas
Campbell, Thomas M., Florida State University
Canon, David, Duke University, North Carolina
Cantor, Louis, Indiana University-Purdue University at Fort Wayne
Cantrell, Gregg, Sam Houston State University, Texas
Cardoso, Jack J., State University College at Buffalo, New York
Carlson, Lewis H., Western Michigan University
Carlson, Paul H., Texas Tech University
Carmical, Oline, Jr., Cumberland College, Kentucky
Carneal, Thomas W., Northwest Missouri State University
Caron, Simone M., College of William and Mary, Virginia
Carpenter, Gerald, Niagara University, New York
Carroll, John M., Lamar University, Texas
Cashin, Edward J., Augusta College, Georgia
Cassell, Frank A., University of Wisconsin at Milwaukee
Cassimere, Raphael, Jr., University of New Orleans, Louisiana
Castel, Albert, Western Michigan University
Castle, David S., Lamar University, Texas
Catton, William B., Middlebury College, Vermont
Cayton, Andrew, Miami University, Ohio
Chambers, Clarke A., University of Minnesota at Twin Cities
Champagne, Raymond W., University of Scranton, Pennsylvania
Charlton, Thomas L., Baylor University, Texas
Cherny, Robert W., San Francisco State University, California
Chesson, Michael B., University of Massachusetts at Boston
Christensen, Lawrence O., University of Missouri at Rolla
Ciardiello, Angelo, Iona College, New York
Clanton, O. Gene, Washington State University
Clark, Michael D., University of New Orleans, Louisiana
Claypool, James C., Northern Kentucky University
Clayton, James L., University of Utah
Clem, Alan, University of South Dakota
Clemens, Paul, Rutgers University at New Brunswick, New Jersey
Clement, Priscilla Ferguson, Penn State University at Delaware County,
    Pennsylvania
Clements, Kendrick A., University of South Carolina
Clowse, Converse D., University of North Carolina at Greensboro
Cobbs, Elizabeth A., University of San Diego, California
Coben, Stanley, University of California at Los Angeles
Colburn, David R., University of Florida
Collier, Christopher, University of Connecticut at Storrs
Collins, Michael L., Midwestern State University, Texas
Conkin, Paul K., Vanderbilt University, Tennessee
Conlin, Joseph R., California State University at Chico
Conrad, David E., Southern Illinois University at Carbondale

Contosta, David R., Chestnut Hill College, Pennsylvania
Conway, P., State University of New York at Oneonta
Cooper, Patricia, Drexel University, Pennsylvania
Corley, Roger W., Northwest Missouri State University
Cornish, Rory T., Whitman College, Washington
Cottrell, Robert, California State University at Chico
Courtwright, David T., University of North Florida
Couvares, Francis G., Amherst College, Massachusetts
Cox, Thomas R., San Diego State University, California
Coy, Richard D., University of Wisconsin at Eau Claire
Cramer, Richard S., San Jose State University, California
Crane, Theodore R., University of Denver, Colorado
Crane, Virginia J., University of Wisconsin at Oshkosh
Crawford, Alastair T., Clarion University of Pennsylvania
Cresswell, Stephen, West Virginia Wesleyan College
Croak, Thomas M., DePaul University, Illinois
Crocker, Helen B., Western Kentucky University
Crouch, Barry A., Gallaudet University, District of Columbia
Crow, Jeffrey J., North Carolina Division of Archives and History
Crunden, Robert M., University of Texas at Austin
Cummins, Light T., Austin College, Texas
Curl, Donald W., Florida Atlantic University
Currey, Cecil B., University of South Florida
Curry, Earl R., Hope College, Michigan
Curtis, George H., University of Missouri at Kansas City
Cutler, Wayne, University of Tennessee at Knoxville
D'Innocenzo, Michael, Hofstra University, New York
Dallek, Robert, University of California at Los Angeles
Danbom, David B., North Dakota State University
Daniels, Bruce C., University of Winnipeg, Canada
Davidson, Roger H., University of Maryland
De Angelis, Joseph, Broward County Library, Florida
De Conde, Alexander, University of California at Santa Barbara
Dekmejian, R. Thair, University of California at Los Angeles
Dennison, George M., University of Montana
Dethloff, Henry C., Texas A & M University
Devine, Michael J., Illinois Historic Preservation Agency
Dierenfield, Bruce J., Canisius College, New York
Dillon, Rodney E., Jr., Broward County Historical Commission, Florida
Divine, Robert A., University of Texas at Austin
Dobson, John, Iowa State University of Science & Technology
Dorsett, Lyle, Wheaton College, Illinois
Doutrich, Paul, York College, Pennsylvania
Drake, Frederick C., Brock University, Canada
Drake, Richard B., Berea College, Kentucky
Dufour, Ronald P., Rhode Island College
Dulaney, W. Martin, University of Texas at Arlington
Duncan, John D., Armstrong State College, Georgia
Dunkak, Harry, Iona College, New York
Dyson, Lowell, United States Department of Agriculture, District of Columbia
Eagles, Keith, University of Waterloo, Canada

Ecke, Melvin W., Georgia State University
Eckert, Edward K., St. Bonaventure University, New York
Eckes, Alfred, Ohio University
Edmonds, Anthony O., Ball State University, Indiana
Edsforth, Ronald, Massachusetts Institute of Technology
Edwards, Lillie J., DePaul University, Illinois
Effland, Anne B. W., United States Department of Agriculture, District of Columbia
Eidson, William G., Ball State University, Indiana
Elkins, Alfred, independent scholar, Bronx, New York
Ellis, Richard E., State University of New York at Buffalo
Ellis, William E., Eastern Kentucky University
Emley, Glenn A., Indiana University-Purdue University at Fort Wayne
Engelmann, Larry, San Jose State University, California
Erickson, Nancy L., Erskine College, South Carolina
Erlebacher, Albert, DePaul University, Illinois
Ernst, Joseph A., York University, Canada
Esposito, David M., Bucknell University, Pennsylvania
Esposito, Jacqueline R., Penn State University, Pennsylvania
Essin, Emmett M., East Tennessee State University
Esslinger, Dean, Towson State University, Maryland
Etulian, Richard W., University of New Mexico
Everman, Henry E., Eastern Kentucky University
Fallaw, W. Robert, Washington College, Maryland
Falzone, Vincent J., University of Texas at Tyler
Farrell, David R., University of Guelph, Canada
Fass, Paula S., University of California at Berkeley
Feinman, Ronald L., Broward Community College South, Florida
Fellman, Michael, Simon Fraser University, Canada
Felt, Jeremy P., University of Vermont
Fenwick, Millicent, retired United States congresswoman, New Jersey
Ferling, John, West Georgia College
Farrell, Henry C., Jr., East Carolina University, North Carolina
Ferris, Norman B., Middle Tennessee State University
Findling, John E., Indiana University Southeast
Fischer, Roger A., University of Minnesota at Duluth
Flynt, Wayne, Auburn University, Alabama
Folsom, Burt, Murray State University, Kentucky
Ford, Linda G., Keene State College, New Hampshire
Forgie, George B., University of Texas at Austin
Formisano, Ronald P., University of Florida
Foster, Richard Henry, Idaho State University
Fowler, William, Jr., Northeastern University, Massachusetts
Frank, Carl M., Edinboro University of Pennsylvania
Fredrickson, George M., Stanford University, California
Fried, Richard M., University of Illinois at Chicago
Frost, Richard, Colgate University, New York
Fuller, Justin, University of Montevallo, Alabama
Furgol, Edward M., Naval Historical Center, District of Columbia
Gabel, Christopher R., United States Army Command and General Staff College, Kansas
Gagliano, Joseph A., Loyola University of Chicago, Illinois

Gallay, Alan, Western Washington University
Geer, John, Arizona State University
Geissler, Suzanne B., Upsala College, New Jersey
Gelfand, Lawrence E., University of Iowa
Gerber, David, State University of New York at Buffalo
Gifford, Jack J., United States Army Command and General Staff College, Kansas
Giglio, James N., Southwest Missouri State University
Gildrie, Richard P., Austin Peay State University, Tennessee
Gillette, Howard F., Jr., George Washington University, District of Columbia
Gilley, Billy H., Louisiana Tech University
Gilroy, Stephen, Manhasset High School, New York
Glass, Brent, Pennsylvania Historical and Museum Commission
Glassberg, David, University of Massachusetts
Glatthaar, Joseph T., University of Houston, Texas
Glen, John M., Ball State University, Indiana
Godbold, E. Stanley, Mississippi State University
Goings, Kenneth W., Rhodes College, Tennessee
Goldberg, Joyce S., University of Texas at Arlington
Gomolak, Louis S., Southwest Texas State University
Goodstein, Anita S., University of the South, Tennessee
Goodwin, Ralph W., East Texas State University
Gordon, Jean, University of North Carolina at Greensboro
Gould, Lewis L., University of Texas at Austin
Gowaskie, Joseph M., Rider College, New Jersey
Gragg, Larry D., University of Missouri at Rolla
Grant, Curtis R., California State University at Stanislaus
Grant, H. Roger, University of Akron, Ohio
Grantham, Dewey W., Vanderbilt University, Tennessee
Graves, Gregory R., California State University at Northridge
Gray, Ralph D., Indiana University-Purdue University at Indianapolis
Graybar, Lloyd, Eastern Kentucky University
Green, George N., University of Texas at Arlington
Greenberg, Cheryl, Trinity College, Connecticut
Greenberg, Karen J., Bard College, New York
Greene, Jack P., University of California at Irving
Gregory, Ross, Western Michigan University
Grinde, Donald A., Jr., University of California at Riverside
Grivas, Theodore, California State University at Sonoma
Grob, Gerald N., Rutgers University, New Jersey
Gross, Donald A., University of Kentucky
Gross, Jimmie F., Armstrong State College, Georgia
Grossbart, Stephen R., University of Florida
Grundy, Martha Paxson, Case Western Reserve University, Ohio
Guarneri, Carl, Saint Mary's College of California
Gugin, David A., University of Evansville, Indiana
Guidorizzi, Richard P., Iona College, New York
Gustafson, Merlin, Kansas State University
Guy, Duane F., West Texas State University
Hahn, Dan F., Florida Atlantic University
Hale, Jon F., University of Oklahoma
Hale, Myron Q., Purdue University, Indiana

Hall, Mitchell, Central Michigan University
Halperin, Rick, Southern Methodist University, Texas
Haney, Richard C., University of Wisconsin at Whitewater
Harrell, David, Auburn University, Alabama
Harrington, Richard M., Virginia State Library and Archives
Harris, Bob, Heritage Park, Pinellas County Historical Museum, Florida
Harris, Dennis E., Sonoma State University, California
Harris, William C., North Carolina State University
Harrison, Richard A., Pomona College, California
Harstad, Peter T., Indiana Historical Society
Hartnett, James R., York College of Pennsylvania
Hauser, Robert, Penn State University at McKeesport, Pennsylvania
Hawes, Joseph M., Memphis State University, Tennessee
Hawks, Graham P., Western Michigan University
Hawley, Ellis W., University of Iowa
Hay, Robert P., Marquette University, Wisconsin
Healy, David, University of Wisconsin at Milwaukee
Heidler, David S., Salisbury State University, Maryland
Heim, Keith M., Murray State University, Kentucky
Heim, Virginia H., Southern College of Technology, Georgia
Heintze, Michael R., Clemson University, South Carolina
Henderson, Dwight F., University of Texas at San Antonio
Hendrickson, Kenneth E., Jr., Midwestern State University, Texas
Henig, Gerald S., California State University at Hayward
Hevener, John W., Ohio State University at Lima
Higham, Robin, Kansas State University
Hill, Patricia Evridge, Lander College, South Carolina
Hobbs, Joseph P., North Carolina State University
Hodges, James Andrew, College of Wooster, Ohio
Hoffmann, William S., Saginaw Valley State University, Michigan
Hoff-Wilson, Joan, Indiana University
Holbo, Paul S., University of Oregon
Holley, I. B., Jr., Duke University, North Carolina
Hoover, Dwight W., Ball State University, Indiana
Hopkins, George E., Western Illinois University
Horne, Gerald C., University of California at Santa Barbara
Horowitz, David A., Portland State University, Oregon
House, Lewis, Southern Connecticut State University
Howe, Daniel, University of California at Los Angeles
Howland, Nina D., United States Department of State, District of Columbia
Hoxie, R. Gordon, Center for the Study of Presidency, New York
Hoye, Timothy, Texas Women's University
Hubbard, Preston J., Austin Peay State University, Tennessee
Huebel, H. R., Southern Connecticut State University
Hughes, C. Alvin, Austin Peay State University, Tennessee
Humphrey, Carol Sue, Oklahoma Baptist University
Hunt, James B., Whitworth College, Washington
Hunter, Leslie, Texas A & I University
Huston, John W., United States Naval Academy, Maryland
Imholte, John Quinn, University of Minnesota at Morris
Immerman, Richard, University of Hawaii at Manoa

Ingham, John N., University of Toronto, Canada
Ireland, Robert M., University of Kentucky
Isaac, Paul E., Lamar University, Texas
Isaacs, Joakim, Marymount College at Tarrytown, New York
Isetti, Ronald E., Saint Mary's College of California
Israel, Jerry, Simpson College, Iowa
Isserman, Maurice, Hamilton College, New York
Iverson, Joan, State University of New York at Oneonta
Jackson, Kenneth, Columbia University, New York
Jamieson, Perry D., Office of Air Force History, District of Columbia
Jensen, Richard, University of Illinois at Chicago
Johannes, John R., Marquette University, Wisconsin
Johansen, Dorothy, Reed College, Oregon
Johnson, Curtis D., Mount Saint Mary's College, Maryland
Johnson, John W., University of Northern Iowa
Johnson, Judith R., Wichita State University, Kansas
Jones, Allen W., Auburn University, Alabama
Jones, Daniel P., New Jersey State Archives
Jones, Helen F., St. Bonaventure University, New York
Jones, Landis, University of Louisville, Kentucky
Jones, Richard, Russell Sage College, New York
Jordan, Laylon Wayne, College of Charleston, South Carolina
Juricek, John T., Emory University, Georgia
Karamanski, Ted, Loyola University of Chicago, Illinois
Kazin, Michael, American University, District of Columbia
Keenan, James P., III, Montclair State College, New Jersey
Kehl, James A., University of Pittsburgh, Pennsylvania
Keller, Clair W., Iowa State University
Keller, Frances Richardson, San Francisco State University, California
Kellerman, Barbara, George Washington University, District of Columbia
Kelly, James C., Virginia Historical Society
Kennedy, David M., Stanford University, California
Kennedy, Michael J., University of Wisconsin at Whitewater
Kennedy, Susan Estabrook, Virginia Commonwealth University
Kern, Louis J., Hofstra University, New York
Kerr, James Richard, Southern Illinois University at Edwardsville
Ketcham, Ralph, Syracuse University, New York
Keuchel, Edward F., Florida State University
Kindig, Everett W., Midwestern State University, Texas
Kirkendall, Richard S., University of Washington
Klein, Milton M., University of Tennessee at Knoxville
Klein, Stanley B., Long Island University, C.W. Post Campus, New York
Klement, Frank L., Marquette University, Wisconsin
Klonoski, James, University of Oregon
Klotter, James C., Kentucky Historical Society
Knee, Stuart, College of Charleston, South Carolina
Knox, J. Wendell, University of Texas at Arlington
Kocis, Robert, University of Scranton, Pennsylvania
Konig, David T., Washington University in St. Louis, Missouri
Kornbluh, Mark, Washington University in St. Louis, Missouri
Kousser, J. Morgan, California Institute of Technology,

Kraig, Beth, Pacific Lutheran University, Washington
Kremm, Diane Neal, Central State University, Oklahoma
Krenn, Michael L., University of Miami, Florida
Kukla, Jon, Historic New Orleans Collection, Louisiana
Kumor, Georgia, Cleveland High School, Washington
Kuroda, Tad, Skidmore College, New York
Kuzniewski, Anthony J., Holy Cross College, Massachusetts
Labbe, Ronald M., University of Southwestern Louisiana
LaFeber, Walter F., Cornell University, New York
Lambert, C. Roger, Arkansas State University
Landers, Helen, Broward County Historical Commission, Florida
Langworthy, Carol DeBoer, College of St. Catherine, Minnesota
Lanier, Osmos, Jr., Armstrong State University, Georgia
Larkin, John A., State University of New York at Buffalo
Larsen, Lawrence H., University of Missouri at Kansas City
Lass, William E., Mankato State University, Minnesota
Lee, David, Western Kentucky University
Lee, J. Edward, University of North Carolina
Lee, Jean B., University of Wisconsin at Madison
Lehmann, Terry J., Angelo State University, Texas
LeLoup, Lance T., University of Missouri at St. Louis
Lemons, J. Stanley, Rhode Island College
Levstik, Frank, Kentucky Department for Libraries and Archives
Levy, Peter, York College, Pennsylvania
Lewis, Gene D., University of Cincinnati, Ohio
Liddle, William D., Southwest Texas State University
Linden, Glenn, Southern Methodist University, Texas
Lindgren, James M., State University of New York at Plattsburgh
Little, John E., Princeton University, New Jersey
Litwack, Leon F., University of California at Berkeley
Livingston, Jeffery C., California State University at Chico
Logsdon, Joseph, University of New Orleans, Louisiana
Longenecker, George, Norwich University, Vermont
Lotchin, Roger W., University of North Carolina at Chapel Hill
Lovin, Hugh T., Boise State University, Idaho
Lowe, Richard, University of North Texas
Lowe, William C., Mount St. Clare College, Iowa
Lowther, Larry, Central Washington University
Lozier, John W., Bethany College, West Virginia
Lucas, M. Philip, Cornell College, Iowa
Lugar, Richard G., United States Senator, Indiana
Lytle, Mark H., Bard College, New York
Mackey, Howard, Lamar University, Texas
Mackey, Thomas C., Kansas State University
Main, Gloria L., University of Colorado at Boulder
Manson, J. Marilyn, Kansas State University
Margulies, Herbert F., University of Hawaii at Manoa
Marszalek, John F., Mississippi State University
Marten, James, Marquette University, Wisconsin
Martin, James Kirby, University of Houston, Texas
Martin, Thomas S., Sinclair Community College, Ohio

Massmann, John, St. Cloud State University, Minnesota
Mathias, Frank F., University of Dayton, Ohio
Matray, James, New Mexico State University
Matthews, Frederick H., York University, Canada
Mayer, Michael S., University of Montana
Mazzie, Mark G., Arizona State University
McAdams, John, Marquette University, Wisconsin
McAfee, Ward M., California State University at San Bernardino
McCardell, John, Middlebury College, Vermont
McCarthy, Eugene J., former United States Senator, Minnesota
McClung, John B., Pepperdine University, California
McCormick, Richard L., Rutgers University, New Jersey
McCroskey, Vista K., Southwest Texas State University
McDonald, Archie P., Stephen F. Austin State University, Texas
McDonald, Forrest, University of Alabama
McElligott, John F., Eastern Illinois University
McIver, Stuart, author, Lighthouse Point, Florida
McKenna, Marian C., University of Calgary, Canada
McKinney, Gordon B., National Endowment for the Humanities, District of
    Columbia
McLoughlin, William G., Jr., Brown University, Rhode Island
McPherson, James, Princeton University, New Jersey
McWilliams, John C., Penn State University, Du Bois Campus, Pennsylvania
Melendy, H. Brett, San Jose State University, California
Menk, Patricia H., Mary Baldwin College, Virginia
Merrill, Dennis, University of Missouri at Kansas City
Meyer, Donald, Wesleyan University, Connecticut
Meyer, Howard N., Columbia University, New York
Mickel, Ronald E., University of Wisconsin at Eau Claire
Middleton, Stephen, North Carolina State University
Miller, Daniel R., Calvin College, Michigan
Miller, Glenn E., Franklin and Marshall College, Pennsylvania
Miller, Lynn H., Temple University, Pennsylvania
Miller, Randall M., Saint Joseph's University, Pennsylvania
Miller, Sally M., University of the Pacific, California
Miller, Worth Robert, Southwest Missouri State University
Moody, Bradley, Auburn University at Montgomery, Alabama
Moore, James T., Virginia Commonwealth University
Moore, Newell S., Middle Tennessee State University
Moore, William Howard, University of Wyoming
Morgan, H. Wayne, University of Oklahoma
Morice, Joseph R., Duquesne University, Pennsylvania
Morse, Andrew N., Pace University, New York
Morton, Joseph C., Northeastern Illinois University
Moses, Norton H., Eastern Montana College
Muir, Malcolm, Jr., Austin Peay State University, Tennessee
Muller, H. Nicholas, III, State Historical Society of Wisconsin
Mullins, William H., Oklahoma Baptist University
Murphy, Frederick I., Western Kentucky University
Murphy, Paul L., University of Minnesota
Mutersbaugh, Bert, Eastern Kentucky University

Myers, John L., State University of New York at Plattsburgh
Myres, Sandra L., University of Texas at Arlington
Nall, Garry L., West Texas State University
Nash, Michael, Hagley Museum and Library, Delaware
Nelson, Anna K., American University, District of Columbia
Nickell, Frank, Southeast Missouri State University
Noe, Kenneth W., West Georgia College
Noll, Mark, Wheaton College, Illinois
Nugent, Helen Jean McClelland, Franklin College of Indiana
Nybakken, Elizabeth I., Mississippi State University
O'Connell, Daniel J., Iona College, New York
Odom, E. Dale, University of North Texas
Olwell, Robert, Mount Saint Mary's College, Maryland
O'Neil, Floyd A., University of Utah
O'Neill, William L., Rutgers University, New Jersey
Ostrower, Gary B., Alfred University, New York
O'Toole, James M., University of Massachusetts at Boston
Owens, Estelle, Wayland Baptist University, Texas
Pacheco, Josephine F., George Mason University, Virginia
Parker, Joseph B., University of Southern Mississippi
Parsons, Judith, Sul Ross State University, Texas
Pastor, Robert, Emory University, Georgia
Paterson, Thomas G., University of Connecticut at Storrs
Patterson, Robert, Armstrong State College, Georgia
Paulsen, George E., Arizona State University
Paz, Denis, Clemson University, South Carolina
Peek, Ralph L., University of Florida
Peltier, David P., Ohio Northern University
Penick, James, Jr., University of Alabama at Birmingham
Perlman, Mark, University of Pittsburgh, Pennsylvania
Peskin, Allan, Cleveland State University, Ohio
Peters, Donald F., Niagara University, New York
Peterson, F. Ross, Utah State University
Petillo, Carol M., Boston College, Massachusetts
Petracca, Mark, University of California at Irvine
Pickens, Donald K., University of North Texas
Pilant, Charles A., Cumberland College, Kentucky
Pinkham, Harold A., Jr., Salem State University, Massachusetts
Platt, Hermann K., St. Peter's College, New Jersey
Potts, Louis W., University of Missouri at Kansas City
Prescott, Gerald, California State University at Northridge
Presser, Stephen B., Northwestern University, Illinois
Price, Glenn W., Sonoma State University, California
Prince, Carl, New York University
Proctor, Samuel, University of Florida
Pruett, John H., University of Illinois at Urbana
Pugach, Noel H., University of New Mexico
Ramsey, B. Gene, Southeast Missouri State University
Randall, Richard S., New York University
Rapson, Richard L., University of Hawaii at Manoa
Rasmussen, John P., California State University at Stanislaus

Rawley, James A., University of Nebraska at Lincoln
Raymond, Harold B., Colby College, Maine
Reagan, Patrick D., Tennessee Technological University
Reeve, Thomas V., II, Cypress College, California
Reynolds, Donald E., East Texas State University
Rhoads, James B., Western Washington University
Richard, Carl J., University of Southern Mississippi
Ridings, William, Jr., attorney, Pompano Beach, Florida
Rieselbach, Leroy N., Indiana University
Riforgiato, Leonard R., Penn State University, Shenango Valley Campus,
    Pennsylvania
Riker, William, University of Rochester, New York
Ringelstein, Albert C., East Carolina University, North Carolina
Robertson, David, University of Missouri at St. Louis
Robichaud, Paul, Catholic University of America, District of Columbia
Robinson, John L., Abilene Christian University, Texas
Rodriguez, Junius P., Auburn University, Alabama
Rogers, William W., Florida State University
Rolak, Bruno J., retired professor, Houston, Texas
Rolater, Fred S., Middle Tennessee State University
Roller, David C., Bowling Green State University, Ohio
Rommel, John G., Trinity College, Connecticut
Rorabaugh, William J., University of Washington
Rosenzweig, Roy, George Mason University, Virginia
Ross, Robert L., University of Northern Iowa
Rothschild, Eric, Scarsdale High School, New York
Rowe, David L., Middle Tennessee State University
Rubenstein, Bruce A., University of Michigan at Flint
Ruddy, T. Michael, Saint Louis University, Missouri
Ruggiero, John, St. Francis College, Pennsylvania
Russell, James M., University of Tennessee at Chattanooga
Rutland, Robert A., University of Tulsa, Oklahoma
St. John, Jacqueline D., University of Nebraska at Omaha
Sanders, Elizabeth, New School for Social Research, New York
Savage, Robert L., University of Arkansas at Fayetteville
Schafer, Judith K., Tulane University, Louisiana
Schaffer, Donald D., Broward Community College North, Florida
Schapsmeier, Edward L., Illinois State University
Schapsmeier, Fred, University of Wisconsin at Oshkosh
Scharff, Virginia, University of New Mexico
Schiffman, I., California State University at Chico
Schlafly, Phyllis, author, Alton, Illinois
Schmidt, Winsor C., Memphis State University, Tennessee
Schneider, Robert W., Northern Illinois University
Schnell, Kempes, State University of New York College at Brockport
Schnittman, Suzanne, independent scholar, Rochester, New York
Schonberger, Howard B., University of Maine
Schott, Matthew J., University of Southwestern Louisiana
Schulman, Bruce J., University of California at Los Angeles
Schutz, John A., University of Southern California
Schwantes, Carlos A., University of Idaho

Scott, Roy V., Mississippi State University
Seavoy, Ronald E., Bowling Green State University, Ohio
Sellen, Robert W., Georgia State University
Sessions, Gene, Norwich University, Vermont
Shapiro, Samuel, University of Notre Dame, Indiana
Sharp, James Roger, Syracuse University, New York
Shriver, Phillip R., Miami University, Ohio
Siegel, Katherine A. S., St. Joseph's University, Pennsylvania
Silverman, Henry, Michigan State University
Simpson, Brooks D., Arizona State University
Sims, George E., Belmont College, Tennessee
Sims, Robert C., Boise State University, Idaho
Singal, Daniel J., Hobart and William Smith Colleges, New York
Sinsheimer, Bernard, University of Maryland
Sitkoff, Harvard, University of New Hampshire
Skeen, C. Edward, Memphis State University, Tennessee
Skelcher, Bradley, Delaware State College
Skemp, Sheila, University of Mississippi
Sklar, Kathryn Kish, State University of New York at Binghamton
Slaski, Gene, Penn State University, Allentown Campus, Pennsylvania
Slaybaugh, Douglas, St. Michael's College, Vermont
Small, Milton, Boise State University, Idaho
Smallwood, James, Oklahoma State University
Smith, Alan M., California State University at Hayward
Smith, David C., University of Maine
Smith, Geoffrey S., Queen's University, Canada
Smith, Paul II., Library of Congress, District of Columbia
Sochen, June, Northeastern Illinois University
Socolofsky, Homer E., Kansas State University
Somers, Walter R., Ball State University, Indiana
Southwell, Priscilla, University of Oregon
Sparks, Randy J., College of Charleston, South Carolina
Spear, Allan, University of Minnesota
Spencer, Donald S., State University of New York at Geneseo
Spetter, Allan, Wright State University, Ohio
Spragens, William C., Bowling Green State University, Ohio
Sproat, John G., University of South Carolina
Stamatopoulos, Tina, University of Akron, Ohio
Starr, Raymond, San Diego State University, California
Steely, W. Frank, Northern Kentucky University
Steiner, Dale R., California State University at Chico
Steirer, William F., Jr., Clemson University, South Carolina
Stephens, Otis H., University of Tennessee at Knoxville
Stephenson, Charles, Central Connecticut State University
Sterling, Keir B., Harford Community College, Maryland
Sterling, Robert, Eastern Illinois University
Stevens, Kenneth, Texas Christian University
Stevenson, Marshall F., Jr., Ohio State University
Stewart, Peter C., Old Dominion University, Virginia
Stidham, Ronald, Lamar University, Texas
Stoler, Mark, University of Vermont

Stonesifer, Roy P., Jr., Edinboro University, Pennsylvania
Sutton, Robert M., University of Illinois at Urbana
Sutton, Robert P., Western Illinois University
Sutton, Walter A., Lamar University, Texas
Sweeney, James R., Old Dominion University, Virginia
Synnott, Marcia G., University of South Carolina
Tallant, Harold D., Georgetown College, Kentucky
Taylor, Alan, Boston University, Massachusetts
Taylor, C. James, University of South Carolina
Taylor, William L., Plymouth State College, New Hampshire
Terborg-Penn, Rosalyn, Morgan State University, Maryland
Terreo, John, Montana Historical Society
Thomas, Mary Martha, Jacksonville State University, Alabama
Thomas, Norman C., University of Cincinnati, Ohio
Thompson, Gerald, University of Toledo, Ohio
Thornton, J. Mills, University of Michigan
Towey, Martin G., St. Louis University, Missouri
Towne, Ruth W., Northeast Missouri State University
Trefousse, Hans L., Brooklyn College, New York
Trelease, Allen W., University of North Carolina at Greensboro
Tricamo, John, San Francisco State University, California
Trow, Clifford W., Oregon State University, Oregon
Tucker, David M., Memphis State University, Tennessee
Tyler, Bruce M., University of Louisville, Kentucky
Unger, Irwin, New York University
Unger, Nancy C., San Francisco State University, California
Vandal, Gilles, Université de Sherbrooke, Canada
VanderMeer, Philip R., Arizona State University
Van Dusen, Albert E., University of Connecticut at Storrs
Van Ee, Daun, Johns Hopkins University, Maryland
Van Tassell, Richard, York College, Pennsylvania
Van Vugt, William, Calvin College, Michigan
Vaughn, William Preston, University of North Texas
Ver Steeg, Clarence L., Northwestern University, Illinois
Wall, Joseph F., Grinnell College, Iowa
Walroth, Joanne R., Illinois Historic Preservation Agency
Walsh, James P., Central Connecticut State University
Waltman, Jerry, University of Southern Mississippi
Wandersee, Winifred D., Hartwick College, New York
Ward, Harry M., University of Richmond, Virginia
Ward, Marilyn S., independent historian, Dallas, Texas
Weaver, David R., Saginaw Valley State University, Michigan
Webb, George E., Tennessee Technological University
Weiner, Marli, University of Maine
Weis, W. Michael, Illinois Wesleyan University
Weisbrot, Robert, Colby College, Maine
Welch, June R., University of Dallas, Texas
Werner, John M., Western Illinois University
Whisenhunt, Donald W., Wayne State College, Nebraska
Whitaker, James W., Iowa State University
White, Ray, Ball State University, Indiana

Whitehurst, G. William, Old Dominion University, Virginia
Wiggins, Sarah, University of Alabama
Williams, Lee E., II, University of Alabama
Williams, Oliver P., University of Pennsylvania
Wilson, Benjamin C., Western Michigan University
Wilson, John F., University of Hawaii at Manoa
Winnik, Herbert, St. Mary's College of Maryland
Wojcik, Patricia, political activist, Pompano Beach, Florida
Wood, Forrest G., California State University at Bakersfield
Wood, Gordon S., Brown University, Rhode Island
Woodruff, Judy, *The McNeil-Lehrer News Hour,* Virginia
Woods, James M., Georgia Southern University
Wright, Conrad E., Massachusetts Historical Society
Wunderlich, Roger, State University of New York at Stony Brook
Wyman, Mark, Illinois State University
Zappia, Charles A., San Diego Mesa College, California
Zeidenstein, Harvey, Illinois State University
Zelman, Donald L., Tarleton State University, Texas
Zimand, D., Northwestern University, Illinois
Zlomke, Susan, University of Oklahoma
Zophy, Angela Howard, University of Houston at Clear Lake, Texas
Zophy, Jonathan W., University of Houston at Clear Lake, Texas
Zoumaras, Thomas, Northeast Missouri State University
Zuckerman, Michael, University of Pennsylvania
Name withheld, Penn State University, Pennsylvania
Name withheld, University of Notre Dame, Indiana
Name withheld, University of Pittsburgh, Pennsylvania
Name withheld, Texas A & M University

SELECT BIBLIOGRAPHY

— ★ —

In our bibliography we are listing only general books on the presidency and works pertinent to presidential polling. We are not including the numerous biographies on each of the forty-one presidents and the histories of the periods in which they served.

Bailey, Thomas A. *Presidential Greatness: The Image and the Man, From George Washington to the Present.* New York: Irvington Publishers, 1978.

Barnett, John, ed. *Directory of History Departments and Organizations in the United States and Canada, 1990–1991.* Washington: American Historical Association, 1990.

Boller, Paul F., Jr. *Congressional Anecdotes.* New York: Oxford University Press, 1991.

———. *Presidential Campaigns.* New York: Oxford University Press, 1985.

———. *Presidential Anecdotes.* New York: Penguin Books, 1982.

Connelly, Thomas L., and Michael D. Senecal, ed. *Almanac of American Presidents from 1789 to the Present.* New York: Facts on File, 1991.

DeGregorio, William A. *The Complete Book of U.S. Presidents.* New York: Wings Books, 1993.

Famighetti, Robert, ed. *The World Almanac.* Mahwah, N.J.: World Almanac Books, 1996 and prior years.

Filler, Louis, ed. *The President Speaks: From McKinley to Lyndon Johnson.* New York: G.P. Putnam's Sons, 1964.

Frankel, Noralee. *Directory of Women Historians.* Washington: American Historical Association, 1988.

Frost-Knappman, Elizabeth, ed. *The World Almanac of Presidential Quotations.* New York: Pharos Books, 1993.

Kennedy, Lawrence F., chief compiler. *Biographical Directory of the American Congress, 1774–1971.* Washington: U.S. Government Printing Office, 1971.

Murray, Robert K., and Tim H. Blessing. *Greatness in the White House: Rating the Presidents, Washington Through Carter.* University Park: Pennsylvania State University Press, 1980.

Neal, Steve, "Our Best and Worst Presidents." *Chicago Tribune Magazine*. January 10, 1982.

Rossiter, Clinton. *The American Presidency*. New York: New American Library, 1962.

Schlesinger, Arthur M., Sr. "Our Presidents: A Rating By Seventy-five Historians." *New York Times Magazine*, July 29, 1962.

Spragens, William C., ed. *Popular Images of American Presidents*. New York: Greenwood Press, 1988.

Whitney, David C. *The American Presidents*. Garden City, N.Y.: Doubleday, 1969.

Wright, John W., ed. *The Universal Almanac*. Kansas City, Mo.: Andrews and McMeel, 1995.

INDEX

———— ★ ————